Pinkham Pioneers

By Madeline Utter

Pinkham Pioneers

By MADELINE UTTER

Copyright 2006 by Madeline Utter

Library of Congress Catalog Number: 2006933390

ISBN 1-931291-57-8

Published in the United States of America

First Edition

ALL RIGHTS RESERVED
No part of this publication may be reproduced, stored in a retrieval system, or transmitted in any form or by any means without the prior written permission of the copyright owner or the publisher.

STONEYDALE PRESS PUBLISHING COMPANY
523 Main Street • P.O. Box 188
Stevensville, Montana 59870
Phone: 406-777-2729

CONTENTS

Foreword 7
Early Days Recollections by Darrell Roose 9
Map of Place Names on Pinkham Ridge 10
Tribute 11
Introduction 12
Homestead Facts 14
History Notes 15
Poem: Pinkham Pioneers 16
Will and Nanny Workman 17
Poem: Pioneer Women 22
Thatchers and Della Young 23
Calhoun Brothers 24
Remember When 25
Will Stacy 26
Almeda Stacy 28
Harles Bergette 30
Andrew Stacy 33
Sylvester Stacy 36
Dora Stacy-Combs 40
James (Bill) Stacy 44
Stacy: Pinkham Bluff Song 47
Pyles and Brewer Stuart 48
Tom and Tilly Moore 48
James Queen 49
William Payne 50
Pluid Homesteads 52
Receet for Washing Clothes 56
O'Brien Family 57
Frank Slick 61
Kinney Family 63
Charles Workman 66
Alta Kinney Workman 68

Great-Grandmother Alta Workman	70
Wayne Workman	71
Lynn Workman	76
Sid Workman	76
Harry Workman	78
Chuck Workman	81
Dan Anker	84
Sid Workman – Stories	92
Sid Workman – Employment	98
Pinkham Creek Road Closure – 1924	104
Patrick Kearney	109
Poem: "Perly Waters of Pinkum Crick"	111
Roberts and Young	112
Pioneer Home Remedies	114
Abe and Sarah Cook	116
Elmer and Ovella Roberts	119
Milo and Mattie Leib	123
Maude Leib	124
Joseph Hamilton Leib	125
John Leib	128
Leib – John Leib Talks About the Tie Industry	130
Alice Wilson-Leib	132
Marie Leib-Roose	133
Leib Cemetery	135
Poem: When Boys Wore Bibs	137
Grandad Dan Utter	138
Cecil Utter Family	140
Lee Utter – Interviewed in 1996	149
Lee and Madeline Utter – Senior Citizens of the Year	152
Poem: Utterlee Haven	155
Esther Utter-Carvey	156
Caldwell and Carr	158
Camp 32 and Pinkham Falls	160
Water	165
Pioneer Privies	166
Poem: Pioneer Privies	169
Poem: WPA Special	171

Poem: Saturday Night Bath	172
Victor Banks	173
Finch Family	175
Jim and Thena Jenkins	177
Armstrong Family	179
Floyd and Agnes Sederdahl	179
Gene McWhirter	183
Poem: This Is The Bridge	184
Tom Wilson Biography	187
Poem: At The Picnic	190
Eureka Journal Notes – 1911	191
School History – Herrig	191
School History	192
Hunsinger	193
Lula Mikalson – Teacher and Homesteader	195
Remembering Pinkham School	198
Ethel Long – Teacher	200
School Picture (1930-31)	203
School Notes and Pupils – 1945-46	204
Madeline Rost Utter – Teacher Reminisces	204
School Christmas	207
Teacher Gets Married	209
School and Gathering Place	210
Poem: Changes	216
Changes	217
End of an Era	219
Moose Horn Club	222
Pinkham Veterans	224
Poem: Peace of Pinkham Creek	226
About The Author	Back Cover

Foreword

If it weren't for its unique setting as one of the most remote, if not *the* most isolated and thereby among *the* most remote of western places claimed by homesteaders in the opening decades of the Twentieth Century, the story of the settling of Pinkham Ridge in the heavily-timbered mountains of northwestern Montana would be just another story of the migration of eastern-based, poverty-stricken Americans to new opportunity in the West. It is much more than that, however, as our author – Madeline Rost Utter – explains. This is the dramatic story of people out of the West Virginia hill country – hillbillies they were called there – who came West with precious little and survived, one generation after another for two, three, four and sometimes five generations in succession under conditions that very well may have been more arduous, more challenging and ultimately more isolated from the mainstream of America, and even their own general area, than what the initial pioneers to the Pinkham Ridge country had left behind in West Virginia.

This is a story of perseverance. Of resourcefulness. Grit. And survival, one generation to the next, of family and friends and neighbors succeeding in the face of overwhelming odds when considered in relationship to a land that, when these immigrants first came, had not yet found its time of plenty. A wonderfully beautiful if not totally hospitable land, Pinkham Ridge lies to the west of the small town of Eureka, and just south of the tinier settlement of Rexford, whose original townsite now lies under the water of the Koocanusa Reservoir on the Kootenai River.

My conclusion after following the story of the *"Pinkham Pioneers"* – presented by the author in a matter-of-fact manner that lays the stories of these pioneers to the Pinkham Ridge country out, family by family and individual by individual – is that the integrity of her story in and of itself precludes any notion of melodrama. This is the raw, flesh-and-blood story of the human spirit confronting all that's thrown at it as it faces life at its fundamental level, one-on-one against almost over-whelming circumstances. Plus, the story is a triumphant record of what the human spirit can achieve when it wills itself to succeed, to persevere from hope to fulfillment. This is the powerful story of a group of people who, as we learn as the author describes, not without some lament I might note, their story from the beginning to the end of the pioneering era – a fact, literally, that not only came to the Pinkham Ridge people but to every other pioneering era in the American West.

One of the things that makes Madeline Rost Utter's story so powerful is that it tells the story of a place and its people that truly remained, up to just the most recent of times, in a pioneering status far longer than any other place in the American West. And, to our gain, it is told from a perspective *within* its unique community – the first such internal *voice* to do so. Other writers have told some aspects of the Pinkham Ridge story when writing about Montana history, but always from a point-of-view outside the Pinkham community. Madeline, herself, *is* part of the story of the Pinkham pioneers. And its transition from pioneering days to settled days is a contemporary story; its transition is even now, today, in the early years of the Twenty-first Century, being fulfilled. Some of the last of the Pinkham pioneers whose stories are told within these pages are still alive. Some of them, indeed, are friends of mine, old schoolmates with whom I shared the privilege of growing up as a neighbor and classmate at Lincoln County High School in Eureka. My early years were spent in the Trego area just south of Eureka, a landscape adjacent to and just to the south and east of Pinkham Ridge. I know personally that what Madeline has put together within these pages is the story as it played itself out. The saga of the resourceful Pinkham pioneers was legendary even in my youth; today it is one that has grown to Homeric proportions. This is a tale, ultimately, of a time and place, and its people, that has become larger than life itself . . . it is a story that, as you will find as you go through the pages of Madeline's text, transcends time and place and circumstance. It's a story we can all enjoy because it's one that, in its powerful truth, is more compelling and ennobling than one anyone could possibly make up. . .

>					Dale A. Burk
>					Stevensville, Montana
>					October 20, 2006

"EARLY DAYS 1880" – TRAIL TO PINKHAM CREEK
By Darrell Roose

There was no Eureka at that time, just old Tobacco or Mill Springs. The trail came down about the same as Highway 37 to south of the Pine Grove Ranch, then it went across the Tobacco River, on a bridge. That was the only bridge across the river at that time.

After crossing the bridge, the trail went over the hill to east end of Black Lake, then followed the lake up to the Black Lake Ranch west.

If you look across the Black Lake now, you will still see parts of the old trail. It went though the barnyard of the ranch, and over the hill to Blower Lake (the east side), then over the hill and down to the "Shenger Flats".

This crooked, up and down trail went over the hill to the west to Twin Lakes, then a little farther south was the "Lane Lake," which they call "Dale Cook Lake," then on to the "Hunsinger Place" at the north end of Twin Lakes just between the two lakes, then on to the "Fluharty Place" on the north end of the big lake. This trail went on up to "Sandy Place."

Just west was another homestead. The trail turned left there to go up the hill to Pinkham Creek Falls, a woman (Della Young) homesteaded it. It continued on up to Thatcher Homestead before going on up Pinkham Creek. (Ella Sanford had married Harry Thatcher).

One day, Orie Fluharty went through my Grandad's barnyard. He was riding one horse and leading a packhorse. My Grandad asked him where he was going, "He said up to Twin Lakes." After he left my Grandma asked, " Who was that?" My Grandad said "It's old man Fluharty going to Twin Lakes. He has a wife and four kids. That man's crazy. There's not a chance in the world ever getting a road up there." (Now look at all the roads!)

As time went by, a wagon road was built. It came from Eureka on the Black Lake Road. They went over the hill from the south end of Black Lake to Twin Lakes and on up to Pinkham. Later they built the road that they travel on now (2003).

There was also a trail from Old Rexford to Pinkham by way of Mud Lake.

This was told to me, Darrell Roose, by my Grandad John Shenefelt, Black Lake Ranch.

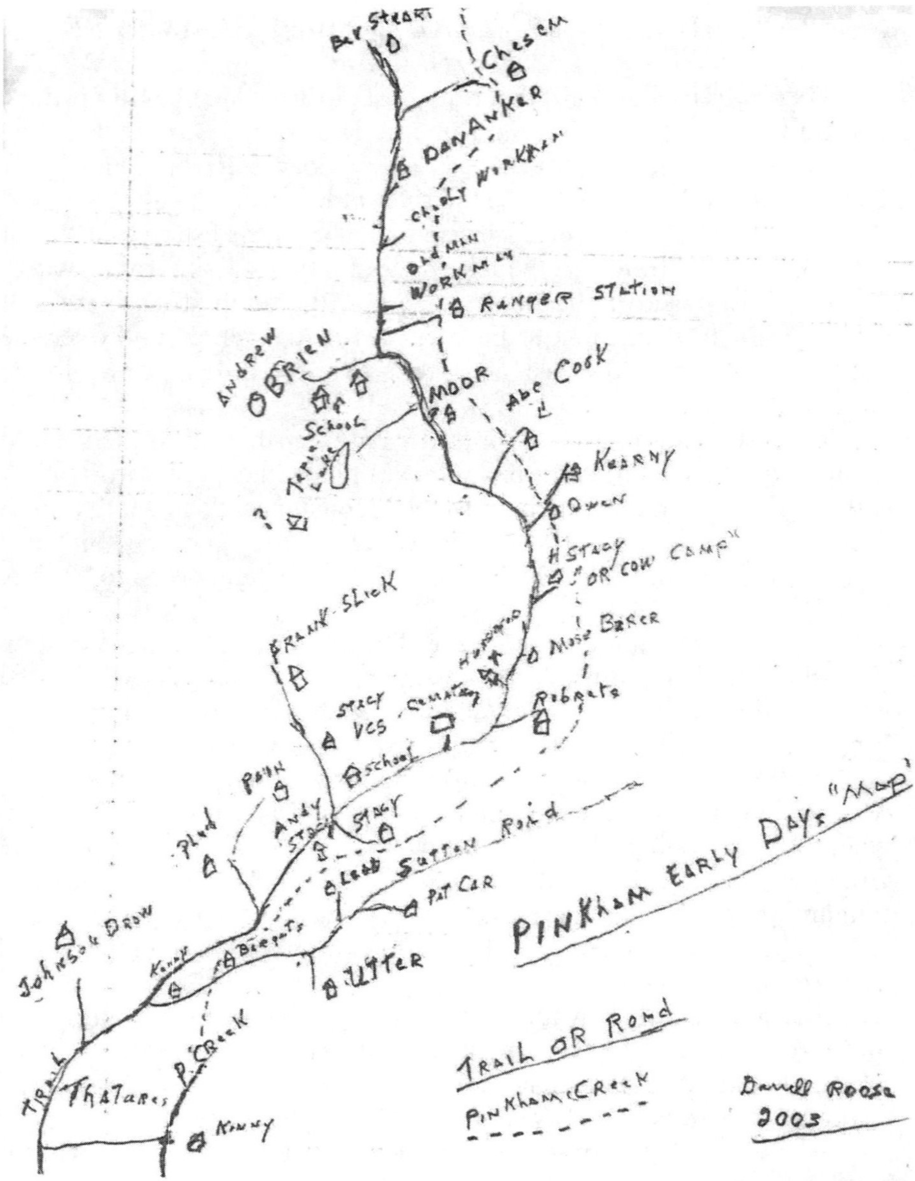

Chesem
DAN ANKER
CHARLY WORKMAN
OLD MAN WORKMAN
RANGER STATION
ANDREW OBRIEN
School
MOOR
Abe Cook
Kearny
Owen
H STACY "OR COW CAMP"
FRANK SLICK
Mose Baker
STACY
VCS
Cemetery
Roberts
school
Andy STACY
STACY
Sutton Road
Pat Car
Johnson Draw
Kenny
UTTER
P. CREEK
TRAIL
Kenny
PINKham EARLY DAYS "Map"
TRAIL OR Road
PINKham CREEK
2003

TRIBUTE

This book is a tribute to the early pioneers who came to settle up Pinkham Creek. It spans about fifty years from 1900 to the 1950's, a lifetime of struggle for some people. They came with very little except high hopes of living in paradise. It tells of individual families and their struggle for survival in the wilderness, a wild mountain area with cold, snowy winters and hot, dry summers. There were a few folks who had the tenacity to stick it out during the lean years and survive hardships. Others gave it up and moved on to greener pastures.

This book is based on information gleaned from records in the Lincoln County Courthouse in Libby, Montana, and from personal interviews with descendants of the original Pinkham Pioneers.

There are remnants of pioneer families still living in the community and surrounding area. It was from these that the story unfolded of bygone days. This collection of family histories was told with nostalgia, humor and some sadness. It reveals the forbearance of ancestors and their determination to make things better for the next generation.

Sid Workman contributed interesting historical stories as well as others. Lee Utter, my husband, was a good critic and helped me keep my facts in line. Donna Sederdahl Gentry helped immensely by putting it all on computer. Emogene Boslaugh gave good advice and edited as she read. Then there were those who gave me encouragement – I thank you all!

Changes came after World War II for an easier way of life for those living up the 'Crick.' Servicemen came home from the World War II to settle down and raise another generation in a more modern world.

INTRODUCTION

Pinkham Creek is located in the mountain area of the northwest region of Montana. It starts at the base of Pinkham Mountain and flows in a northerly direction until it joins the Kootenai River from Canada below the little village of Rexford, Montana. The river is now Lake Koocanusa behind Libby Dam on the Kootenai River. The lake name is derived from parts of the three names: Kootenai, Canada and U.S.A.

In early discovery days about the time Montana became a state of the union in 1889, a trapper by the name of Pinkham followed the Kootenai River up from Libby north toward Canada. He stopped at the mouth of a little creek to set up camp and look the country over.

Pinkham liked what he discovered: primitive forest filled with wild animals, streams with beaver and various species of fish in the river. This was the spot where he chose to build a rustic log cabin. He brought his wife, Hannah, and adopted daughter, Grace, to keep him company. Thus the little creek soon became know as Pinkham Creek. Pinkham Mountain was also named for this family as water drainage from these mountains formed the creek as well as other tributaries downstream. Lydia Creek might have been named after another famous Pinkham and her famous elixir (Lydia Pinkham's Elixir).

It is not known what happened to Mr. Pinkham but a news item in the Tobacco Plains Journal December 17, 1904, stated: "Mrs. Pinkham of Libby is visiting old-time friends in the Plains. She formerly owned the ranch upon which the old town of Rexford was built." There is no record of a homestead filed by Pinkham in Lincoln County but at that time it was part of Flathead County. The 1910 census listed Hannah Pinkham as a widow and her grandson (last name Robinson) was living with her in Libby. The Pinkhams had no other children. Mrs. Pinkham was well liked and helped in the area as a midwife and nurse with many of her own home remedies.

There were Indian trails that followed up the creek as it meandered down from the hills. One of their favored camping spots was near the lakes that formed a multiple shore line along meadows. These were later called Twin Lakes by pioneers. Early pioneers witnessed Indians camping, hunting and picking huckleberries farther up the drainage. The redmen liked to trade moccasins and such for white man tools. They also took hides as payment. Indian women also traded huckleberries for bright colored skirts and shirts.

Another spot where Indians camped was farther up the Pinkham drainage near bubbling springs that formed a marshy area and a little lake. This was known as Teepee Lake by homesteaders. Early settlers recall seeing Indians camping there with tepees set up for family abodes during summer time hunting forays.

It was the Indian trails and game tracks that Will Workman followed up the creek when he first came to the wilderness. He picked a spot along the creek far away from civilization for his homestead. Here he could hunt all year around for meat to feed his family while saving the hides to sell or trade.

HOMESTEAD FACTS FROM LINCOLN COUNTY CLERK AND RECORDERS OFFICE

To get the ball rolling on Pinkham pioneer history, here are a few facts gleaned from records held at the Lincoln County Clerk and Recorder's office in Libby.

According to the records, the first one to prove up on a stone and timber claim on upper Pinkham was Moses Brewer, who got a patent in 1916 on 160 acres in Section 18. The next spring, April 1917, Alfred Hunsinger had a patent recorded for 120 acres, followed closely in June 1917 by Joseph Henry Stacy for 160 acres, all in Section 18.

In December of 1917, Charles William (Bill) Workman patented 80 acres in Section 28. Then in April 1918 a patent for 160 acres was given to William Clyde Hunsinger in Section 19. These patents were first recorded in Flathead County and signed by Woodrow Wilson, then sent to Lincoln County after the counties were divided.

A patent to Laura Belle Bertge (Bergette) was recorded in July 1919 for 40 acres in Section 6 and 80 acres in Section 7. John Maurice Harrington received a patent for 160 acres December 1920 in Section 9. In December 1921 a patent was issued to Sylvester Stacy for 100 acres in Section 8 and 60 acres in Section 9.

It was May 12, 1922, that a portion of the William Stacy homestead was deeded to School District 18. That same year, February 1922, Albert Kinney proved up on his homestead and received a patent for 160 acres in Section 6. Also in 1922 Milo Leib was issued a patent for 90 acres in Section 8.

The next recording was in 1924 when July Patrick Carr got his patent for 80 acres in Section 6. That same time Amos Arvis Kinney was issued a patent for 160 acres in Section 6, with 40 acres deeded to Cecil L. Utter and 40 acres to Harry and Ella Thatcher. Then in 1925 Frank Slick got a patent on 160 acres in Section 9 and in 1926 William Stacy was issued a patent for 160 acres in Section 8. In October 1927, Cora Croft got a patent for 25 acres and turned it over to Harles Bergette for taxes.

Andrew O'Brien proved up on 160 acres in Section 28 and in 1925 was issued a patent. Pat Kearney received a patent in 1922 for 40 acres in Section 29 and 80 acres in Section 30. Daniel Anker was given a patent for 80 acres in Section 34 in 1924.

A homestead usually consisted of 160 acres, or a quarter section of land. There were no dates recorded of when a person filed a claim to the land they wanted to homestead. Certain requirements, such a living on the place and making improvements, were mandated before a patent deed could be issued. A fee was also charged for closing costs, which were hard to come by for many and delayed the actual recording. It was also a long ways to Libby and would probably include a train ride both ways.

These statistics take in only part of the homesteads of those on Pinkham. It will take more trips to Libby to search records of other sections down the creek below the existing schoolhouse.

History buffs may also get in on the search as well as those now living on a part of these old homesteads.

HISTORY NOTES
By Madeline Utter

At the top of the South Eureka hill, the Pinkham road continues southwest (left) off the Black Lake Road to the Pinkham-Rexford Y, then left to follow Pinkham Creek Valley about fifteen miles to Pinkham Mountain. Well-timbered but isolated, and with a mere track for wagon road, its settlers had little contact with the outside.

By 1903 Mr. and Mrs. Will Workman and family were homesteading far up the creek, and Wm, Sr. and Almeda Stacy in 1905 were much farther down. The first school was held in a little one room log cabin for Workman children. The young teacher boarded at Workmans.

When O'Briens came, a bigger building was needed to hold both large families. On land donated by Wm. Stacy and Andy O'Brien, schoolhouses were built near each home for their children and those of their neighbors. The lower 'Stacy' school and the upper 'O'Brien' school were both in School District 18 with the same board governing both.

Nancy Jane Roberts (Mrs. James) and Ida Workman, sister of Charlie Workman, served often as midwives, along with other efficient women.

As was to be expected in an isolated community, many alliances took place between these families. The seclusion of the mountain area with little contact with the outside world, plus the mutual struggle for survival, bound the homestead families into a tight knit group. It was only natural for young folks to choose a partner from a similar background. Most of these commitments lasted a life-time and brought the families even closer.

When two large families were combined into one household, it made the situation confusing to outsiders. For instance when Jim Roberts and "Sis" Young tied the knot, each with several children, stepsisters and brothers were brought together. Then when stepbrother

Rome Roberts and stepsister Fanny Young chose each other as mates, it bound the family tighter.

Other families were brought together through marriage. When Leo Utter took Bessie Workman as his wife, and his sister Myrtle Utter married George Workman, a brother to Bessie, it made their children double cousins. This happened again in the next generation. Sidney L. Workman wed Alice Combs and Bob Combs married Ellagene Workman, Sid's sister, so their children were double cousins. This also made a connection to the Stacy family through Dora Stacy Combs.

Hopefully, the personal stories in this book will help clear up confusion of family connections of Pinkham people.

PINKHAM PIONEERS

The pearly waters of Pinkham Creek lured the pioneer
Some came from West Virginia to make a home here
Word spread and more came from far away and near
They were happy with water, abundant timber and deer

Folks filed for timber and mining claim along the crick
Using cross cut saws they built log cabins to make it stick
Then moved in their belongings including feather tick
Midwives delivered babies and took care of the sick

A few went to town by shanks mare and others rode
Men worked together to clear and build a wagon road
They sawed down trees and hewed ties to make a load
Then used a team to haul them down to the railroad

Most of the pioneers had their own milk cow
To raise pigs for bacon, they needed a brood sow
For eggs they had chickens they raised somehow
To have a garden they broke the sod with a plow

Raising a garden for winter food was a necessity
They stored vegetables in a dug out cellar or pantry
Pioneers planted rhubarb, transparent, and crab apple tree
Pie crusts made from bear grease was a woman's specialty

It took a lot of tenacity to prove up on a homestead
Pioneers literally lived off the land and tried to get ahead
They helped one another by sharing, families had to be fed
Some couldn't persevere so to other places they fled
by Madeline Utter

WILL AND NANNY WORKMAN

The first family to settle on upper Pinkham Creek was that of Charles William and Elizabeth Frances (Nanny) Workman. They left Greenbrier County, West Virginia, in 1903. They came by immigrant train as far as Whitefish, where the tracks ended. Settlers were allowed two boxcars to move their belongings, one for livestock and one for household goods and family members.

Families were prepared to live in the boxcars about a month before they found another place to live. The Workmans had six children on the train; Katie and Lula were young teens, Charlie, nine, then came Sidney, George and Ida, the toddler. (Ben, just older than Charlie, had died in West Virginia with a deadly childhood disease.) The boxcar was crowded with pads and feather ticks for sleeping eight with children sharing a bed. Will took Charlie with him to sleep on a pad in the boxcar of animals and other gear.

Will wanted to settle in the wilderness far away from civilization so he could hunt bear. Their hides were worth money, and it would help support his family. While looking for the right place, he rode his horse farther north to the little town of Hayden on the Kootenai River. There he found a job building a branch line of the railroad into Canada. He also found an empty settler's cabin in the Iowa Flats area.

The Workman family moved by team and wagon from Whitefish to the Tobacco Valley, which took two days. They made overnight camp at Spring Creek, the half way camp for many travelers. That winter the older children attended the Iowa Flats school..

When spring came, Will was out scouting around on horseback in the surrounding hills for his hideaway. He'd heard that Pinkham Creek ran down from a remote area, so he followed the Indian trails up the drainage. He noted that two women were building cabins near Pinkham Falls and other land looked to be promising, but he wanted farther away from civilization. While riding through virgin stands of timber – pines, firs, spruce and tamarack with a few cottonwoods along the creek, Will watched for signs of wildlife. There were deer to be seen as well as bear sign, but no beaver dams in the creek. They would show up in later years.

At the end of a long days ride, Will was looking for a place to camp for the night. He'd passed by a meadow with several springs (this would eventually be the O'Brien homestead) to look further up stream. He found a spot with big trees for shelter and a small meadow for his horse to graze. Next morning, Will explored some more and found a grove of trees the right size for house logs, not far from the creek. That was the place he chose to build a cabin for his family.

It was a five day trip on horseback to Kalispell, the county seat, to stake a timber and stone claim for 160 acres. That was a two day ride each way plus a day for business. Will spent the summer sawing down trees and erecting a three bedroom cabin while Nanny and the children raised a good garden where they were. The older children again attended the Iowa Flats school. Ted was born in 1905 and Cora was born in 1907 in Fernie, B.C., when Will was working for the railroad again.

Will provided his family with meat as deer were plentiful and easily shot on his trips to Pinkham. He had a reliable 33 carbine breakdown model that could be easily carried on horseback. He was a true sportsman as he believed in giving game a chance by giving a piercing whistle that either startled the deer to stop and listen or to bound off. This also saved ammunition as Will had a clean shot if the deer stopped. He had ammunition left over. He returned bullets for $2.00 to Bill Fewkes store to go on grocery bill.

Before moving his family up Pinkham Creek, Will built a stone boat or go-devil as some called it. It was a sturdy platform nailed on small logs tapered in the front like a sled to not dig into the ground. It was narrower than a regular wagon or team pulled sled, so that it could easily be pulled up the trail behind a single horse. The boat would haul heavy barrels, trunks and a cook stove that was too heavy and cumbersome for a pack horse. It would be pulled up hills, then go like the devil on the down side. It was right handy to haul barrels of water from the crick on washday, or bring a bear home without damaging the hide. The stone boat also made it easy to haul rocks from the garden patch, or field to be dumped elsewhere.

Every chance he got, Will would work on the trail to widen it for a team and wagon. He sawed down trees here and there or pried out a rock. During the winter, when snow was on the ground, was the easiest to travel the trail. A team could pull a sleigh loaded with ties to the railroad landing without much difficulty as it was mostly down hill. The general store in Rexford was the 'shopping' center for most anything a pioneer would need and close to the railroad round house as well as the tie landing. When the O'Briens moved up the crick in 1910, there were many more hands to help improve the road.

Will hunted bear in spring and fall when pelts brought the best price. The meat wasn't wasted as roasts were like pork and scraps ground up for sausage. Bear grease was also rendered for many uses. When firm, it made good pie crusts and biscuits besides greasing leather boots and harnesses to make them supple and waterproof. Bear grease also was used to make candles by dipping a string in melted fat and cooled after each dip. Soap was made from bear grease, wood ashes and lye.

The Workman family lived in their log cabin just two years before disaster struck. This is the tale of the house fire as told many years later by Ida and Cora. Will was in control of the situation or it would have been much worse.

"We were all snug in bed one cold winter night when we heard Dad holler: "Everybody up and get dressed. The house is on fire! Put your coats on and go to the barn. Take something with you." As he was talking, he was doing. The pail of water was not enough to put the fire out on the roof next to the stove pipe so he threw the bucket out into the snow.

He gathered up his gun and bullet pouch and handed them to Charlie. He told him to put them in the horse feed box and come back – run! Will lit the lantern and handed it to George. "Take this to the barn and hang it on a nail so it won't get tipped over." Then he started putting stuff in the dish pan, a coffee pot, coffee, tea, salt and pepper shakers and what dishes he could grab up to fill it. He gave it to Sid to carry.

Mama dressed baby Cora and wrapped her in a blanket. When Charlie came back, he carried Cora, clutching her rag doll and took Teddy by the hand to the barn. We girls took things too. Ida picked a pillow off the bed and Mama gave her sewing basket with yarn, thread and needles to Bessie to carry as she followed the parade to the barn. Mama and Lu each grabbed a corner of a feather tick, bedding and all, and dragged it out the door and down to the barn. Mama told us kids to get on it and stay there!

She went back to help Dad. He had grabbed the washtub off the outside wall and was filling it with what ever he could. She made sure to put in the wash board and a bar of soap. Charlie grabbed the handle of the tub and dragged it over the snow to safety. Dad threw chairs out the door for boys to take. It wasn't safe to get too close to the inferno, but another feather tick was there for mama and Lu to drag to the barn. Dad was tuckered and had worked up a sweat even if it was cold. We huddled in the barn 'til morning."

"When we looked at the smoldering ruins, there was the black iron cookstove standing by itself! Dad also found black iron fry pans, spider kettle, the iron Dutch oven and a butcher knife with no handle. He found the bucket out in the snow to milk the cow. What little she gave, as she was drying up before another calf, we slurped up for breakfast. Dad moved the chickens into the barn then took a shovel to clean out the chicken house down to the clean dirt. Then we moved in there for a while."

After the fire and when the cold snap had passed, Will rode his horse to town. He found a place near Black Lake for the family to stay temporarily. They also brought the cow and chickens. Older children attended Black Lake school until the term ended. Will bought bolts of cloth to replace things that burned. White sheeting was not only used for bed sheets and pillow cases but also for white shirts, blouses, petticoats, aprons. A bolt of dark blue serge was needed for pants and long skirts for girls and Nana. Blue chambray was a necessity for shirts and blouses too. These were all cut and sewn by hand, plus buttonholes.

That summer Will re-built a home up Pinkham. This time he used rough boards sawed from Frank Slick's sawmill that had just been set up on the Thatcher place. He traded logs for lumber to build. Besides a combined kitchen, living area in the middle, there were two bedrooms on each end. The privy was still out back and water carried from the crick.

The Workmans were concerned about schooling for their growing children. Lula had been helping her younger siblings to read and write but when she married a railroad boss named Angelo in Fernie, B.C., they thought of getting another teacher. They offered board and room to a young girl just out of high school. A little log cabin was used for the school room, the first school on Pinkham. All six students were Workmans: Charlie, Sid, George, Bessie, Ida and Teddy.

Ida also told of the annual treks to Hot Springs, Montana. Although her dad was a strong six-foot-tall man, he became afflicted with arthritis and suffered through the winters. Each spring when school was out, Will would take his family by team and wagon to make the three week trip, a week each way and one to stay. "After Dad had soaked in the smelly mud and drank the stinking water he felt better and was ready to go to work again."

"We would pile the wagon full of stuff for camping. Feather beds and tents made soft seats for us to sit on. Mom always took her sour dough starter and dried meat to go in gravy. She made hotcakes in the spider over a campfire and buttermilk biscuits in the Dutch oven. A crate of live chickens was put in the back along with a new born calf. Our cow followed along behind and was milked twice a day. We had scrambled eggs most every day but when a hen quit laying Mom just wrung its neck and made a big pot of chicken and dumplings. She also skimmed the cream from the milk that sat overnight and put it in separate crock with a cover. The jolting of the wagon each day churned the cream into butter for us to use. We camped outside of Hot Springs so cow and horses could graze and boys could hunt rabbits."

Ida and Cora also told about stocking Pinkham Creek with fish. Will liked to fish but there were no fish above the falls as fish migrated up from the Kootenai River that far before they were stymied with a rock wall. To remedy that Will stopped in Creston and picked up a barrel of fingerlings at the fish hatchery. It was a large wooden barrel made of staves glued together and held with iron rims. There was a bunghole in the lid for air. Will dumped the barrel of brook trout in the creek at home on Pinkham. The fish grew and multiplied for good fishing in later years. Ida was the fisherman and Cora liked to eat crisp fried pan size fish.

Ida took after her dad by growing taller than her siblings and acting like a tomboy. She also liked to go on hunting trips with the guys. One time her dad sent her home from hunting camp with a bear carcass. She 'drug' it home behind her horse but didn't take care to watch out for rocks or brush. By the time she got home with it, all the hair was worn off one side which ruined the hide for sale.

Will was the first to prove up on his homestead and meet the qualifications. The family lived there full time; they had a field to raise hay and a garden. He paid the required amount to Flathead County and received a patent signed by Woodrow Wilson dated December 29, 1917. It said he "had secured a Homestead to actual Settlers on Public Domain in conformity to law." Will had filed to the State of Montana in 1910 for water rights on Pinkham. He was the first one of the homesteaders to do that too.

The family grew up and found spouses. Charlie married Alta Kinney and Sid married Hila Moore, both daughters of Pinkham homesteaders. George chose Myrtle Utter and Bessie mated up with Myrtle's brother, Leo Utter. Ida wed Bill Weewick and Cora tied the knot with Trustin Wagner. Ted went west to Washington, then to California with his family.

Katie married Bill Siphon from Fortine. He had been employed by U.S. Forest Service to spy on Pinkham people as they were under suspicion of setting fires and other sculduggery. He found a lovely girl and enjoyed good times with country folks.

    Ida and Cora both helped to serve as midwives for Alta when she gave birth to her sons, Wayne, Lynn, and Sidney. The grandparents, Will and Nanny, lived long enough to welcome their grandsons into the world. Nanny died in 1918, and he followed in 1920.

PIONEER WOMEN

Pioneer women needed to be both sturdy and strong
To bear babies, bake bread and work hard all day long
To milk the cow twice a day and churn butter all along
Make meals from scratch and sing babies a bedtime song.

Pioneer women did laundry the hard way, it's a trick
First she chopped wood with an ax to build a fire stick
Then she heated a caldron of water carried from the crick
She boiled the white clothes while stirring with a stick.

She bent over washboards with home made soap so slick
When hanging them on the line to dry, she gave them a flick
Braided rag rugs she cleaned by beating them with a stick.
Is it any wonder she complained that her back had a crick?

Flat irons were kept on the wood-burning stove at the back
Because ironing day followed wash day and that's a fact.
They ironed sheets, pillowcases, apron, shirt and slack
The fire in the stove cooked beans and heated up the shack

Even pioneer kids had chores to do their share of the work
They carried in wood, took out slop to the pigs and
didn't shirk
Some had to feed chickens and gather eggs all before dark
They swept floors, set table, washed dishes as growing
up work

The Pioneer woman was not retarded or a fool.
To get things done she made a simple schedule
She raised her children by The Golden Rule
She taught them herself or sent them to school.

                                        by Madeline Utter

HARRY AND ELLA (SANDFORD) THATCHER
AND DELLA YOUNG

Back in the beginning when Pinkham Creek drainage was a wilderness area, two staunch pioneer women started a new life on the western frontier. Ella Sandford and Della Young came when a new century had just begun. Lower Pinkham had been settled by homesteaders but there were only horse and game trails above Pinkham Falls.

The two women each filed a stone and timber claim for a homestead when Flathead County covered the whole northwest corner of Montana. Their land joined each other. Della took 160 acres that included the Pinkham Falls while Ella was up the creek. They built cabins of rough lumber near the creek for water and near their joining boundaries for fellowship.

Both homesteads were blessed with verdant timber stands of Ponderosa Pine, with Douglas-fir and Western larch mixed in. Della lived in her rustic cabin a few years but never proved up on her homestead. She sold to Bonners Ferry Lumber Company, which then turned it back to the government. Now the scenic wonder of Pinkham Falls is on USFS land. The big pines stood for many years with the narrow one lane road winding through the forest and around the trees.

Ella Sandford became Mrs. Harry Thatcher before she filed her patent on the homestead in November of 1916. She played a prominent part in the early history of the Pinkham settlement. Ella never had children of her own, but she was interested in a good school in the community. When the new lower school was built, she served as clerk of the school board for 15 years.

Another Pinkham pioneer, Frank Slick, set up his sawmill along the creek on the upper Thatcher homestead. The mill was run by steam-powered engine and put out lumber to build more homes in the area as well as the new school buildings. The mill also provided work for local people including Harry Thatcher.

Ella Thatcher served the community as a midwife besides being a good neighbor to every one. She helped deliver many babies at home in the Pinkham hills. Among them were Chuck and Ellagene Workman, who was named after her. Harry T. Workman was born at their place, with a doctor in attendance, after they moved to town. Now Harry Thatcher had a namesake, too.

Back in the early days road work was by volunteer labor. Road graders with wheels and a blade between were pulled down the road by two teams of horses. Men with forks or shovels came behind to pick rocks out of the roadway. Harry Thatcher once made the remark that now we pick the rocks out but some day we'll be putting rocks back in.

Ella Thatcher liked to pick huckleberries and would go with the Workmans to camp out for a few days in the summer. Ella was in her 70's when she went on such a trip where she rode a colt to Camp Tuffet on Sutton Ridge. Little Jack Workman was on a burro and others on horses when a big hailstorm blew in, pounding them with hailstones as big as two-bit pieces. Ella piled off and shoved Jack under a huge log for protection. They still brought their huckleberries on home to can.

In 1931 the Thatchers sold their Pinkham homestead to Amos Kinney and moved into Eureka for retirement. They still kept busy as Ella raised a good garden. Harry worked as a bartender and swamper at Jim's Place. He also watched out for Pinkham teenagers who weren't yet of drinking age.

They kept in touch with many friends of the Pinkham Creek community as their interests were still with folks up the creek. They both were buried at the Tobacco Valley Cemetery.

CALHOUN BROTHERS

The Calhoun brothers both took up homesteads in the Pinkham drainage. None of their relatives lived in the vicinity in later years for family information. Records in the Lincoln County Courthouse show that Alva Calhoun got a patent June 12, 1922, for his place in Section 5. Then, in 1935, taxes went delinquent. The place was deeded to Alta Workman in 1943, then to Victor and Pearl Workman in 1953.

The Calhoun homestead home was a log house built near the main road and a nearby spring for water. (This place became known as the silk stocking place when the Charlie Workman family wintered there.) According to the 1920 Census taken of the Pinkham area, Alva was listed as a farmer from Iowa and his wife from Finland. Their son was born in Montana. As proof of his farming ability, Alva planted a prolific orchard on the sidehill across the road from the house. It was protected from sun on frosty mornings, then exposed to afternoon sunshine.

Alva's brother, Albert, was listed as head of the household and a sawmill operator. His place was up on the hill along the Sutton Road. Family members were a wife, Lois, from Kentucky, a 6 year old son, Marion, born in Kentucky and a daughter, Florence, 4 years old, born in Montana. There was no record of either family in the 1930 Census.

(The 1920 Census of School District #18 listed Pinkham population as 115. Population report in 1930 Census was 75.)

REMEMBER WHEN

Remember when your only transportation was in a wagon or sleigh pulled by a horse or riding it yourself to go shopping or visiting.

Remember when you walked two or more miles to school carrying your cold lunch in a lard pail and when your writing tablet cost a nickel and pencils were two for a penny.

Remember when the only light you had to read by was a kerosene lamp or a candle and that the family sat around the table to share it.

Remember when milk came from a cow instead of a carton in the store, that you churned your own butter and bread you ate was what you baked.

Remember when the stove you cooked on was called a range and it was stoked with wood cut by a crosscut saw, then split with an ax and carried to a wood box.

Remember when you grabbed a bucket and went to a well or spring to fetch a pail of water, then drank when thirsty from a family dipper hanging nearby.

Remember when you packed many pails of water to heat on the stove in a boiler to do laundry, clothes were scrubbed on a washboard, bleached with lye or bluing, starched heavily, then hung on a clothesline outdoors to dry.

Remember when the following day the sad irons were heated on the stove, the ironing board set up and starched clothes were sprinkled with water and ironed.

Remember when babies were born at home with the help of a midwife or neighbor and that diapers were made of washable material.

Remember when home remedies were castor oil, mustard plasters or home made chicken soup.

Remember when you did all your Christmas shopping from a Sears or Montgomery Ward catalog.

Remember when you made up your own entertainment with games such as spin the bottle, I spy, drop the handkerchief, tag or hide and seek.

Remember when in the night you used the chamber pot under the bed or took a trek in the dark out to the little shack out back. When snow was deep and frost was on the seat you still had to go when nature called.

Remember when you were a wee wee tot and mama put you on the cold cold pot then told you to wee wee whether you wanted to or not.

If you remember all these and more – then hey! You were born back in the good old days!

WILL STACY

It was in 1905 that William and Almeda Stacy came from West Virginia to settle in Montana. Since they were hillbillies at heart, they chose the Pinkham Creek area and soon felt right at home. Their homestead spanned the creek and crossed the wagon road that skirted a large hill. When more people came from West Virginia, it soon became known as Virginia Hill.

The children of Will and Almeda: Victoria, Henry, Julius, Sylvester, Laura Belle, Cosby and Andrew, all grew up in West Virginia. Most of them came to Montana and some of them took up homesteads on Pinkham near their parents. Those that filed for homesteads were Laura Belle Stacy-Bergette, Andy, Ves and Henry. Not all proved up on their place and put down roots.

Will Stacy was a tall strong man and a willing worker. To carve a homestead out of the wilderness it took a lot of tenacity as well as hard work. Will and Almeda made a good team as they worked together to make their dreams come true. They were farmers at heart and that was their goal – to make their homestead a productive place.

Although they had only primitive tools to work with, Will knew how to use them. After selecting a building site next to the little branch creek with a garden spot nearby, he set to work falling trees to clear the area. He was adept with the ax and spent the first summer chopping uniform trees to make house logs. By fall, a little two room log cabin with a sod roof sat nestled in the timber ready to move into for the winter.

Will worked all winter chopping down trees to build a barn and clear more garden space. The shelter was built in two sections with a covered space between. That way horses could have a part and cows the other with a place for buggies, wagon and sled parked in the center out of the weather. A hayshed was added in later years.

In the spring, Will spaded up an area to plant a garden. The following years he expanded the garden by plowing the sod under with the help of a horse. With back-breaking work, the garden flourished and became quite productive. A photo taken in 1915 showed the proud results with the family.

Will was always workiing at something. He helped farmers and ranchers down in the valley to put up hay the hard way, then trade for livestock and feed them.

The Will Stacy family garden.

Will also worked with his neighbors to build a wagon road up the creek. More homesteaders were moving in and they all wanted improvements and better roads was a priority for wagon and buggy traffic. Will was part of the road gang to fall trees with a cross cut saw and limb with an ax, to dig out rocks with a pick-ax and level off with a shovel.

There were more children in the community and a larger school was needed. Will didn't have much schooling himself, but he wanted his grandchildren to have the advantage of "book larnin." He helped tear down the little log school to make room for a new one. The logs were moved and used for a house on the homestead of Jim Roberts, just up the creek. Will deeded the land to the School District 18.

Will and Almeda also had the biggest and best orchard of anyone up the creek. Across the Slick Gulch road from the school was an ideal slope for fruit trees to get afternoon sun. Here they planted several varieties of apples, plum and pie cherries which produced prolifically when blossoms didn't get frosted in the spring. Besides bears, school children liked to help themselves to juicy apples now and then.

The couple lived to see their dreams come true up the creek surrounded by their expanded family. Almeda died March 28, 1923, and Will died February 15, 1928. They were both buried in Tobacco

Valley Cemetery.

ALMEDA STACY

When Almeda Stacy came west with her husband Will; she had high hopes of living in a paradise in the mountain wilderness of western Montana. She knew it would be hard going at first but she and her husband were hard workers and intended to make their dreams come true.

The first year would be the hardest, when they literally had to live off the land with no house for shelter. All their worldly goods they brought with them on the train, had to be put on horses to be taken up Pinkham Creek to their stone and wood claim for a homestead.

The most essential items were packed by horse such as a bed roll, change of clothes, gun, ax, knife, matches, frying pan, coffee pot plus a few staples like coffee, (tobacco), flour, salt and sugar. Meat for the pan was waiting in the forest for the hunter to claim. Deer was plentiful as well as bear, pine squirrels and wild chickens, but no fish in the creek as yet.

During the summer Almeda made do with camp fire cooking outdoors and putting up with a wickiup for shelter. A wickiup is a temporary protection from elements, put up from what ever is handy. Thick needled heavy spruce limbs slanted against a clay bank or placed on cut poles makes a fairly good shelter from rain and gives shade from sun.

Almeda was also good at finding edible plants in the wilderness to vary their diet. Wild onions, sage and mushrooms were some of her favorite seasonings. Service berries, elder berries and chokecherries were free for the picking and a welcome variety to their diet of wild game. Thus she made do until she could have a garden of her own in a mountain paradise.

This pioneer woman was thankful that her children were grown up, and she didn't have little ones to care for. On wash day she could soak their work clothes in the creek for a while then scrub them clean on rocks. She placed them on bushes to dry in the sun or hung them on tree limbs to drip dry. It was still back breaking work and she was glad for no diapers to do too.

Somehow, Will managed to get a milk cow from one of the farmers in the Tobacco Valley. It was Almeda's job to take care of it and do the milking. One of the problems was keeping track of the cow so it wouldn't wander off, since there was no fence. Part of the problem was solved by putting a bell on the cow for daytime tracking, and tying it up nearby at night. She didn't mind milking twice a day, but where was she to keep all the milk? She used a clean dish towel to strain the milk from the milk bucket into all the clean pans or crocks she had. Then setting them in the little creek branch covered with a lid, kept it cool and fresh. When cream raised to the top she skimmed it off to use in their coffee, cooked cereal or over fresh-picked berries. Sour cream and sugar was used as a topping for hot cakes or biscuits. Almeda looked forward to having chickens to lay eggs too.

By fall, the house was ready to move into. It was only a log cabin with two rooms but it was a comfortable dwelling and a big step up from camping out all summer. There was no more sleeping on the ground when nights were getting colder and no more huddling around a campfire wrapped in a blanket to keep warm. There was a cook stove where Almeda could stand up to cook and, also take the chill off inside the cabin. And a roof over their heads to shed rain or snow in the winter. They felt as snug as a bug in a rug and ready to face Winter!

Almeda wrote to her family and friends back in West Virginia telling them of their plans and progress toward their dreams of making their own paradise in the wilderness. She told their daughter Laura Belle to come with her husband and youngin' and have a homestead too. There was plenty of timber land all around next to them that wasn't claimed yet. The only others were a couple of women about two miles down the creek and Workmans, also from West Virginia several miles up the creek. Now that she had a house, Almeda was looking forward to sharing it with her young grandson, Oakey Perkins.

She urged Laura Belle to bring extra things with her on the train such as a huge iron tub to heat wash water over a fire by the creek and things to plant in the garden. She especially wanted roots for rhubarb, gooseberry and red currants besides shoots for a lilac bush. Also needed were garlic bulbs, onion sets, seeds, etc., and if LauraBelle came in the spring, she could help plant the garden, then share the produce.

They not only planted a garden, they put down roots for a life time.

Almeda Stacy's "Receet" for Spring Green Salad

When plants are growing lush and tender in spring pick leaves from dandylion, pig weed, lambsquarter etc. Wash in cool water, shake off excess drips and put in bowl. Make salad dressing of 1 cup sour cream, vinegar and sugar to taste. Drizzle over greens.

For wilted greens fry 2 or 3 slices of bacon, drain and cool. Add vinegar and sugar to the drippings in pan and stir. Dump pan of clean green into hot pan to wilt, turn to wilt other side. Add crumbled bacon to greens and toss. Serve hot with more vinegar to taste.

HARLES BERGETTE

Harles Bergette recalls pioneer days of Pinkham. His mother, Laura Belle Stacy, came from West Virginia with her parents, Will and Almeda Stacy, other brothers and sister and husband, Mr. Perkins and baby son Okey. Her husband stayed in Montana only a short time when he decided he wanted to go back to West Virginia and left wife and son to live with her parents.

Laura Belle filed a claim for a homestead alongside of Will and Almeda's claim, just down the creek. Her brother, Andy, filed for a claim on the other side of the creek. All had cabins built not too far from one another. Okey spent most of his time with his grandparents.

Then John Bertge, a Frenchman from Bangor, Maine, came to work in Frank Slick's sawmill. He met Laura Belle and married her. They lived on her homestead and started raising a family. Harles was born Aug. 11, 1907, and Ressie was born in 1911.

A space was cleared around the little log cabin on the creek bank for a garden spot, apple trees and rhubarb plants. A cellar for storing vegetables was dug into the bank with a door frame made for entering. (This door frame is still there, though the roof is caved in. Apple trees still bear fruit).

Harles remembers how each spring he and Ressie would sit on the high bank to watch logs go tumbling by to Slick's sawmill down below on the Thatcher place. Frank Slick had a dam up the creek near the O'Brien place to collect logs during the winter. In high water logs would be flushed out in a boiling muddy mass to the mill pond below. All living along the creek could hear the rumble and roar of the logs.

Harles started his first year of school in 1913 with Mrs. Hunsinger as teacher. (One of the teachers or school clerk wrote the name Bergette instead of Bertge, thus changed the spelling of their name.) School was in a little log building on his grandpa's place. He remembers them tearing down the logs to move them up to the homestead of Jim and Sis Roberts to be reassembled and then built on to for more room.

Miraculously, to Harles, he entered a brand new school in 1915 with Mrs. Hunsinger still the teacher. Harles had been so busy doing "boy things" that summer he hadn't realized they were building a new school and painted it white!

Harles claims there were no beavers in the creek then, but lots of fish for a boy with a willow fish pole, string and a bent safety pin for a hook. It was also a good place to swim and play. There were plenty of deer around, pheasants, wild rabbits and red squirrels in the trees, but no gophers.

Harles helped his mother on wash day by dipping buckets in the creek for water to fill her washtubs. Laura Belle had a huge black cast iron tub with legs set down by the creek. She would build a fire under it to heat the water. After scrubbing clothes on the washboard and rinsing and wringing by hand, she hung the clothes on bushes and tree branches to dry.

When Ressie started to school she followed Harles across the foot log spanning the creek and up to the schoolhouse. They raced home for lunch to be back to school and play with the Leib kids and others who had their lunch. Harles always had to look out for his little sister, which he didn't really mind.

In 1914, John Bertge was working to improve the Pinkham road with Frank Slick. John was the powder monkey who was to blow rock on the hill near Twin Lakes. He set off six sticks of dynamite but one didn't blow. As he went to check, it blew up and took two fingers off his hand besides face damage. He later became blind due to the blast.

Harles helped his dad log their homestead. The logs were hauled by team and sled during the winter down to Slick's mill. It left big tamarack stumps in what was to be their field. Some stumps were blown out with dynamite to make a bigger garden plot and a place to build a barn and hay shed for the horses.

The little log cabin seemed to grow smaller as children grew older and now another baby was on the way. Lumber was hauled up from Slick's mill for a frame house to be built farther up from the creek. The house was built by the same man who also built a house for Ross and Dora Combs on the same floor plan, only longer. The Bertge house was 18'x 24' with an upper story for sleeping quarters. Narrow stair steps went up from near the outside kitchen door. The 10' kitchen had a partition dividing it from the living room. There were two stoves – a heater in the living room and a wood range in the kitchen on the other side of the wall. A T was put in the stovepipe to share the one going on up and out the roof. Harles huddled by the stovepipe upstairs to keep warm in cold weather.

The whole house was made of sturdy rough lumber. There was no insulation on the walls but sheets of building paper were used under the shiplap on outside walls. The paper came in rolls. Roofing was boards laid on rafters then sheets of tarpaper with more boards nailed on top. There were three tall double pane windows in the house, none on the north or west side.

It was a cold house. When temperatures got below zero fires had to be kept going constantly. Ice still formed on water buckets and water spilled on the floor turned to ice. In other words their whole water system froze up! The house was finished the fall of 1924.

There was a hand-dug well with pick and shovel near a slight gully close to the house. Over the top was a small well house with a pitched roof and a wood floor. It was used a food storage with perishables like cream and butter stored in crocks under the floor next to the cool water in the well.

Violet decided to be born on December 16, 1924, when the temperature dropped to 40 below zero. Harles drove to town the day before but on this morning when his mother told him to go get Sis Roberts the Model T Ford refused to start. Harles hiked over to the main road to catch a ride with Bert Kinney, who was hauling his kids to school in a canvas covered sleigh pulled by a team of horses. Bert went on up to get Sis Roberts and bring her back to help Laura Belle.

Harles remembers going to dances held in people's homes from when he was a kid. All the furniture would be moved outside in the summer time to make room for dancers inside. Everybody liked the fun of square dancing. Jim Roberts was fiddle player, while Fanny Young and Ovella Roberts played banjos. Other musicians were involved at times to change about.

Laura Belle Bertge recorded her claim on the homestead for patent in July of 1919. In 1925, the year after the new house was built, the Bertges sold 60 acres, including buildings, to Cecil Utter. After the Bertges moved to town another son, Johnny, was born. Their old Pinkham homestead is the place where Lee and Madeline Utter call home.

Harles and Helen were married in October of 1927 in Eureka and lived in a three-room cabin along Spring Creek. They eventually bought a house on the hill from Myrtle Peters and then traded it to Amos Kinney for a place on Pinkham. Harles traded his Model T Ford with hard rubber tires to Cecil Utter for a cow. They also had chickens and Harles would balance a basket of eggs on his horse "Appy" to take to town and trade for groceries. They had three children, Delores, Dennis and Bessie.

During World War II they moved to the coast near Portland, Oregon, where both Harles and Helen worked shipyards. "They moved back to Pinkham in 1946 in time for all three children to attend the last year of school being taught by Miss Madeline Rost. Harles attended first school sessions in this building and his kids the last.

DEWEYVILLE DRIVEL – DECEMBER 3, 1904

Several new settlers have gone in upon the head of Pinkham creek, and are making improvements. The distance to this place by the present traveled route is about 12 miles, but the new residents there propose to cut a road to a connection with the Lampton road, which will make the distance to Eureka three or four miles less. – *Eureka Journal, October 29, 1914*

October 29, 1914 - John Brettge*, a resident of the Pinkham creek country, was seriously injured while working on the Pinkham-Eureka road. He was dynamiting loose shale rock and had fired two shots, one of which held fire. He went over to the spot, and just as he reached it the second blast occurred and Brettge was hurled into the air, a piece of rock went through the palm of his hand, his face was peppered with powder and small rock, and his arm broken in two places.

As quickly as possible he was brought to Eureka and placed under the care of Dr. Bogardus. He was found to be in a very critical condition, being in danger of losing his entire eyesight.

The accident was a very unfortunate one, not only for the victim, but for his wife and several children. A slow improvement in the patient's condition has been reported during the past few days.

(The name was changed from Brettge to Bergette)
The 1920 Census name was spelled BURGETT, John

ANDREW STACY

Andrew Stacy, younger son of Will and Almeda Stacy, grew old enough to file for a homestead. He was small in stature, and he built his hut to his size.

Andy chopped down a few trees and limbed them for logs to build the structure. He put up a shelter about 12' by 16' with one small window, a short door and no floor. It was left as packed dirt. His bunk bed was built to fit in a corner and the homemade table and bench sat in the center. The stove had a stove pipe out the low roof. It provided heat, and the flat top a space for coffeepot and frying pan. The hut was built very low, about six feet in the center since Andy was about 5'5" and the door was so short that other men had to remove their hats and stoop to get in.

Andy's claim was on 160 acres of land adjacent to his folks and touching the parcel along the creek belonging to his sister, Laura Belle.

Though Andy's place didn't touch Pinkham Creek it was close enough for his water supply that he carried in a bucket. In those days it didn't matter if the household water froze up in a cold spell. The pail could be set on the stove to thaw out enough to make coffee, or warm up for the wash pan.

Andy was a slow learner with little chance to attend school. He was a willing worker with a strong back if only he could get a good job. Andy joined the U.S. Army in WWI and was put to work in the woods falling spruce trees in the state of Washington. The timber was used in the building of light aircraft.

Andy married Kitty Messler, whose family lived in the Lick Lake area. The couple didn't stay together very long and had no children. Andy stayed a bachelor the rest of his life. He and his brother Jude (Julius) built a two-room log cabin across the creek on their folks place. It was their home base whenever they were on Pinkham.

After the war he came back to Pinkham Creek where he joined others in the struggle for survival. There was hard work involved and one of the jobs was to haul hay for his dad to feed livestock through the winter. The hay was already cut with a horse drawn mower, raked when dry, then piled in little shocks about waist high. It was Andy's job to hitch the team to the hay wagon and haul it home. Since the hay field was the other side of Eureka, Andy got an early start to beat the heat. It was hard, dusty work. It was fork the shocks onto the wagon, arrange it evenly, then move on to the next shock until he had a load. In no time he had worked up a sweat and needed a swig of water from the canvas bag tied to the hay rack.

When home, Andy guided the team up beside the barn where it would be handy to pitch the hay into the haymow. He unhitched the horses and took the harness off and watched them roll in the grass to swipe off their sweat before heading to the creek for water. He would unload the hay in the cool of the morning.

Not all trips to get hay were uneventful. Andy, after getting "likkered" up on moonshine one day, started bragging: On one trip a neighbor woman who seldom got to town needed a ride so Andy stopped by to pick her up. He boosted her sturdy form from behind as she placed her foot on the hub of the wagon wheel to climb on the wagon. She shared the wagon seat with Andy as she adjusted her long skirts and bonnet to shade the sun from her face. Andy let her off in town to do her shopping and pick up the mail while he went to load hay. When Andy was loaded, he stopped in town for lunch and to pick up his passenger. They were both hot and tired with the boring ten

The haying crew at the Andrew Stacy homestead.

miles yet to go. The soft hay was a resting place while the team of horses plodded along the dusty road, knowing their way home. Andy, no stranger to women, described in detail what would be called a 'good roll in the hay' – with no name to be mentioned here.

Times were tough and got even tougher during the Depression. There were no paying jobs to be had unless the Forest Service needed fire fighters. Hot dry weather made the woods combustible, ready to blaze up after a thunderstorm. Men and boys 18 or older were hired on to fight the fire with pick, ax and shovel. (Some boys 16 or 17 lied their age to be able to get a job even it was a cook's flunky or water boy.) Everyone was issued a blanket and fed for the duration of the fire besides paid a minimum wage.

If fires were infrequent, man made fires sprang up in the forest. Different ones were suspected of arson but could never be caught. According to family tales, Andy unknowingly turned himself in for setting forest fires. He went to the ranger station in Rexford to just hang around waiting to be called out. The Ranger asked him, "What are you doing here?" Andy replied, "I'm waiting to go on the fire." "What fire? We don't have a fire now." "Yes you do," said Andy. "There's smoke up on Pinkham Ridge." Instead of going on the fire, Andy was arrested, proven guilty of arson and sent to prison in Deer Lodge for five years.

Andy was another one to use shank's mare (his own two legs) wherever he went. When walking he resembled a road runner bird as he leaned forward with the bill of his cap sticking out front. His hands were held together at his lower back, like tail feathers. His feet, clad in walking boots, did a fast walking trot on his short legs. To hike the ten mile to town from Pinkham, he followed game trails up the draws, over the hills and down for a shortcut, instead of following the crooked road of wagon tracks.

As was the custom of most men, Andy chewed tobacco. His favorite brand, Peerless, was kept in a pouch and carried with him at all times. It was more important than a purse or a billfold.

Andy turned his homestead rights over to Elmer Roberts in 1925 who finished proving up on the place. Elmer procured a patent on August 27, 1930, then had to let taxes go delinquent. Victor Banks paid the back taxes on 100 acres which were filed in his name in 1940.

SYLVESTER STACY
Told by Gladyce to Shirley Lee Casey

Gladyce Stacy Queen Nelson, whose parents and grandparents homesteaded up on Pinkham Creek, remembers the early days and how it all came about. The Stacy family was originally from Wales and France. They then immigrated to the United States. I had an Uncle Henry on my Dad's side of the family, who went to homestead in Canada. So he wrote to my grandparents about what a wonderful place Montana was as he had heard about it. That started it. My grandparents, William and Almeda Stacy, came to Montana about 1906 and the chain reaction was that my Dad and mother, Sylvester and Emma "Lockie" Roberts Stacy were next.

William and Almeda came west from the little town of Welch in McDowell County, West Virginia. They homesteaded 160 acres (Patent 1918) about eight or nine miles out of Eureka on Pinkham Creek. Their first house was a dugout with sod on the roof. Almeda had said "Will, I have to have a big garden." So he made a plot for one. Two other houses were eventually built on their place. William and Almeda's children were all grown before they came west so they didn't raise their family on the homestead. Their children were: Victoria, Henry, Julius, Sylvester, LauraBelle, Cosby and Andrew.

Gladyce's parents, Sylvester and Emma, known as Ves and Lockie, lived in Eureka the first early years. Gladyce remembers her folks telling her, "There used to be an old man by the name of Jimmy Forsyth in Eureka. He had a hack buggy and team of horses. I guess you would call him a cab driver. He'd take Mom and the kids out the Grandpa and Grandma Stacy's place. There was another old man, Dan

Anker that used to visit us. He was supposed to have been a scout for General Custer once."

Sylvester homesteaded on the road to Slick Gulch, not far from William's homestead on Pinkham Creek. They also had 160 acres. Their family eventually included 10 children: Dora, Carl, Elmer, James (Bill), Veon, Doyle, Gladyce, CleElla, Dean and Georgie.

Gladyce explained that her Dad had logged in West Virginia, Greenbrier County, prior to coming to Eureka. He had a logging outfit for hardwood when he was only 21 years old. After coming to Montana, he continued to log in addition to improving his homestead. Sylvester later sold his homestead.

"My Dad logged in a lot of places" Gladyce said. "One time he got a job in Lewiston, Idaho, logging with horses. I had six brothers, some of them were big enough to help Dad. This was about 1924 or 25. And we did have a car. I think it was a 1924 Chevy. Believe it or not, we always had a new car. But Dad built a covered wagon for the trip to Lewiston to be pulled by a team. My sister, Cle Ella, younger than I – we rode in the covered wagon. We insisted on that. Dad had said, "If you want to and if you behave yourselves." And we did.

They returned to Eureka about 1927 and Ves bought a house in town. Then once again moved out on Pinkham Creek on Grandpa and Grandma's place in a second house down in the lower field.

William Stacy donated one acre of ground for the community's little one-room schoolhouse. (It must remain public property, it can never be used for any other purpose.) Pinkham school was located near the fork in the road. All eight grades were taught and Gladyce attended this little school. She recalled, "The teacher taught Doyle and me to spell our name with an 'e' Stacey – but I still spell it Stacy."

"About my grandparents – they were ranchers. Of course they had horses, cows and chickens. Grandpa and grandma raised beautiful gardens and had a lovely orchard. The orchard was just across the road from the schoolhouse. My brother Doyle and I, we'd go up to the orchard to eat cherries. My Grandpa was down at the house below the road, we could hear him, "Get out of there you kids!" I don't think he really cared if we ate cherries or apples but it was something for us kids to do. We'd get down and lay down for awhile and we'd climb back up in the tree. I can still remember those good ripe red cherries."

Their house is not there now. It was made of lumber and Grandpa built a porch the whole length of the house. He'd sit there in late afternoon to rest. They had no electricity or telephones on the ranches in the early days. Gladyce recalled how it was on these homesteads through the years. My mother, Lockie did the washing on the washboard. She was a beautiful washer. I can remember when the boys became teenagers and wore white cords and she washed those on the board. Mom was an immaculate housekeeper; you could have eaten off her floors. My mother worked hard and so did my Dad.

Mom said when Bill was little he had to bring in the wood and kindling. He was left handed but he'd take kindling sticks and make the motion like he was playing a violin in his left hand – the bow. Mom bought Bill his first violin when he was seven years old. He also played for dances. Bill grew up to be an accomplished musician and wrote songs. One of them was about his Pinkham Creek home.

The revenuers and bootleggers were part of the interesting events in this isolated mountainous area. Gladyce remembered a couple of stories.

This is a story about two little sisters, ages five and three. An older brother was supposed to be babysitting these little girls because Mom and Dad would be gone a short time. Instead he decided to go fishing in a little creek that ran nearby. After he had gone, a knock came at the door and the girls answered. There were two gentlemen dressed in suits. They asked if their Dad was home. Of course they said no. Then one of the men stated, "We are revenue men, I hear your Dad has a still. Is that right?" The girls said yes. He asked, "Do you know where he keeps it?" And yes, they would show them.

So the two little girls started out and the men followed. The girls got into a lot of underbrush, sat down and started crying. When the men asked them what was wrong, the girls told them "We are lost. We don't know where the still is. We don't know where our house is." The nice men took the girls back to the house then left. That was the end of that.

The other story: There was a young moonshiner who took a fancy to a girl walking by his house in Eureka on her way to and from high school. He would stop her and talk to her every time he saw her. This went on for six months. At last he invited her into his house for a cup of tea and she knew that he was a moonshiner. Even so – she saw his good qualities. She said "I love him." By the end of the school year they were married.

A bit of work was picking up by then and he went into logging. This couple raised a beautiful family. They were real nice people and a credit to the community all through the years. This happened during the Great Depression. Now this couple has passed on. This goes to say a lot of nice people were moonshiners.

It took a lot of supplies to keep a family the size of Ves and Lockies going. Gladyce said "We went into Eureka to get groceries, George McGlenn – Dad used to trade with him. Sometimes Dad went down to Rexford to Bill Fewkes's country store. We'd go in the car. In the winter Dad would use the sleigh and horses to get staples."

When the Depression hit, it brought really hard times for everybody. Gladyce told how it affected her family. "Grandpa Stacy died in 1919 during the Depression – we lost Grandma a long time before that. So all the rest of my uncles and aunts told Dad that if he'd take care of the funeral expenses, they would give him the ranch. He didn't have money at the time so he mortgaged the ranch. My sister, Dora and her husband Roscoe Combs lived in Idaho. She told Dad she wanted Grandpa's place. Dad said, 'If you pay off the mortgage I'll sign it over to you.' He did and it was a good thing. When the crash hit, they had just started logging with trucks and cats. That was the only time I saw my Dad cry – when they repossessed his equipment. He sold the last team of horses, a beautiful team and paid off a $600 grocery bill he owed. Mom moved into our house in Eureka and put us kids in school. We lived in town, we were now city people."

In the thirties Ves hauled ties from Pinkham Creek to the mill in Eureka – The Brooks and Scanlon Lumber Company. He kept busy – he logged with his own outfit, using wagons in the summer and sleighs in the winter. He had a little place on the Jim Roberts ranch where he kept his horses or whatever. He didn't own it but he stayed there a lot.

Then war came and everyone went to the coast for work. Ves stayed on the coast. When years later he came back to Eureka, he and his brother Andrew batched together. "Some of us kids were nearby," says Gladyce. "We were raising our own families by this time." Gladyce was married to Buck Queen and her kids are Ronald, Lindora, Judy, Teri, Jay and Kathy.

"Dad passed away at age 79. He had been staying with Andy until then. Mom lived in town. She lived to be 86 years old. Mom left the house in town to CleElla and me. We sold it. The house was torn down and the Riverside Park took part of the land."

In 1973 Gladyce married Otto Nelson and they made their home in Libby. Otto was a sawyer in the woods. He worked many years up in the Yaak before his retirement. Gladyce has inherited the trait from her mother to keep a tidy and clean house. Her home is a warm and welcome place for her children, grandchildren and great-grands.

She was born in Eureka July 24, 1919, and spent most of her early years on Pinkham Creek. Gladyce has many memories of neighborly people and the great time she shared with them. It was a way of life that was simple and good.

Pinkham Creek is a picturesque and remote area of Lincoln County that draws the family together for reunions. In 1992 Stacy relatives came from the east coast to west coast to gather at Camp 32 on lower Pinkham Creek. In the year 2002 a family reunion was held at the Pinkham school and camping in the yard.

"Tapestries of Yesterday" The Wonder Stump by Robert L. Graham

Abe Van Horn worked at W.R.Grace (Zonolite) as a cat skinner. From time to time we discussed jobs we had done and things in general, or places we had seen. Once we talked about the Thirties and Forties. Abe mentioned that he had lived in Eureka. He said he knew where he could get good "moon," which was short for moonshine. Abe claimed it was the best he ever tasted. As the story unfolded, he smiled and reiterated how he could drive up the Pinkham Creek road for a ways and park his vehicle. Abe then placed a five dollar bill on a certain stump and then went for a short walk. When he returned sometime later the five dollar bill was gone and in its place was a bottle of "Shine". Abe claimed he had never seen anyone and had no idea who put the jug on the stump but had always wondered about it.

DORA STACY COMBS

Dora was the first-born of Ves and Lockie Stacy before they left West Virginia to come to Montana. Though Dora was still a toddler she liked to be a "little mother" to her baby brother Carl. When more brothers came along (Elmer, Veon, Bill and then Doyle) she was in her element and a great help to her mother. Dora helped care for them when they came down with childhood diseases, but then she was the one to get the dreaded polio. It left her with one leg shorter than the other. Ever after, Dora walked with a decided limp that didn't seem to slow her down. When standing on one foot she balanced on the toe of the short leg.

When her grandfather Will Stacy gave an acre of land for a school in 1911, Dora was one of the first pupils. The next year, she took her little brother, Carl, along with her. She was very careful of her younger brothers and held their hands to help them along over the wilderness wagon trail through the timber. In winter, they trudged through the snow making their own trail.

The little log building used for a school soon became too small for all the pioneer children coming up the creek. In 1915 a new frame school was built on the site and the log school was torn down. Logs were hauled to her Grandpa, Jim Roberts place, then put up again to use for a house.

Some of the pioneer folks were tangled in family feuds and fights back in West Virginia and brought their spit and fire with them. Dora was a little spitfire right from the git-go. She took no teasing or torment from anybody without retaliation. She stood up for her little brothers as well until they could fend for themselves. It was best to be on Dora's good side as she could be a loyal friend, but woe to anyone who got on her bad side.

By the time Dora finished grade school, she had four brothers in the new school, Carl, Veon, Elmer and Bill. Brother Doyle and little sisters Gladyce and CleElla were still too young to go. Dora was a big help to her ma in taking care of little ones, learning to cook and keep a clean house. She also learned to sew on the treadle sewing machine to make dresses for herself as well as her little sisters. Years later, she was to use her sewing skills for her own daughters and make quilts.

By the time the right man came along, Dora was ready to leave home and begin again. Roscoe Combs, a logger, swept Dora off her feet and they tied the knot in 1921.(After Dora left home, Lockie had another baby boy, Dean and another girl named Georgia.)

Their first years were spent following logging operations and living close by. In 1930 they decided to settle down on Pinkham. There were four children: Alice, Robert, Jean and Duaine. They were all to attend the Pinkham school just across the road from their home.

Dora had come back to live on the place of her grandparents, Will and Almeda Stacy. The homestead had been neglected and went to Lee Setser, who paid delinquent taxes and procured a tax deed. Roscoe and Dora did the same when he left the place.

Now Dora had the place of her dreams with a full-grown orchard and a fertile garden spot. She became known for her green thumb as she could produce more than any of her neighbors up the creek. By planting certain plants by phases of the moon, and following the Farmers Almanac, her garden flourished. When weather cooperated, she could even grow cucumbers, corn and tomatoes to ripen. When harvest and canning season came she was an extra busy woman, even though her kids were put to work to help. They didn't want anything to go to waste

Dora was bragged about as the 'best cook up the crick.' She was especially noted for her soda biscuits, light bread, doughnuts and pie crusts made from bear grease. (Bear grease is rendered down to lard just like pork)

One summer Dora was expecting company for Sunday dinner at noon. She got up at the crack of dawn that day to build a fire in the wood cook stove, fill the teakettle with water, and put it on to heat. She then snatched the wire hook hanging on a nail behind the kitchen door, and headed for the chicken house. All the chickens came running to her as she scattered food around. Using the chicken catcher, she slipped the wire around the neck of a nice frying size rooster and held it with one hand as she grabbed both legs together. She then headed to the chopping block at the woodpile. While holding his legs firmly she laid his head on the block, picked up the ax and whacked it off with one blow. While the body jumped around to bleed out, Dora went to get another one to repeat the process until she had enough chickens for a feast.

She took time out to put on the coffee pot and have breakfast while she heated more water and added wood to her fire. The roosters had to be dipped in a large pan of hot water to scald them and loosen the feathers before plucking. Pinfeathers and whispee down were singed off with a blazing flame of paper in the firebox.

After entrails were removed and the chicken washed, it was ready to be cut into pieces for frying. Dora used a sharp knife to do the job right.

By the time chicken was on the stove in the big cast iron fry pan, the oven was hot for her famous soda biscuits made from fresh buttermilk. Her hot biscuits were devoured with milk gravy made in the chicken pan or home made jams and fresh butter.

Dora didn't use a 'receet' as it was called. She just mixed together flour and other ingredients until just about right, then rolled them out to cut on a floured surface before putting in a pan. Same way with heat in the oven, she tested it with her hand in the open oven door, as it had to be hotter for biscuits than for cakes. More wood was put in the firebox if more heat was needed or oven door was left open a crack, if less heat was needed.

To round out the meal, Dora hand churned butter the day before besides pulling and cutting rhubarb to bake pies for the occasion. She had also picked peas fresh from the garden to shell while sitting in the shade. Her linoleum floors had been scrubbed and waxed to a high shine before she could rest.

Dora was fortunate to have an extra shack with a cook stove in it – this was known as her washhouse. It was located between the main house and the water source, making it easier to carry water to heat up in the wash boilers. In summer, it also kept the heat out of the main house and the mess out of her clean kitchen. She also used it during the canning season. The place was ideal for Roscoe to start a batch of hooch on the back of the stove along with a pot of beans for supper. If a Revenuer hove into sight the brewing mash could be quickly taken to the pigpen and dumped into the trough for hog feed. Roscoe also had a hidden still in bushes by the creek. A neighbor boy discovered it while fishing but went right on by as though it never existed. It just didn't pay to be nosey.

Fall was Dora's favorite time of the year. After the first heavy frost it was Christmas tree season. The last of the garden was harvested, cabbage made into kraut and apples in the cellar. Days were getting shorter and cooler. Leaves were changing color and tamaracks turning from green to gold. Temperatures in the 20's set needles on the fir trees so they didn't dry up and fall off when cut. It was time for Dora to sharpen her ax and head for the woods. Small firs growing up after logging made ideal Christmas trees. Perfect shaped Douglas-fir trees were cut down to sell to buyers at tree yards. Trees were sorted to size and tied into bundles before shipped out by train. It took one 12 foot tree to make a bale, two 10 footers, three 8 foot trees, four 6 footers, six 4 footers, and eight deuces. Everyone was paid by the bale and the quality of the tree, which varied through the years. More was paid if trees were hauled to the tree yards than if a truck was sent to the woods by them to pick up trees.

Tree cutting was a family affair. Money earned was used to first pay taxes and other bills before setting aside some to order from a Christmas catalog. All worked together in the woods to cut, drag and load the trees or stack in a pile to be hauled. Alice loved to help her mother and became proficient with wielding an ax. Her specialty was cutting deuces and four footers. She could bend a little tree over with one hand, then whack it off with the other with one sweep of the ax. These thinned thickets made more room for other trees to develop.

One year during tree season, a family heard some pigs squealing in fright. Then there were sounds of loud, angry grunts. Finally, the squealing drifted up the hill on the other side of the creek and dwindled away. When the family got home one wiener pig was missing from the pen and the sow had been in a fight. Bear tracks were found in and around the pen. Earlier, apples left on the tree had been picked by a bear with limbs broken in the process.

Roscoe was killed in a woods accident in 1954. He was following a drag of logs down Virginia Hill to a landing, when the cat turned a corner and a long log swung around and hit him in the head.

Dora was then a widow until she met and married Orval Storie in 1956. He was later killed in Longview, Washington, while jaywalking. Dora's third husband was Sam Knouse. They moved from Pinkham to Libby and sold the homestead to Stan and Beverly Neff in 1984. Their son Steve took it over and it became known as "Cold Comfort Farm."

Dora died in Libby, May 14, 1986, and was laid to rest in the Tobacco Valley Cemetery.

Dora's Soda Biscuits

Fill large bowl about half full of flour; add pinch of salt and handful of sugar and some soda. Swish together with fingers – spoon in lard and mix with hands until texture is right. Add more if needed – pour in buttermilk little at a time until dough is moist enough to form large ball – put on floured table – roll and cut. Place biscuits in large flat pan and bake in hot oven until browned.

JAMES (BILL) STACY

James (Bill) Stacy was born in 1912 to Sylvester and Emma Roberts Stacy who were known as Ves and Lockie. James was soon known as Bill as that is what his grandpa Will Stacy called him. Will and Almeda Stacy had a homestead along Pinkham Creek first, then Ves and Lockie filed for a homestead up the gulch from them to the east. The Pinkham road bisected the Will Stacy homestead and this is where Will donated an acre for a schoolhouse. The road up the gulch turned at the schoolhouse to go up to the Frank Slick homestead above the Ves Stacy homestead. The road became known as the Slick Gulch road.

Bill was the fourth child to be born to Ves and Lockie out of tem children. He walked about a mile down the hill with his older siblings to start school then a mile again up the hill to go home. Bill liked his teacher Mary Rice (21-22) and recalls many good times held at the school house, especially country dances where the little ones slept on coats in the cloak rooms while grown-ups danced the night away.

Grandpa Jim Roberts, Uncle Elmer and Aunt Ovella Cook Roberts, were musicians. He played the fiddle and she the banjo with Abe Cook also on fiddle. They took time out between dances to take a nip of moonshine to keep them in the mood to play all night. At a young age Bill also wanted to play the fiddle. He didn't dare touch his grandpa's fiddle so he rubbed two kindling sticks together to keep the beat. His folks gave him a small fiddle of his own to practice on. He learned to play by ear with the bow in his left hand. Then in later years it was his turn to play for dances and sometimes sing along. Bill also composed a song entitled "Way Up on Pinkham Bluff." Ivan Anderson played guitar with him for dances at the Pinkham school or the Senior Citizen Center. They also played for entertainment at Mountain View Manor nursing home where everybody liked the old hillbilly tunes.

Bill was caught in the great flu epidemic in 1918 along with most other people. Doctor Long prescribed Canadian whiskey for a cure-all and Bill guzzled it down as it was prescribed for kids too. It evidently worked as he lived to tell the tale. Not everybody could get pure whiskey but some had moonshine as a substitute. Bill chuckled at the sight of extra tall "old Doc Long" settling his large frame in behind the wheel of his little Model T Ford. He had to sit hunched over to peer out the windshield with his knees drawn up almost to his chin.

Bill remembered making moonshine along with his dad and others who lived in the Pinkham hills near a cold stream of water. A still he said was built in a variety of ways but the most common was a rock cairn to hold the fire, the boiler set on top with a dome to catch the steam. Cold water was used to condense the steam and run it through copper tubing into a jug or jar. The mixture used determined the type of drink. If fermented fruits were used you had brandy, if rye or corn were mixed with yeast to get it going it turned into rye or corn whiskey, also called moonshine, hooch, or white lightning.

At the young age of thirteen, Bill got his first steady job away from home for the summer. He went to work for Walt Holder as mule horse wrangler. Bill was to grain and water the working teams then keep tabs on them at night while they grazed. He used a lantern as he walked among the animals to check on them. He also had a dependable bay horse that he tied to his leg so he would be jerked awake if he fell asleep on the job. Bill got paid $60 a month and felt rich on payday!

Like most of the other Pinkham pioneers Bill became a jack-of-all-trades and went where the work was. He learned to drive a team at a young age and handle his end of a two-man crosscut saw. At one time he had a job down along the westside of the Kootenai River. He drove a team down the trail (there was no road yet) to where he skidded logs. When he worked as a sawyer he picked a partner who knew how to keep the saw filed sharp, it worked better that way. There was nothing worse than a dull saw to drag a man down and wear him out.

In 1922 the Stacy family went to the West Coast for work. Since they were loggers, that's where they got a job. Ves and four of his boys: Carl, Elmer, Bill and Veon traveled six days in a Model T Ford through

Canada to get to Moses Lake, Washington. There was no road down the Kootenai River and very poor roads in Canada. They camped out along the "trail" each night and ended up near Chehalis before finding work. They found the logging different there as steam rigs were used to load logs on railroad cars to haul logs out of the woods. Loggers were paid $1.87 per day.

Bill was back on Pinkham Creek when he met Lillie Armstrong, who came to Pinkham with her family from California. They were married in 1931, after he courted her by taking her to all the Saturday night country dances. The couple ended up with ten children of their own. They were: James (Jiggs), Jerry, Beryl, Billy, Donald, Dean, Ronald, Marlene, Doreen and Allan.

During WWII the family moved to Washington where Bill worked for Boeing as pot puncher. By 1945 Bill decided he wanted some of the action of war so he joined the U.S.Navy even though he had five kids. He took boot camp training in San Diego but the war was over before he saw any action. He recalled how, during the war, his family lived on rations. The government gave out ration stamps for sugar, coffee, meat, shoes, gas, tires and even whiskey. Each person was allowed so much. If shoes wore out before the next stamp was allowed, you went barefoot. Everyone was careful to make things last, nothing was wasted. Bill noted that gas to go to work was his biggest problem.

After the war Bill brought his family back to Pinkham where his older boys attended school until the school was consolidated with Eureka. Now the younger generation was involved in community activities and dances at the Pinkham school where Bill played his fiddle.

In 1981 Bill and Lillie celebrated their 50th wedding anniversary at Senior Citizen's Center. All ten of their children were there to help celebrate besides a host of relatives and friends. The couple spent their retirement years in Eureka where they frequently attended the Senior Citizen's Center activities.

Lillie died with cancer in 1985, and Bill passed on in 1987 at the age of 76.

PINKHAM BLUFF by Bill Stacy

I never had a pair of shoes
that weren't old hand me downs,
and my daddy's morning coffee
was made from left over grounds
My mommy wore no jewelry
or any store bought stuff
But hope was on the hill top
way up on Pinkham bluff
    chorus:
        Way out in the country
        there's a different way of life
        where a man thinks of his neighbor
        and not his neighbors wife
        Life was far from fancy
        and sometimes mighty rough
        But contentment made it worthy
        Ten miles on Pinkham Bluff

And the only family treasures
was a beat up radio.
but it took us to the place
where we knew we never go.
We never had much money,
but we always had enough
because money didn't matter much
way up on Pinkham Bluff
    chorus

Nearly every winter when
the snow gets on the ground
the roads will all be closed
And Old Bill can't get to town.
As long as he had a little tobacco
and Ma didn't chew much snuff,
Yes them winters didn't seem so long
way up on Pinkham Bluff.
    chorus

BEN STUART, PAYTON PYLES, MOSES BREWER

A bachelor by the name of Ben Stuart built a log cabin on Pinkham Creek up and beyond all other pioneers. His place was along the trail to Pinkham Mountain lookout. He was a tall, slender man but blacksmithing was his trade.

Ben never proved up on a homestead. He was a squatter and lived in his cabin only part time when he wanted to be alone. He worked for the USFS during summer months to keep their mules and pack horses shod. While in Rexford he lived in a small shanty down by the wooden bridge that crossed the Kootenai River to the Island.

Sometimes Ben lived in a shack down across the railroad track in Eureka. He was kept busy shoeing horses as that was a time of horse and buggy days. After he died the Forest Service burned his cabin on Pinkham Creek. They didn't care to have squatters living in the forest.

Ben Stuart was a tall lanky man with a long stride. Since he didn't have a horse of his own, he used shank's mare (his own two legs). He made good time as he strode to town with a pack on his back and a hat on his head. It was 18 miles one way, 36 round trip. Ben was well known to everyone, so at times he would stop to talk or stay for a meal with another pioneer along the way.

When he stayed in town during the winter Ben was known to go to the post office almost everyday. He was intelligent and kept up on current events. He wrote letters to government officials expressing his views and opinions. Ben could be a thorn in the side of USFS local personnel as he had his own ideas of how and what should be done.

Another bachelor staking his claim in the Pinkham hills was Payton Pyles. His cabin was built in the Teepee Lake area along the trail from the Andy O'Brien homestead on Pinkham Creek to the homestead of Joe O'Brien on the Fortine side of the hill. He gave up his bachelorhood when he took Ellen Caldwell as his wife.

People interviewed have little memory of Payton Pyles. He let his homestead go back to the USFS in 1936.

Moses Brewer was another bachelor who filed for a homestead along Pinkham Creek. He proved up on his land that extended on both sides of the creek. His place was eventually purchased by Bert Roe to pasture his cattle during summer months.

TOM MOORE

Tom Moore and Tilly were married in West Virginia before coming to Montana to take up a homestead on Pinkham Creek. They chose

160 acres where Cooks Run empties into Pinkham. It has changed owners several times but old-timers still refer to it as the Moore place. (T35N,R27W,Sec 20)

The Moores came to the area in the early 1900's when the country was still a wilderness. Their house was built by the side of the narrow road, close enough so that no driveway was needed. It was made of logs cut from their land and hand hewed on two sides with a broad ax to make flat walls of the large two story structure.

Everyone going up or coming down the creek passed by their door and shared news of the day. The road was kept open in the winter by passers-by.

The barn was also built by the roadside. An agile person could jump from the passing vehicle right into the barn loft. It was handy for putting hay into the barn, just pull over to the side with the team and wagon and there it was. Tom believed in the less labor involved the better.

He was also not above accepting help from neighbors, be it either a helping hand with work or a hand out. Many a side of venison was handed over with no payment expected to make sure the little ones had meat to eat.

Tom was a tall, slim man known as TeeHee Tom. He had a horse and single buggy that he took to town by himself. He whipped the horse to a gallop with the buggy bouncing on the bumps of the single track road, dust flying. He made the trip faster than any of his neighbors, who he seldom met on the narrow crooked road.

Tom and Tilly had five children. Hila, Druzilla and Elsie went to the upper Pinkham School, when it opened in 1910 along with the Workman, O'Brien and Cook families. Ida and Willie were handicapped and were cared for at home.

Eventually Hila married Sid Workman (an uncle of Sid Workman now on Pinkham). Druzilla married Romeo Garrison from the Yaak and Elsie married Pete Woods, who had land below Pinkham Falls.

Tom Moore registered the patent for his 160 acres on Pinkham at the Lincoln County courthouse in June of 1926. He then sold it to Louis Kenshella in 1929 and moved his family to town to live somewhere on Pinkham Avenue near the railroad.

JAMES QUEEN

Jim and Druzilla Queen also came from West Virginia to settle on Pinkham. They had a cabin across the creek and up the hill from the Tom Moore place. Druzilla and Tilly Moore were sisters.

They had three children, Hazel, 8; Tom, 6; Buck, 4, and Druzilla was expecting another baby. Hazel and Tom also attended the upper Pinkham School. To support his family, Jim got work at the Eureka sawmill, a 15-mile walk from home. Most times he stayed in town during the week, then packed groceries home in a backpack for his family on weekends.

Druzilla gave birth to a baby girl at home on May 3, 1911. Her sister, Tilly Moore, helped care for her and the other children. But Druzilla never recovered her health again.

One morning when baby May was several months old, Tilly came to visit her sister. The children seemed to be alone so she asked Hazel and Buck where their mother was. They told her that she was still in bed asleep, but their mother never woke up. Tilly went in and found that Druzilla was dead.

When Joe and Mary Webb heard about the baby girl on Pinkham with no mother, they offered to take care of her. Jim agreed. At that time the Webbs lived on Rush Lake in the vicinity of Frank Lake. Joe hiked over the hill to Pinkham on a cold fall day after a snowfall to get the baby. He heard the cry of a panther on the way.

The Queen children were on their own a lot while Jim kept his job. One time he sensed that guardian angels had been there with the children. They had tried to build a fire in the cold cabin with sticks, paper and an excess of kerosene. There were burned match sticks around the stove but the fire didn't light. It could have exploded into a house fire.

After two years of hardships, Jim Queen decided to take his family back to West Virginia. When he went to get his two-year-old daughter, May, Mary exclaimed, "You take this baby over my dead body!" So May Queen was raised by the Webbs. Joe had a cousin "Doc" back in Ohio. When he came to Montana to visit he fell in love with May and they were married.

After raising a family and surviving her husband, May resided in the Mountain View Manor nursing home until her death in 1998.

Jim Queen married a widow with four children in West Virginia. They then had four more of their own. Hazel and Buck came back to Montana to visit. Buck decided to stay and married Gladyce Stacy.

This information was gleaned from interviews, various old-timers and Pal Johnson, daughter of May and Doc Webb.

WILLIAM A. PAYNE

One of the Pinkham Pioneers was named William A. Payne. He

called himself Bill but also answered to Billy. Maybe his mother called him Wee Willy. But Billy wanted a home of his own so he came west to file a claim. He picked a spot on a side hill up a draw from Pinkham Creek (now known as Banks Draw) but his place was dry as a bone. Even so, he built a shack and made it his home. Now he was a Hill Billy.

Bill wasn't a man to hew ties for a living even though he was a bachelor with only himself to worry about. He was a small man, about five feet tall, and weighed a little over 100 pounds soaking wet. Neither was he a man to care for livestock, which gave him a pain to even think about.

But Bill could drive an auto and he could be a salesman. So Bill bought a Model-T Ford. He built a big box on the back with compartments for storage of different sized items. He would sell time-tested Watkins products. Bill sent an order to the company in Winona, Minnesota, for the basics to get started, then waited for them to come in on the train.

Thus Mr. Payne became the first Watkins salesman in the area to deliver goods to the customer's door. He had black pepper and red pepper, vanilla and other extracts, dry mustard and sage for homemade sausage or chicken dressing to please all the good cooks. He had red liniment or white liniment for aches and pains, menthol camphor salve for colds and coughs, Old Red Barn salve or petro carbo salve for scrapes and bruises. So Mr. Payne became a pain killer by selling products to alleviate pain.

Bill was a good salesman. He had rather unique qualities that helped. His voice came out in a whisper. He was soon known to his neighbors as "Whispering Willy." When he related the news of the community at his stops it sounded as if he was sharing their secrets. Willy was often asked to share a family meal. He gladly accepted. They could hear more about their neighbors and he wouldn't have to go home and eat alone. Children got to know him. When they heard his Model-T come they shouted, "Ma, here comes Whispering Willy!"

Bill was a fair man to deal with. If a homesteader didn't have the money to pay, which most didn't, he would make a trade. He took jars of home-canned jelly or jam, milk, butter, eggs, a hunk of venison or vegetables from the garden. He even traded for jugs of moonshine

The moonshine started him into another business. Since he sold Watkins products over the whole area including Tobacco Valley and into Canada, it was easy for him to become a Whiskey Runner. He couldn't compete with the big wheels but it was a lucrative business on the side. Whispering Willy wore a long black overcoat as his habitual attire. As he was short and his back was bent, sometimes the overcoat would drag in the snow. The coat had huge pockets where he could stash bottles of booze. Willy was very willing to reach deep down into a pocket to exchange moonshine for greenbacks when approached by certain people while making the trade.

A West Kootenai resident remembered the Watkins salesman coming to their house with his wares when she was a little girl. She liked the free gum he gave to children. Her mother had invited the man to stay for dinner. While he was sitting at the table, the girl snuck up behind him to feel of his hair which she thought was a wig. Her mother gave her the eagle eye and shook her head in time to arrest the motion and save the situation.

Bill was one of those who did go through with proving up on the homestead by 1923 but he didn't stay there. For one reason, his place was so far back in the hills it was hard to get there by winding around through the trees and gullies in good weather. It was impossible in winter snows or in the spring when the ground was soft. He sold it to Charles and Art Lindsy in 1926 who let the taxes go delinquent. Hofert Tree Company got a tax deed in 1947 on the place.

For a time, Bill moved into shacks that were closer to town, those left empty by other folks who had moved on. The last place Bill lived was down near the railroad tracks in Eureka. From there no one seems to remember.

So Whispering Willy was a mystery man. Nobody knows where he came from but his final resting place is in the peaceful Eureka cemetery.

PLUID HOMESTEADS
Sections 4 and 10, T26N, R27W

The Pluid brothers, Ernest, Percy, Chester, Cecil and Frank decided to heed the advice of the saying "Go west, young man, go west." They left Michigan in the first part of the century and traveled by train as far as the Flathead Valley where the tracks ended. The young men were used to hard work and knew how to wield an ax and a crosscut saw. They went right to work on crews to log the town site of Whitefish, thus becoming part of creating the historic stump town.

But they didn't stop there. Rumors were going around that there was work and homesteads available in the Tobacco Valley area. So the Pluids jumped on the train again to head for Eureka, which ended their search for a place to put down roots.

The railroad was buying hand-hewed ties and there was standing timber available on the hills in the area. But most of it belonged to someone else. To get timberland a man had to file for a homestead so that was what the Pluid brothers did. Their claims were in the Pinkham area but not on the creek itself. Percy settled over at Tobacco Siding. Chet Pluid filed for a timber claim in Section 4, near the Billy Payne place. Frank Pluid found a good timber stand up on top of the divide above the Frank Slick homestead. His place was remote up in Section 10 but the brothers worked together to clean out a wagon trail and build log cabins to live in.

These virile young men wanted wives to care for their home and raise a family. For partners they chose young women of pioneer stock who were used to roughing it.

Percy married Ethel Price of Eureka and they had a family of three boys and three girls. Percy never homesteaded on Pinkham. Ernie and Grace had Ernie Jr, Floyd, Effie and Illa, who married Hiram Reynolds. Ernie Jr. was killed when he was bucked off a horse.

Chet picked Nellie Baker and Frank chose Harriet Schultz, whose folks had a homestead near Glen Lake. Both couples tied the knot January 26, 1909, in Kalispell by standing up with each other.

Chet and Nellie had a daughter, Eunice. (Brothers of Nellie were Charlie, Chester, Walter and Billy Baker) After Nellie died, Chet married Lizzie Johnson, a widow with a family of four: Alfred, Albert, David and Josephine. Chet and Lizzie then had Irene, who married Otto Olt. Josephine became the bride of Stub Greene.

Frank and Harriet lived in the wilderness with no close neighbors. Horses provided transportation over rough trails through the trees as they went up and down hill. There were no telephones, radio or mail service. They had each other and many times Harriet was alone when Frank was working away from home. They had ten kids all together but only four grew to be adults.

Frank Lyle died soon after he was born and the next one died an infant also. Don became a teenager before he developed a goiter on his neck. When he was eighteen he went hunting in November with snow on the ground. He shot a buck deer and dressed it out before sitting on a log to rest. When he didn't come home that night they tracked him the next morning and found him where he had bled to death from a ruptured goiter.

Both Zula, three years old, and Delora, one and one half years, died with the flu in 1918. Madge reached school age before she met her demise. She fell out of the barn while playing. Winnie carried her to the house but she soon died of her injuries. The four survivors were Harrel, Winnie (Winston), Jim and Neal who died at the age of thirty-one.

Winnie remembers starting the first grade three times. The first two years he dropped out after about three months when winter set in and it was too far to walk. The third time he started first grade his folks had moved into the Billy Payne place next to Chet's homestead, which was closer to the Pinkham school.

Children from both families walked to school together with the older ones taking off at a fast pace. Josephine stayed back to walk with Winnie and Jim who was also starting first grade. When winter snows came the older ones broke trail for the little ones. They all stood around the huge wood heater at school that the teacher kept stoked with wood to warm frosty fingers and toes.

An incident at school that Winnie recalled happened during the noon hour. The kids were enacting a mock trial and the culprit was found guilty. He was sentenced to hang by the judge. A rope was secured over the top support pole on the front gate and the noose was put around his neck. The teacher happened to ring the bell at this time which interrupted the lynching and saved the day.

Something else the Winnie remembered was the little duck pond between the Chet Pluid homestead and the Billy Payne place. It was a great pond to play on the ice or to learn to swim in summer or build a raft to float. Older siblings or cousins always watched out for younger ones.

Winnie remembers coming down with the German measles and being confined to his bed under the stairway in the two story Payne log house. The contagious disease was passed from child to child and family to family. There were no immunizations to prevent catching it in those days but once you survived you were immune and wouldn't get it again.

The Pluids were all able loggers and progressed with the times. At first they started with crosscut saws to log homesteads. After the trees were down they used the ax to trim off limbs almost to the top, which they left on for stability. The top limbs kept the log from rolling while a broad ax was used to trim all four sides to make a straight edge. Thus the log was made into railroad ties when cut into 8 1/2-foot lengths with the saw. This was a two man operation to run the crosscut saw.

The ties were then loaded onto a wagon pulled by a team of horses to the railroad landing. The ties were unloaded by hand, one man on each end to stack them on the ground or sometimes to load them into a railroad car sitting on the siding. This was all hard work and took them several days to get a load and bring groceries from town with the paycheck. Storekeepers would give credit to those who needed food for their families before payday.

Progress was made when small sawmills became popular. The circular saw was powered by a gas engine. It could cut much straighter and faster than a man making them by hand. They still used crosscut saws for falling trees, then skidded them to a landing with horses where logs were bucked (sawed) to the right length. The logs were then rolled onto the carriage with cant hooks to be pushed on a roller into the saw to be cut full length. A man was needed besides the sawyer to catch the slabs from the saw and pitch them onto a slab pile. The cut tie was loaded on the wagon or in time, a truck to haul a load into town. Some logs were large enough to turn for another tie.

Chet Pluid purchased a portable sawmill that was used on their homesteads and moved to a different setting in the timber. Thus the skid trails were shorter for the horses to pull the cut trees. A teamster for the horses was one of the first jobs that a ten or twelve year old could do. Some of the horses could almost do the job by themselves and the youngsters soon learned to keep out of the way of a moving log. Another job for the young was stacking slabs. Frank Pluid soon became known as a master with the cant hook at a sawmill.

After their own homesteads were logged off, the Pluids moved the mill to other places and made more settings. They moved their families along with them to be closer to home so they could drive their horses to work.

Chet Pluid proved up on his homestead and got his patent May 13, 1926. Then it was registered in the name of Russell (Stub) and Jo Greene December 6, 1954, and Jim Hurst in 1960. Since then it has been broken into smaller portions.

Frank Pluid proved up on 100 acres, then turned it over to Horace Sampson in 1926. Sampson was a grocery store owner in Eureka. Later it was sold to Tom and Charles Finch, then to Van Finch.

The only record of Ernie Pluid having land on Pinkham was when he paid the taxes on 40 acres that was originally homesteaded by Lula May Mikalson. This then gave him a tax deed to a place in Section 4 next to Chet. He later sold it to Basil Buckmaster then others down the line owned it including Bill and Edna Gwynn for Christmas tree stumpage.

The Pluids passed their love of logging and working in the timber down to the next generation. Times were changing and new inventions made things easier. Gas powered chainsaws were used to cut down trees, first a cumbersome two man saw then a lighter one-man model. Trucks were used for hauling and Caterpillars to skid. Horse logging became almost obsolete.

After World War II there was a great demand for lumber to build homes for returning veterans. As someone said, "You could find a small sawmill behind every stump." The loggers were now "gypos" getting their own timber, their own sawmills to cut cants or ties and trucks to haul with.

A cant is a timber cut four inches thick that can be sawed again to make 2x4's. A good sawyer at a mill could saw a tie or two from a log and saw a cant also. Cants were also made from the top of a tree too small for ties.

Winnie got his first truck by trading his pickup to George McCully for a 1939 truck with an 11-foot flat bed. This is what he used to haul ties to the railroad and cants to the large sawmills to be cut into 2x4 studs and planed. Gas was then 20 to 25 cents per gallon. When hauling off from Pinkham, he sometimes met the Pinkham school bus driven by Lee Utter. The road would accommodate only one way traffic so each driver had to get off the road on their side to pass. The load of cants or ties would still scrape the side of the bus.

Winnie ran the saw in the mill for Columbus Clark for a while, which had many good sets on Pinkham. He was also a partner with Fred King in a sawmill. They had seven men working at the mill when they got into a good timber stand up Pinkham and took out 10,000 ties from one set. Later Winnie got his own sawmill and bid in competition for small timber sales put up by the Forest Service. By this time, Winnie and Ada had sons of their own old enough to help with the work using bigger and better equipment.

"RECEET" FOR WASHING CLOTHES

1. bild fire in backyard to het kettle of rain water.
2. set tubs so smoke won't blow in eyes if wind is pert.
3. shave one hole cake lie sope in bilin water.
4. sort things. make 3 piles. 1 pile white, 1 pile cullord, 1 pile werk britches and rags.
5. stur flour in cold water to smoth, then thin down with bilin water.
6. rub dirty spots on board, scrub hard. then bile. rub cullord but don't bile – just rench and starch.
7. take white things out of kettle with broomstick handel. then rench, blew and starch.

8. spred tee towels on grass.
9. hang old rags on fence.
10. pore rench water in flower bed.
11. scrub porch with hot, sopy water.
12. turn tubs upside down.
13. go put on cleen dress – smooth hair with side combs. brew cup of tee

– set and rest and rock a spell and COUNT BLESSINGS.

O'BRIEN FAMILY

Andrew Jackson Benjamin Harrison O'Brien and wife Sarah Frances Georgia Jane had fifteen children but used shorter names on them. There were nine boys and six girls with all of them born in West Virginia. Their son Edward and family stayed there instead of moving to Montana.

When word got back to Greenbrier County, West Virginia, that there were homesteads available in Montana the O'Briens were all ears. A son, Dow (Lorenzo), eighteen years old, came to the Pinkham Creek drainage to check out the rumors. He wrote back home to inform his family that it was the perfect place to be.

Pat, the youngest son, describes life on the homestead: "As you know we left West Virginia in March 1910. Dad was going to stop in eastern Montana, but the conductor on the train we were on advised him not to as the Indians were pretty mad at the whites and still doing some fighting.

"William 'Bill' Workman wrote my folks of the new country and of a homestead that was relinquished, had a good little meadow and a small cabin. So we moved up on Pinkham Creek. The road was just 2 ruts for a wagon, narrow and crooked, fourteen miles from Eureka where we got off the train. The 160 acres had beautiful big timber and lots of good clear pure water. The folks were pleased with the place.

"We lived in the 14'x16' cabin and a large tent the first year while getting logs ready for a house which was built in 1911. The house was two storeys with four rooms downstairs. On the homestead we finally got land enough cleared (Mother helped too) to get a deed (in 1925). Dad gave 1 acre for a school that was built in 1912 or 13."

Leo O'Brien, son of Dow, relates that the school also served as a church. His grandfather Andy O'Brien taught Sunday school and also served in place of a Catholic priest when one was not available.

Leo also says that the house was built of hewed logs that fit squarely on top of each other. All the men and boys of the family helped with this project of sawing down trees with a crosscut saw then hewing them to size with a broad ax. The house was built below the road down by the creek.

The project of the women and girls was to provide food for the crew. Jane, who was half Cherokee, was a good hunter. She shot the game, cleaned it out and dragged it home with a horse. It took a lot of meat to feed the family. There were usually four or five deer hanging up at a time to be used. There was no designated hunting season then.

(According to old school records there was a school held at upper Pinkham in 1910. It was in a log cabin and the teacher was Estella Milnor from Troy. She boarded at the Bill Workman home. In February 1911, County Superintendent F.D. Head transferred a teacher from Fortine District 14 to Pinkham District 18. Trustees appointed by the County Superintendent were C.W. Workman, Henry Stacy and Frank Slick. Clerk was Mrs. N.E. Workman. The school had twenty pupils.)

When the O'Brien family moved into the community the little log cabin school was bursting at the seams. Frank Slick sawed rough lumber in his sawmill and planer to build a new school on land donated by O'Briens in 1912. Enrollment jumped to thirty registered children.

Jim, the eldest son, brought his wife with him to Montana, but she was a delicate lady and didn't care for being a pioneer and roughing it in the wilderness. They soon moved on to where there was more civilization. They went down to the steamboat town of Jennings on the Kootenai River in its heyday of over one thousand people. There Jim became the town constable. This is a story told about him:

"Jim O'Brien was town constable of Jennings. One day he took a prisoner down on the train to Libby. He was going to put him in jail but as they were coming up the street from the river the prisoner started to run. Jim shouted to him to stop. The prisoner kept running so Jim fired a shot at him. The shot missed and hit a nearby high board fence, ripping off one of the boards. When the shot was fired, the prisoner froze in his tracks. Jim growled, 'If you move, I'll fill you so full of holes you won't hold water.' Needless to say, the constable took his prisoner to jail."

John O'Brien gave up frontier life and took his family back to West Virginia to more civilization in 1921. While in Montana, John and his wife operated one of the seven saloons in Gateway, a booming town on the Kootenai River near the Canadian Border.

Howard O'Brien migrated to Alberta, Canada, after working as a lumberjack in Montana for a few years.

Dow O'Brien with his team of horses.

Joseph O'Brien decided to stay in Montana. He filed for a timber and mining claim over the hill a couple miles from his dad in Section 25. He proved up on his claim and had it recorded in 1924. Joe was a lumberjack from way back. After he helped his dad clear land and build a house, he now had his brothers help him build a house of his own.

Joe was also an accomplished moonshiner. He learned back in West Virginia and brought his skills to the hills of Montana. He could cook up a batch of corn "likker" in a short time for local parties or to trade. Joe was one of those who "boot-legged" across the border into Canada.

When the Bonners Ferry Lumber Company came to log off this part of the country, Joe hired on as a lumberjack. His skills soon became known to the company so he became a river boss on the Kootenai log drives from Canada down on the river to Libby and beyond. The last area to be logged of big timber was at Camp 32 on lower Pinkham Creek. The Bonners Ferry Lumber Company bought out all the homesteaders in that area for the timber. After the logs were taken the land reverted to the government and is now managed by the U.S. Forest Service.

Joe sold his homestead to John Kinshella and took his family out west near his brother Jim. His homestead finally went to Quirk Cattle Company when they secured a tax deed in 1940.

Ben and Dow O'Brien, as young single men, helped their folks prove up on their homestead. Younger than they were Della, Nora, Howard, Malinda, Richard, Patrick, and Pearl. Andy and Jane still had quite a family growing up at home even with the older boys grown up with families of their own.

Malinda O'Brien married Levi Young, another young man on Pinkham. Mary O'Brien married Joe Webb. They adopted Mae Queen and lived in Rexford for many years.

Dow was paired up with his dad on a crosscut saw one day while falling timber up on the hill, when Andy slipped and fell. He broke his leg. Dow gave first aid as best he knew how. He pulled the leg to get it lined up and snapped the bone in place. He strapped two straight limbs of trees along his leg for stability, then found more sturdy branches to make a travois. With Andy loaded on, Dow pulled him down the hillside to home. When Andy was taken by team and wagon to the doctor in Eureka, his leg was ready for the cast. The doctor told Dow he did a good job for his dad.

Dow married Blanche Baillargon, a French Canadian. They stayed in the area while Dow worked as a lumberjack for the various sawmills. They had six children who went to school in Eureka.

Dow moved his family to the Black Lake area in 1930 where they took over a homestead. They proved up on it together as they raised their family. The younger ones attended school there. Dow entered grain and produce from his farm at the Lincoln County fair. In later years he retired to Rexford until his death.

The children of Dow and Blanche were Leona, who married Clay Benefield; Frank married Trudy Woods of Pinkham; Fred married Ruie Peterson from Whitefish; Leo married Shirley Stark of Eureka; Louie married Beverly Bernhard; and Richard married Pat Howard from Libby. Della married Lon Smith and Nora married Ed Smith, brothers who homesteaded near Black Lake as farmers. Martha married Ray Nelson from Kalispell. Their great grandson became funeral director in Libby (Niles Nelson).

Dow's younger brothers, Ben and Pat, went farther west to be near their other brothers. Ben eventually came back when he retired and is buried in the Tobacco Valley cemetery near Eureka alongside his mother.

Pearl, the youngest in the family, wanted to become a teacher and go on to school. But her mother was declining in health from bearing too many children and living a life of hard work, so Pearl took care of her instead. They lived in Eureka until Jane's death in 1925 at the age of forty-four. Pearl then left with her dad to go west to Vancouver along with others in the family.

Andy kept his homestead on Pinkham but when times got really tough, he let the taxes go delinquent. Sylvester Stacy paid back taxes in 1947 and took possession of the place. He then sold it to Charlie and Alta Workman, who passed it on to their son Chuck and Vivian Workman in 1960. They built a house above the new wide road close to a spring for water. They also moved the school house up there. Some young folks held a party there one night and the school house caught fire and burned.

This information was furnished by Leo O'Brien.

FRANK SLICK

By the time Frank Slick came seeking a homestead around 1910 most of the bottomland was already taken along the creek. After exploring the area he found the perfect place up a draw to east of the Will Stacy homestead and above Sylvester Stacy. There was a bubbling spring of water forming a small stream flowing down through a flat and then on down the canyon. This eventually became known as Slick Crick flowing down Slick Gulch.

After filing a claim for this prime piece of ground he built a little log cabin near the spring with primitive tools. Right from the start he saw the possibilities of the place and the potential growth of the community. Everyone had a good stand of timber to harvest but they were doing it the hard way with crosscut saws and a broad ax to shape the logs. Frank decided to get a sawmill – not a small one but a big enough to saw logs into dimensional lumber.

To do all this he needed power – if he got a steam engine he needed a steady flow of dependable water like what was in Pinkham Creek. Frank approached Harry and Ella Thatcher, who had a homestead situated on the creek. Together they made a plan that would benefit the whole community. Those living up the creek could fall their timber, cut it into lengths and skid it to the creek to wait for high water. Spring run off would carry logs to the millpond!

The sawmill operation was highly successful. Frank added a planer mill to have lumber also. Fellow homesteaders were his mill workers as well as the suppliers of logs for the mill. They were soon using the left over slabs; bark side out to build shacks and sheds on their home places.

Frank, a natural leader, saw the need of a better road and organized the pioneers into a road construction crew. The wilderness trail, which followed the path of least resistance up the Pinkham valley, was as crooked as a snake with ups and downs that were hard on a team of horses pulling a load of lumber or ties. Trees had to be cut down with crosscut saws to make the road wider, and then limbed with an ax. Good logs were saved for the mill but brush was piled up and burned.

Frank was the one to get a contract from the county to rebuild the Pinkham road. Making the road bed was the biggest challenge. Stumps in the way had to be removed, either by digging around them to loosen dirt and then pulled out by horses, or blasted out with dynamite. Big rocks were also blasted to break them up for removal. A team of horses pulled a slip (a tool shaped like a large sugar scoop with two handles on the back to hold onto like a plow) to scrap off the road and smooth it down. Larger rocks that would catch a wagon wheel were removed with a heavy fork or shovel by man handling. The slip peeled off the high spots and filled in the low spots of the road.

Back in the beginning, there were no bridges built. Those living across the creek forded it unless water was too high to cross during spring runoff. The road was built around points in Twin Lakes as a simple method of construction. It wasn't until the 1950's that the road was straightened and widened by county bulldozers and graders when dump trucks hauled fill dirt to cross the points of the lake.

In dry summers, white clay dust plumed from horses feet to cover wagon occupants with a dust coat. In wet weather, clay mud clung to horses feet and wagon wheels. In really bad spots, slabs were laid across the road and made a bumpy corduroy ride. In winter, snow was plowed off with a team of horses pulling a homemade V made out of planks. The driver would stand on the cross beam on the wide angle, horses hitched to the point to pull.

Clint Slick came to file a homestead claim beside his brother up the gulch. Together they worked on their homesteads to prove up on them. They cut timber to clear the meadow below the spring for a hay field. They built a big log barn for horses and a milk cow, with a hayloft above. The brothers built a dam below the spring to form a pond – then stocked it with fish. It also served as irrigation water for the field. Clint kept at it only a few years, then sold out and left the country.

Frank Slick used lumber from his own mill for the first frame house in the Pinkham area. It was a large two-story house with two big bedrooms upstairs as well as two bedrooms at the back of a large kitchen, plus a living area with room for a couch! Frank also piped gravity flow water from the spring to a kitchen sink with faucets. The outside boasted two wide porches, one on the south and one on the west. Painted white, it looked like a mansion of a well to do family. Dora Slick and her daughter, Zelda, had it easier than others, but still had the old outhouse.

When the community grew enough to require two school buildings (1915) Frank was awarded the contract to supply the lumber for both the upper and lower schoolhouses from his mill. He also served on the school board as chairman and was re-elected several times. As a promoter of progress he was a good influence in the community, but he was not all work and no play. He and his wife were also involved in social events at the school and elsewhere. Sometimes he would act as caller for square dances.

Frank would get the guys together in winter after a long cold spell to cut ice blocks from his pond and beaver ponds along the creek. The ice was stored in sawdust filled ice houses made from slabs. During hot summer months, ice could be used to make ice cream or cool the icebox usually kept on the north side of the house.

In 1930 Frank supplied lumber to build a garage in the school yard for Mrs. Long's car and a barn for horses on the end of it.

Frank was a chain smoker and rolled his own cigarettes. His health failed and he developed emphysema. He sold his homestead in 1936 to the Finch family and moved to Eureka with his wife and daughter.

KINNEY

Albert and Grace Kinney moved their family from Michigan to Montana around 1908 or 1909. They came by train with their belongings to Whitefish, where their eldest son Amos got a job in the Great Northern roundhouse. Other sons were Loyd and Basil; the three daughters were Emily, Alta and Lily.

Albert filed for a homestead on land across Pinkham Creek from the Thatcher homestead extending west. The Gut Creek road now bisects the original homestead. Albert received his patent on 160 acres February 1922.

Proving up on the homestead was a family effort. They built a log cabin on the high creek bank and cleared space for a garden. They planted lilac bushes near the house with apple trees and rhubarb plants growing in the garden. A barn for the horses and milk cow was another necessity for life in the wilderness.

Times were tough in the 1930s and people had no money to pay their taxes. Albert and Grace Kinney had to let their place go to the county. Myrtle Peters paid back taxes in 1936 and the homestead became hers. She sold to Fred Hannah in 1938, who sold it again to Gene McWhirter in 1940. Since then the place has been divided into smaller parcels.

Albert became disabled and grew progressively worse. He and his wife lived in town until their death. Grace died in 1944 at the age of sixty-nine and Albert died in 1945 at seventy-three years. They both are buried in Tobacco Valley Cemetery.

While still working in Whitefish, Amos Kinney filed on a homestead farther from the creek and higher on the hill south of his folks. He would catch the train to travel back and forth to Eureka and walk to Pinkham. In 1910 during a fierce forest fire, the train came only as far as Fortine and Amos walked from there.

Amos was courting Ora Caldwell, who lived about a mile up the hill on the other side of the creek. It was a difficult walk all winter when snow was deep so he popped the question and she accepted.

The newlyweds lived in a frame house of rough boards that Amos had built. They also made a clearing for a garden space, rhubarb and apple trees. Amos dug out a spring on the hillside and built a wooden shoot to bring water closer to the barn where it filled a stock watering trough. Water was packed in buckets from there for household use.

The couple had four children. Archie, Ervin, Dorothy and Albert named after his grandfather. Archie and Ervin built a summer bunkhouse for themselves. All of them walked to attend the Pinkham school. When Bert became school age, they moved down on the ten-acre piece from the Mikelson homestead, which was on the main road.

Amos registered his patent for 160 acres in April 1924. That same summer he sold forty acres to Cecil Utter. Then in 1931 he sold forty acres to Harry and Ella Thatcher. Floyd and Agnes Sederdahl bought eighty acres in 1944 then sold it to Pete and June Klinke in 1957. The land produced good Christmas trees for many years.

Amos and Ora Kinney moved to town in 1938 where Bert finished grade school and graduated from high school. Amos had hacked ties by hand with a broadax on Pinkham but now he had an easier job. He worked for Columbus Clark hauling slabs from the mill with a team of horses.

Ora died in 1969 at the age of seventy-four. Then Amos died at age eighty-three in 1975. They are both buried in Tobacco Valley Cemetery. Their son Bert then lived in their home as a bachelor for many years until moving to the Mountain View Nursing Home in 2004.

Archie Kinney took Lola Armstrong as his first wife; they divorced. Oneda Tiffany became his third wife. Archie moved his family from place to place but spent his last years in Troy.

Ervin Kinney went to work in the Fisher River area where he sawed logs with Lee Utter for Ralph Burlingham. Ervin married

Beatrice Burlingham. They mostly lived in Eureka where they raised their family. After Beatrice died of cancer, Ervin married Edna Smith DeShazer, a widow.

Dorothy Kinney met Herman Owens while he was in the CCC camp at Troy. He came with his buddy Joe Carr by train to visit his family on Pinkham. Kinneys and Carrs were close neighbors as well as cousins. Herman and Dorothy were married in 1935.

The couple lived in the Slick's mill shack down by the creek while Herman hacked ties for Joe Carr. The shack was made of boards, tarpaper and more rough boards including the roof. One winter there was four feet of snow and cold. They were listening to the battery operated radio when they looked up and saw the roof on fire around the stove pipe (there was no ceiling) Herman dashed out and shoveled snow to put the fire out.

Later, in 1953, Herman bought the Thatcher place from Harles Bergette. The four Owens boys, Raymond, Jerry, Clyde and Herb, caught the school bus. They raised 4-H heifers to sell, helped put up hay and raised a big garden. Then in 1955 they sold out to George Haden and moved to town.

Davey Robinson filed for a homestead of 160 acres in Section 6 next to Albert Kinney. Davy cleared about five acres of land and dug out a spring for water. He also built a barn and a log cabin with a shed roof with a porch facing east, he made a stone chimney at the end of the cabin.

Davey made these improvements but left without proving up on the place. Cecil and Mae Utter lived there in 1922 and their son Lee was born there. The lilac bush by the cabin grew to be huge and blooms prolifically each spring.

Loyd Kinney, youngest son of Albert Kinney, filed for a patent on forty acres of the place about 1924. The other 120 acres reverted to the government. It was then later traded to Jim Hurst to be subdivided.

Loyd Kinney married Marie Ingram and they had two children, a boy and a girl. They sold their forty acres to Cecil Utter in 1948. Then in 1968 it became the property of Lee Utter. Now Lee owned the cabin in which he was born in 1922.

The place has been logged several times. At one time a chute was built on the steep side hill to propel the logs down the slope through the Thatcher place to Frank Slick's sawmill. The place has also produced excellent Christmas trees.

Uncle Dan Utter lived in the cabin for a while and remodeled it. He took down the logs and extended the frame addition and made a snug little cabin. The last to live there were some hippies from California who wanted to rough it in Montana. They took out the ceiling to expose the rafters and removed insulating boards to reveal rough boards. When it got below zero in January, they moved out. The cabin is still standing but vacant.

Hiram Kinney, a brother to Albert, came to visit relatives homesteading on Pinkham. 'H', as Hiram was called, was a carpenter and built several houses on Pinkham as well as Eureka. He was an influence in persuading his friends, the Armstrong family, to move to the Pinkham community. He bought part of the homestead of Lulamay Mikalson which was later sold to Ernie Pluid.

He had a son, Gerald, who settled in Eureka with his wife and family. His daughter, Agnes married George Evins, a rancher near Eureka.

Charlie Workman homestead cabin, built in 1913, with the addition built in 1925. Note the telephone pole and wire connecting to the U.S. Forest Service phone system.

CHARLES WORKMAN

Charles Workman, homesteader at age twenty, was following his father's footsteps. His homestead was across the creek, his cabin was built that same year, and he spent so much time 'courting' that his dad suggested he take along a sack of flour to pay his board. The courting was effective and on Christmas Eve 1913 Charlie married lovely Alta Kinney, daughter of Mr. and Mrs. Albert Kinney who had a homestead lower down the drainage.

Fall of 1914 Charlie helped his dad and other neighbors build three dams: one at Will Workman's homestead, one above the Moore place, and one below Pinkham Falls. That winter they cut, skidded, and decked logs, waiting for high water when the logs were rolled into the stream to roll and tumble down to the Kootenai River with lots of help from the men who followed them. At other times, ties were hewed out with broadaxes and floated downstream to be sold to the Great Northern.

Charlie became a father in May of 1915 when William Wayne was born at the home of Grandma Workman, who with her daughter, Ida, served as midwives; Wayne's birth is remembered as the year of the big log drive. Victor Lynn was born 1917, Sidney 1919. Like other homesteaders Charlie had to live seven months a year there, and clear more land; but he worked out the other months, sometimes for the Forest Service, one summer packing for the Geological Survey in the Bob Marshall. That year, he proudly brought home a buckboard from Kalispell and later got a 1917 Model T. In 1925 Charlie bought a new Star and took the family to Leavenworth, Washington, and Lula Grace was born, all of which made Charlie proud and happy; in 1927 back on Pinkham, Ellagene was born in August, and Charles Arthur in 1929. Five years later Alta started her third family, Harry T. 1933, Roger James 1935, and John A. (Jack) 1938.

In 1929 Charlie went to work steady for the Forest Service as packer on the Rexford Ranger District. Bob Byers was Ranger, then Charlie Powell came 1930. Charlie packed supplies to twenty-six lookouts during fire season, with an average of nine mules in a pack string, headquarters at Rexford. The outpost stations like the Pinkham Work Center near Will Workman's, or Big Creek cabin were a haven of rest for packer and mules. First stop up Pinkham was Mud Lake lookout, later moved to Black Butte; thence on to the Virginia Hill tree tower (the lookout attendant had a tent on the ground), and spend the night at the work center. (Beyond was the Pinkham Patrol Tower, Pinkham Mountain lookout, Warex, McGuire and Tree Point Nine-A on Beartrap, then circle back to Rexford). Every two weeks Charlie visited each lookout with supplies, mail, news and companionship, sharing their meals and beds. Back in Rexford the mules were shod by Ben Stuart, the village blacksmith, and all tack repaired. Later, miles of telephone wire were packed up on mules to the mountain tops, then strung back down, attached to trees with insulators; these required frequent checking. For Webb Mountain lookout, lumber and other supplies were mule-packed in, as well as furnishings as needed for all the lookouts.

Charlie was a small man but carried himself proud, standing out in a crowd with his cowboy boots and big western hat. One of his joys was driving big new cars and smoking a cigar. Charlie went hunting every fall right up until he was 78; that fall of 1971 he suffered a stroke up in the Bob Marshall Wilderness on a hunting trip with daughter, Lula, and her husband, Randall Richmond. He was brought out by helicopter; since then he had mostly lived with son, Wayne, or daughter, Lula. Spring of 76 Charlie was in the Richmond home when it burned, but Lula got him out; since then his sister, Ida Davis, cared for him on his home place on Pinkham. Charlie wore new cowboy boots constantly – ready to mount the great white steed which came for him on August 10, 1976.

ALTA KINNEY WORKMAN

Alta Kinney Workman was a beautiful bride with dark brown eyes and long brown naturally curly hair. These traits she was able to pass on to her children. Alta was a loving and devoted mother to her nine children. She taught them to be responsible for their actions at all times and to tell the truth.

Alta was a pleasant pioneer woman with many capabilities. She kept house and set a table with nourishing food. Charlie liked his beans and coffee so most times there was a pot o' beans simmering on the stove and the coffee pot handy. If there was no bread baked when he came home from pack trips unexpected she quickly fixed a batch of cornbread.

Alta was adept at outdoor work. She could saddle a horse to ride or hitch up a team to drive, as that was her transportation. She raised a garden of root vegetables for food to go along with ever-available venison. There was also the cow to milk twice a day, chickens and pigs to feed. Wood was to split to keep her cook stove going. These were all chores she did until her sons were big enough to help. Then there was the everlasting laundry!

Washday started the day before, with water packed by the buckets to fill a boiler, that sat on the back of the cook stove. The stove reservoir was also filled, so water could be heating while cooking breakfast. Clothes were sorted as to light and dark. When water was hot, it was dipped out into washtubs. Whites such as dishtowels or diapers were boiled separately to get stains out, then scrubbed on a rub board in a tub. Rinse water was in another tub, and clothes had to be wrung by hand each time. Then it came time to lug them out to the clothesline, to hang up to dry. On a good day, diapers would be dry by the time dark work clothes were ready to hang out. Wash water was then used to scrub porch and steps, before being dumped out on shrubs or plants to water them. Water was precious when packed in then out again, and was used in as many ways as possible.

The family also went on huckleberry picking trips. The berry patches were not too far from their place up Pinkham Creek. They could saddle up the horses and ride up the trail to Pinkham Mountain, and pick berries the same day. Camping gear was put on a packhorse for camping overnight and picking berries again the next day. They all picked and shared camp work to make it an enjoyable family campout. Back home Alta would make delicious berry pies and canned the rest in sauce and jams for winter.

Alta was a promoter of education. She taught her children to be obedient and to respect the teachers. She also made sure her children attended regularly and got to school on time even if she had to take them to school herself with a horse and buggy.

Teachers welcomed the Workman children and appreciated the good example they set for other students. They also felt free to discuss school issues or problems with Alta as a parent or a school trustee as she served several terms on the school board. Alta was even generous to offer her home and hospitality to a lonely teacher living by herself in the teacherage.

When the Workman children graduated from grade school and were ready for high school they either batched in a rented house in town or lived with relatives who had moved into Eureka. They were all given a chance and were encouraged to get a high school education.

Alta was also a fun loving person. She liked to socialize with neighbors and the schoolhouse was the community social center. She helped teachers plan Halloween parties, Christmas programs and school picnics where everyone came to have fun and be together. The pioneer life was not all work and no play.

Music and dancing was some of their favorite things to do. Alta was not a musician but she loved to dance and could be the life of the party. Everyone came to the dances; no one was too old or too young. They all took their turn to bathe in the washtub and put on their finest duds for the party. When little ones got tired of all the excitement they were put to bed in a corner with coats and blankets.

The hillbilly band was made up of local people who had an instrument and could play. There were fiddles, banjos, guitars and mouth harps to keep everybody on the floor or tap their toes to the beat. Square dances were called like "Birdie in the Cage." "Dive for the Oyster, Dig for the Clam," or the "Waltz Quadrille." Alta's son Sid learned to call for square dancing and he also played the mouth harp. His favorite piece to play was the "Irish Washer Woman" for those fast on their feet.

Alta laughingly liked to tell the tale of a young teacher doing a lot of dancing when a fellow slightly "likkered" up from sampling the moonshine outside came in to "liven" up the party inside. He drew a string of firecrackers out of his pocket and lit them with a wooden match he struck with his thumbnail then tossed them in the hall. The teacher was on the dance floor and at the first pop she shot up in the air away above her partner and came down facing someone else. At the next pop she did the same thing and continued until all the guys were watching to see who would be the next to grab her. It certainly livened up the party! It gave everybody a good laugh except the teacher.

In later years Alta was inflicted with Parkinson's disease and became bedridden during the last years of her life. She died at home on Pinkham in 1969 at the age of seventy-three and was buried in a family plot in the Tobacco Valley Cemetery.

ALTA WORKMAN (My Great-Grandmother)
By Karmen Starling

It was early in the morning. The wind was howling and the air was bitter and cold. The school was about six miles away and there were still all the kids to pick up. Alta Workman, my great-grandmother, hitched up the team of horses to the buggy and started on her school bus route. The water in the creek was especially high and some planks on the bridge were missing. The only kids she had so far were a few of her own. She let them off at the bridge and proceeded to go across. It was only when she was half way across that the bridge broke from beneath her. Everything was in the water. The horses were being drug down by the buggy. With great effort and a lot of struggle, she finally managed to unhitch them and get to shore.

This was only one of the many experiences she had during the time she drove the school route. In order to keep the kids warm, she would heat bricks and stones and wrap them up and lay them by the kid's feet. She used a kerosene lantern for light. One day when it was extremely cold, she made sure all the kids were warm, but ended up freezing her own big toe.

My great-grandmother and grandfather were some of the first homesteaders in the Pinkham area near Eureka. They built a home at a time when there were no conveniences. Their way of transportation was a team of horses and a buggy on narrow trails. There was no such thing as running water or electricity. Grandpa worked for the Forest Service and was sometimes away for months at a time. Grandma was kept busy at the house. They had nine children. She bore all but two without the presence of a doctor.

At that time of homesteading, people had to prove up the land. They had to do a certain amount of clearing and prove they could make a living off the land. Grandma, who had her share of work in the house, also had her share outside. She and the older boys did a lot of hard physical labor in preparation for actual ownership of the land.

Grandma loved the outdoors and she often took advantage of outdoor recreation. Camping and fishing were the favorites. Once while camping, Grandma was sleeping next to a log. A sound woke her up in the middle of the night. She saw something, and by reaction, hit the animal only to find her hand filled with porcupine quills.

Early homesteading and later the Depression didn't make it easy for Grandma. Feeding a family of eleven was a tough job. Every year they would go huckleberry picking and camping at a cabin for a couple weeks at a time. They would go by horseback and bring the berries to the cabin where Grandma would can them. Then they would pack everything back up and ride the ten or twelve miles back home. It was one of Grandma's goals every year to can 100 quarts of huckleberries and 100 quarts of venison.

I remember standing by my Grandma's bed visiting with her. I was only one little girl out of one huge family. I remember there were always a lot of people around, and all of these people belonged to the same family – her family. Even though my memories are very few, my mother remembers more than I, and even so does her father and his brothers and sisters. She lived at a time when there were no cars, but before she died there were men on the moon. She had to cope with a lot of tough situations and handled them very well. I find that my great-grandmother is a fine example to follow.

WAYNE WORKMAN

William Wayne Workman was born May 18, 1915, to parents, Charlie and Alta Workman. This blessed event took place at the homestead of his grandparents, Will and Nana Workman. His Aunt

Ida helped his Grandma Workman serve as midwife for this first born son. This baby was also the beginning of another generation to settle upper Pinkham Creek. Wayne was a cute towheaded toddler of two with baby blue eyes and naturally curly hair, when baby brother Victor Lynn was born May 31. Then another brother Sidney Leroy joined the family May 9, just two years later.

Wayne tells his own childhood story in an autobiography while he was in high school.

AUTOBIOGRAPHY OF WAYNE W. WORKMAN
CHAPTER I

I was born May 18, 1915, on my grandfather's ranch about seventeen miles south of Eureka. There my mother lived for a year while my father was working up in Canada. When he came back we moved to town. It was in the spring of 1917 now and another brother came into the family. The next year we went back to the ranch where we stayed a couple of years.

CHAPTER II

I was six years old now and it was time for me to go to school. We had a big dog which we called "Brownie." He always went to school and back with me carrying my lunch pail both ways. He would carry in wood, and water and anything we might give him to carry. My father moved to town next winter and I went to the second grade here in town. I didn't like to go here as well as at my own school because I didn't have as many friends at first. Gradually I began to like it better.

CHAPTER III

The next summer we motored out to Chehalis, Washington, where some of our relatives were living. There I went through the sixth grade. From there we moved to Leavensworth. I went through the seventh grade there then. The next year we came home, which was in Eureka. I finished the eighth grade here.

CHAPTER IV

My mother was living on the ranch when it was time for me to start to high school so I moved into a little house and started batching. I didn't like the idea very well but it worked out all right. The subjects I was taking were: General Science, English I, Algebra, and Manual Training. I made only three and a half credits that year due to the fact that I made only a half a credit in Algebra.

CHAPTER V

The next fall my mother moved to town which surely made me glad that I wouldn't have to batch again. This year I took Algebra, World History, English II and Geometry, making only three credits this year – one half in Algebra and one half in World History.

CHAPTER VI

My Junior year I believe is the one I most enjoyed so far. I only had six and one half credits when I started my Junior year so I thought I'd better take five subjects. I tried five but found it was too much for me so I dropped Physics. Now I am taking English IV, Civics, Bookkeeping, and Commercial Geography. Of all my classes I like Commercial Geography the best.

This has been an entertaining year for me, first we had the Junior Play by the name of "It Won't Be Long Now." Then we had the Junior class paper which carried the name of the "The Lincolnion." Now for another entertainment we have the Inter Class Track Meet. In a few weeks we will have the event of the year the Junior Promenade.

Wayne was just 16 when he went to work for the USFS. It was a summer job as a lookout attendant on McGuire Mountain. His dad was the packer and a regular visitor when he brought up supplies. Wayne was on duty both night and day, to watch for forest fires during the hot, dry summer of 1931. It was double trouble when lightning struck all around the mountains.

Unlike the Pinkham Mountain Lookout which had a 65 foot tower, McGuire Lookout was built on the rocky peak with rocks as a foundation. It was 12x12 on the bottom with a cupola on top and windows all around. A ladder went up inside from the living quarters below. The cupola held instruments for detecting the location of fires, and a telephone for reporting them to the Rexford Ranger Station.

It was during one storm that his younger brother, Sid, was allowed to spend the 4th of July week at the lookout. It worked out well, as Wayne needed extra help. Both boys took their responsibility seriously. Sid tells the story:

"My parents homestead was approximately 13 miles away from the lookout, which was accessible only by trail. My mother decided I was old enough (I was 12 at the time) to ride the trail by myself to spend the 4th with my brother. I took an axe, a raincoat, a couple of sandwiches and a canteen of water. It was a dry trail, and I needed to be prepared. My horse was a good walker, he could travel 3 ½ to 4 miles an hour on the trail. I was almost to the lookout, after 4 hours on the trail, when a hot electric storm moved in. Just as I arrived, my brother had located a fire quite some distance down McGuire Creek.

"It was arranged over the phone, that Wayne take my horse to the fire, and I stay at the lookout. Wayne took his firepack (shovel and axe) with extra food, refilled canteen and bedroll in case he had to spend the night. Well, I stayed the rest of that day, the 3rd, 4th and about noon on the 5th before Wayne returned. I reported about three times a day by phone to Rexford District as was required by a lookout. In the meantime, the weather changed and four inches of snow fell on the mountain. It helped put out the fires, but Wayne was cold and wet when he got back. We visited a few days before I took the trail home."

Later that summer, Wayne had another visitor. This one was not welcome. Wayne had seen bear sign around the lookout area. He got to taking his .30-30 rifle with him when he went to the spring for water, or go to the "can." Then the griz got rough as he circled around for days, peering in widows, rattling the frames and pushing at the door. Wayne was literally a prisoner. He was given permission by phone to lower the boom and get rid of the danger. Wayne waited for the right shot and fired from the door. Then someone came by with a camera to take his picture with the bear.

In 1935, Wayne, twenty years old, married Ellen Maude Baker, who was seventeen years old. (Maudie was a cousin to Lee and Esther Utter.) The couple spent their summers manning lookouts together on the Warland District. Winters were spent in cabins close to where Wayne could find work in the woods. Their children were Alma Lee, Rodney and Patricia. When jobs started opening up on the West Coast during World War II, Wayne took his family out there. He worked in the woods near Forks, Washington.

When Wayne came back to Montana, he was divorced. He went to work for his brother, Chuck, who had a sawmill. Wayne skidded logs in the woods and made new skidding roads for logging. His second wife was Lois Carvey Persson. She had five kids, then together they had two more girls, Carla and Ann. They made their home on Pinkham, about thirteen miles from town. The school bus went right past their door and, eventually, mail was delivered.

Wayne left this world when he died at home in his easy chair November 5, 2002. He was cremated and his ashes scattered over the Pinkham Creek area, which he always called home.

Wayne Workman with the bear he killed at McGuire Lookout.

LYNN WORKMAN
By The Tobacco Valley News – 1997

Lynn Workman recently celebrated his 80th birthday with family and friends at the Pinkham schoolhouse, where he once attended school. Lynn was born on the Workman homestead on Pinkham Creek on May 31, 1917, to Charles and Alta Workman.

He and his brothers rode horseback six miles to school. One year his mother was their bus driver with a covered bobsled and team of horses.

"As a kid I enjoyed hunting, fishing and horseback riding," Lynn said. "Horses were our main mode of travel in those early days."

Lynn's family included nine children, seven boys and two girls. All are living except a brother who was killed in a truck wreck. Their father was a Forest Service packer and their mother kept busy looking after the kids. After graduating from Lincoln County High School in 1934, Lynn worked for the Civilian Conservation Corps (CCC) from 1935 to 1941. From 1942 to 1945 he worked for the Kaiser Company in the shipyards at Vancouver, Washington.

Lynn returned to Montana and worked in the woods, mostly falling timber. He, also, helped build Hungry Horse Dam. In the 1960's he owned his own sawmill in the area. He finished his working career with the Forest Service and retired in 1983.

Lynn married Peggy Speyer on June 23, 1941. "We have enjoyed 56 years together," Lynn said. Lynn and Peggy have five children, most of whom still live in the area. Lynette Starling works for Big Sky Exxon and is also fair board secretary; Richard lives in Roundup and is a logger; Susan Evans is a Lutheran schoolteacher in Aurora, Colorado; Mike is a real estate broker in Eureka; and Vic is a realtor in Whitefish. They also have ten grandchildren and four great grandchildren. "We are very proud of them," Lynn said.

Lynn's hobbies include woodcrafts, fishing and hunting. He is a member of the Holy Cross Lutheran Church.

"I plan on spending my remaining years in Eureka among friends and relatives," he said. "I like Eureka because I've lived here most of my life. To me it's home."

SID WORKMAN

Sid Workman was born in a log cabin on the bank of Pinkham Creek on May 9, 1919. He said he began his life as near to a native as could be. Sid's grandfather, Charles, came from West Virginia in 1902 and was the second person to settle on Pinkham.

Sid grew up on his father's homestead in upper Pinkham Creek southwest of Eureka. Before his school days he said he vividly remembers riding the school bus his mother, Alta, drove. "It was a team of horses pulling either a buckboard wagon or a covered sleigh in winter," he said. "My mother would heat bricks and wrap them in burlap to help keep kids feet warm on the six-mile trip."

He said his early home life holds a warm spot in his heart. "We were a close-knit family, being taught love and respect from the ground up," he said. He finds a lack of respect missing in some families today.

Charles and Alta Workman had nine children, seven boys and two girls.

At age five, Sid started the first grade, but the county health nurse examined him and said it would be best to wait another year because he was a bit too skinny.

Sid's father moved the family to Washington state for a temporary logging job and first grade was interrupted once more.

After the third try at Pinkham Creek School, he was promoted to second grade. The second grade teacher jumped him to fourth grade and the fourth grade teacher pushed him into the sixth grade, but then he had to spend two years in the seventh grade.

Sid started high school in Eureka in 1934. "Out-of-town students had no transportation," he said. "Some lived with folks close to the school and some rode horses or lived in rented cabins. Two buses ran then – one from Gateway and one from old Rexford."

He remembers seeing the high school burn in March of 1935. "There were tears and weeping by those witnessing the 4 a.m. fire," he said. "Nothing was saved."

School was resumed in the Roosevelt building for the next term and a half, and there was adequate room for both schools.

Sid said football was his favorite sport, and he lettered in it three years. In 1937, the Eureka team won seven straight games, the best in the district at that time. In 1987, the team was honored at half-time of the homecoming football game on their 50th reunion.

After graduation in 1940, Sid began working for the United States Forest Service as a lookout fireman and other forest-related jobs. He enlisted in the United States Army Air Corps in August of 1941. "FDR was building up the defense units by drafting at that time prior to World War II," he said.

He came home on leave in February of 1943 and married his childhood sweetheart, Alice Combs. From that marriage came four children, Lee, Steve, Sandra, and Sydney Lu.

Twenty-six months of Sid's military duties were served in the states, and the remainder overseas in the European Theater. He served in Paris, London, Frankfurt, and Glasgow, Scotland. He was discharged on December 7, 1945, from General Jimmy Doolittle's 8th Air Force.

Sid returned home on the USS Enterprise and went to work sawing timber with a crosscut saw for the J. Neils Lumber Company at the Warland Camp. He followed woods work, sawmilling, forestry work and truck driving all in this general area. He retired in 1981.

Sid said for recreation he loves all aspects of the outdoors. Stream fishing and ice fishing are his favorite pastimes. He is also very fond of deer hunting, especially whitetail bucks. "In my time I have hunted more than a few," he said. He also enjoys mountain lion hunting with a hound. Hiking and horseback riding are also favorites of his, and he enjoys sharing all this with those who settle in the valley.

Sid and Alice, his wife of fifty-two years, and their children, were baptized and became members of Holy Cross Lutheran Church in 1957. Sid has held several offices in the church, including Sunday school teacher and visiting shut-ins and administering communion when needed.

His future plans are to continue living in the Tobacco Valley and loving and enjoying everything this valley has to offer, "which is many-fold." He also said his thirteen grandchildren take up a lot of his time.

"I like this valley and all who live here," he said "We are one large family where everyone cares for everyone else."

He has continued to witness this attitude through the Depression, three wars and the recent influx of new people.

HARRY T. WORKMAN

Harry T. Workman was the seventh child born to Charlie and Alta. He was the eldest of the third family of three with Roger and Jack following along as the youngest. Lula, Ellajene and Charles, Jr., known as Chuck, were already school age with Wayne, Lynn and Sid of high school age.

Harry's childhood memories include the family moves twice a year. There was no longer an upper school open to attend so kids were all going to the lower Pinkham school. To be closer where kids could walk to school, the Workman family moved down the creek in the fall and back up again to the homestead in the spring.

At the opening of school in September the Workman children rode horseback the seven miles to school. There was a horse barn with a manger for feed at one end of the garage to keep the horses out of the weather, ready for the return trip. This building on the back of the school grounds did dual duty for horses and parking a teacher's car, if the teacher had one. The owner of the horses furnished the feed and cleaned out the barn after them.

The Workmans were paid a stipend by the school district for transportation to school. In hard times this helped buy beans and flour for bread. They usually moved into a vacant homestead house where the stoves and maybe other furniture were left behind. One of the places they spent the winter in was the Jim Roberts place about a mile above the school. Another was Jim Harrington's homestead a mile up the Slicks Gulch Road. When the Cecil Utter family moved elsewhere for a winter, the Workmans stayed there. There were just two rooms downstairs and one long room upstairs for the large family. The boys slept upstairs and the girls had a curtained-off corner of the main room. There was a barn for livestock and a chicken coop ready to use.

The Workmans finally bought the Calhoun homestead, which was about a mile below the school. This place was a four room frame house and by building on two more bedrooms, it made a comfortable house. There was also adequate water from a spring near the house. This place was known as the Silk Stocking place as the door was tied shut with a silk stocking (nothing of value to steal).

Before moving down about Thanksgiving time when winter snow started falling, the Workmans were extra busy. Spuds to be dug, garden vegetables put up and canned in jars then packed along with jars of huckleberries. Hogs had to be butchered after weather turned cool. Then hams and bacon cured while sausage was made from scraps and packed down in crocks.

On moving day, chickens were caught before daylight from the roost to be put in crates and hauled in the wagon or sleigh if snow was on the ground. Feed was also loaded in, with the milk cow tied to the back. Alta or one of the boys usually drove the team of horses – Lightning or Madam Queen while Charlie rode and led his pack string down the road. If a winter was mild the extra horses could graze on Old Baldy or other wind swept hills as there was open grazing at that time. In bad weather, loose hay had to be hauled and fed to animals.

Essentials to be moved besides bedding and clothing were water buckets and wash pan, milk pail, and pans, dishpans, teakettle, coffee pot, large iron fry pans and other cooking utensils. Breakable dishes were wrapped in hand towels or dish towels along with kerosene lamps and packed in washtubs or boiler. The washboard, flat irons, and ironing board had to be taken too. Not many chairs had to be moved as home made benches were left along the walls in most houses.

In the spring around Easter, when the snow melted down on upper Pinkham, the moving process was reversed. Now, empty jars were taken back to be refilled. Baby chicks were ordered, piglets purchased to raised for butchering, and garden seeds bought to plant. The kids were back on horseback to finish out the school term. While riding along they had opportunity to see wild animals along the way, but didn't feel threatened. They depended on their horses to get them safely back home again. At least once a year they would stop at the tree lookout station on Virginia Hill to climb up and look the country over.

Now that the Workmans had a permanent winter home down the creek, the three boys had a little less than a mile to walk to school. Their trek took them past the place of Mr. Banks both ways. One day they spied a pair of burros in with the goats. This phenomenon had to be investigated!

The boys stopped to check it out. Sure enough, Mr. Banks had swapped milk goats for a pair of burros. They were broke to ride besides being used as a team to work. Not only that, but they were just the right size for boys to hop on their back! This would take some wheeling and dealing, as times were tough and the boys had no money to buy anything. With permission from their folks, they made a deal with Mr. Banks. Since he could use a saddle horse to ride, and his legs were too long for the burros, he agreed to trade for their mare, Lightning, and the deal was made.

Harry remembers how he and his brother got right to work on building a cart for the burros to pull. They used old discarded buggy wheels, a tongue, scrap boards and put them together for a usable rig. This cart full of boys pulled by the burros became a familiar sight on the Pinkham road. After moving back up the creek, the burros brought the boys to school. At Christmas time they pulled the sleigh to bring in the tree for decorating.

Harry attended the one room Pinkham school for seven years and then rode the school bus to Eureka for eighth grade and high school. Madeline Rost Utter was his last teacher on Pinkham and Lee Utter was the driver of the yellow Dodge eighteen-passenger school bus. Since the bus came up to the Workman homestead there was no need now to move. During hunting season Lee was lenient in letting the boys have their guns on the bus to upper Pinkham so they could hunt over the weekend.

Harry followed the family trait of working for the U.S. Forest

Service. During summer months he worked out of the Warland District on trail crews. At the Ant Flat District he was taking pack mules to lookouts on the mountains. In the summers of 1952-53 he was working in Glacier National Park.

Harry took time to court and marry Claire Biegler before being drafted by the U.S. Army in 1956. Claire followed him to the Army base at Fort Ord, California. When Harry was sent to Germany, Claire and their son Bill went too. Harry served two years in the Army, then came back to Pinkham. Their family grew with Darla, Alta, Randal and Larry. When they were all in school Claire became the driver of the 56 to 60 passenger Pinkham school bus that was owned by the Eureka School District.

In 1964 Harry started packing and guiding for Lloyd West, who took hunting parties into the Bob Marshall Wilderness. By 1970 Harry applied for his own license to take hunting or fishing parties into the wilderness. Claire became camp cook and his family, the helpers. Their headquarters are at Buck Horn Ranch up Pinkham Creek on the former Dan Anker homestead. They use about twenty-five head of horses and mules for pack trips into the wilderness or take smaller local trips. They also have range stock branded W2 that are pastured out in summer and fed hay in winter.

CHUCK WORKMAN

Bill Workman's Eulogy at his Uncle Chuck Workman's funeral November 6, 2002, read by Marty Kaarre:

We lost a big man a few days ago. Actually, he was a small man with about 200 lbs. of heart. My Uncle Chuck was one of the most kind, caring, and honest men I knew. He was also one of the toughest. Here was a man who faced many serious injuries and illnesses his whole life, and you would never hear him complain. Even with "The Fourth Horseman" bearing down hard at him he never backed down. Instead of feeling sorry for himself his only concern was for how those he would leave behind would cope.

Being kind to your fellow man was always easy for Chuck. If he had it, time, money, and material possessions, were yours if you needed it. It didn't matter if you were a relative, friend, neighbor, or total stranger, he really would give you the shirt off his back. I don't know if you would want it, because he always claimed he only took a bath once or twice a year. I think that Chuck was the model for the phrase "generous to a fault."

I was luckier than most, in that I got to spend a lot of time with Chuck. My times with him started back when I was just a young boy, and we got very tight. I used to go down and visit them a lot and stayed at their place many times. I remember watching Perry Mason on TV and giving Aunt V. a hard time. We used to fish in the crick, hike up to McGuire or old Trail 20 looking for wild chickens and rode many miles chasing cows. When I got a little bit older, we spent a lot of time hunting and getting wood. In later years we made many trips into the Bob Marshall and Great Bear Wildernesses. As you know, horses, packing, camping, fishing, and hunting were a big part of his life. He got such a kick out of me packing mules for the Forest Service as he, his dad, and some brothers had all done before me. All these times were special to me, while they were happening, and even more so now.

Another thing about Uncle Chuck is he really liked having his little fires. If we were fishing we would have to stop and have a fire. When we were chasing cows and stopped to give the horses a blow, we would have a fire. Of course, any time we were getting wood or hunting, we would stop and have a little fire. It got so that the last few times we went hunting, I think hunting was just an excuse to get a little walking out of the way, so we could build our little fire and talk. I know I'll never build another one of my fires without remembering Uncle Chuck.

I also remember a pack trip that Chuck took up the South Fork some years ago. Chet Apeland, Chuck, and a Baptist preacher (who I won't call by name because he is still around) stayed the night at Gail's and my place at Spotted Bear before they headed out for ten days. The day they took off was a real nice day, sunny and warm, so consequently, they left various items like over shoes, coats, and slickers in the truck. An hour after they left it clouded up and rained and snowed for ten days. They showed up at the house at the end of the trip looking like a bunch of frozen prunes. Chuck told me you never saw three fellows in so much misery having so much fun, and it wasn't like you could cuss the weather anyhow with a preacher in the bunch.

Besides all the miles of trail we rode, we also had some good times on the road. We ran his Christmas trees down to Wyoming several times, and this gave us lots of time with each other. Chuck was good company when he was awake, though he could spend more time sitting up straight asleep than anyone I knew. He wasn't fond of driving either, and I always started out driving. I was still driving when we got home. One time we were flying down the freeway with dad's old stock truck when a mallard flew out of the borrow pit and hit the side of the truck.

He flopped up on the front of the hood, square in the middle. Since the old truck only flew at 55, we got passed by a bunch of folks before we could find a place to pull over and get the duck off the hood. We were chuckling about the looks we were getting from all those people that noticed our realistic looking hood ornament. Like Chuck said though, "It ain't everyone can bag a duck with a truck!"

The quality of the rigs I drove also gave me many, many more hours with Chuck. I spent a lot of time at his place taking advantage of his shop, his tools and his expertise while always mechanicing on my rigs. Of course, this also meant heading for the house for a cup of coffee ever so often, some of the thousands of cups I've drank with him through the years.

Well Chuck, I know you have gone to a better place and all I can say is it must be an awesome place. I say that because you and me saw the best places down here. I hope they got a good horse for you to ride and I hope there are some nice fish to catch. I hope there is a big old bull running around for you to chase and a little wood scattered around for your fires.

So long, pard, till we meet again,

Bill

Dan Anker, who had been a scout for General George Armstrong Custer.

DAN ANKER
Former Pinkham Resident was Scout for General Custer
By Madeline Utter

The 100 year anniversary of the Battle of Little Big Horn brings back recollections of a former Pinkham resident who purportedly had been a scout with General Custer. Dan Anker, for many years a bachelor resident of Pinkham told his neighbors that he had been sent back to Cook with a message just before that last disastrous battle on the Little Big Horn. Thus he earned the title, "The Last of Custer's Scouts."

Dan came from English ancestry and called himself "Johnny Bull." He cut a striking figure atop his famous white horse Trapper, even in his twilight years. And this is the way his is remembered by friends and neighbors on Pinkham.

Uncle Dan, as he soon became known in the neighborhood, was reported to have had a wife and two daughters in his early life. As local forks heard the story, Dan came home one time to find the cabin burned and no trace of his family.

It must have been around 1900 that Dan first came to the Tobacco Plains area before moving to Pinkham. The book *"Tobacco Plains Country,"* stated: "Dan Anchord, (sic) also a veteran of the Civil War, had a squatter cabin in the Fallon-Patrick area, and often helped with haying and other work at Quirks in the early days. He later moved to Pinkham Creek, where he ran a herd on the Quirk cattle range several summers before his death."

Uncle Dan built his cabin above and beyond the Will Workman homestead, with dry rough lumber from the Slick sawmill on Pinkham. As soon as his one-room cabin, about 14x20 in size was finished, he had a housewarming, as was the custom in those days. Ida Workman, then a teenager, remembers playing the accordion and mouth harp for the dance music while Jim Roberts played the fiddle. Her brother Sid called the squares and circle two step. It was only natural that Ida felt disappointment in not having a chance to dance.

Dan was a good neighbor and liked being with kids. Whenever he went to town, he brought home candy to distribute to kids along the way. They looked forward to seeing his white horse Trapper coming their way. One of the Workman boys remembers riding a calf that Uncle Dan had penned up. The calf got caught in the fence and the boy got scared! That was one thing he didn't want Uncle Dan to find out about.

Another favorite pastime of Uncle Dan's was thinking up nicknames for his friends and neighbors. Jim Roberts, who was tall and lanky, he called "Rawhide." Billy Payne had developed a whiskey whisper from drinking his own moonshine, so he was known as "Whisperin Willy." Goldie Craft was named "Dead Eye Dick," (He had one bad eye.) Grace Kinney was "Buffalo Gal" and "Physics" was a nickname for a midwife and herb doctor on Pinkham. (Sis Roberts)

Then there were a few other interesting names like: "Heap Big Fly Speck" for father and "Little Fly Speck" for his son. Sidney E. Workman was "Two Tie Sid" and Ida Workman was fondly called "Heidi." Thus individuals of Pinkham Creek became characters in the pages of history.

More information on Dan Anker was found in recordings of the census. The 1900 census recorded that Dan Anker and his wife, Delia, lived in Kalispell, had been married six years, no children. The 1910 census of School District 13 found Dan boarding with Osloskis' near Eureka as a widower. In 1920 Dan was recorded living on Pinkham

Creek as a boarder of Dan and Cecil Utter, who were also single men at that time.

Dan Anker passed away in 1926 at the age of seventy-five and his body was placed in the Tobacco Valley cemetery. Uncle Dan's (honorary uncle) homestead is now owned by Harry Workman. His family of five children lived in the original cabin for several years and they still use it for a bunkhouse for the boys.

Uncle Dan would be gratified to know that part of his labor is still preserved.

AGED INDIAN SCOUT PASSES
(July 1, 1926 – Eureka Journal)

At Rexford last Friday occurred the death of Daniel H. Anker at the age of 73 years. The body was brought to Eureka for preparation for burial and funeral services were conducted from the Gompf Funeral Home Sunday afternoon by Rev. W. Smith.

Daniel Anker was a native of England and came to this country when a small boy, and when about the age of 14 left his home in Wisconsin and began to shift for himself in the Great West. One of his first big jobs was that connected with buffalo hunting, having joined one of the big hide expeditions at which he worked until he had earned enough to purchase a pony, saddle and outfit of his own. Much of his early life was spent on the great frontier as a scout in the Indian wars and he took a prominent part in the winning of the west. His efforts, however, to secure a pension at various times proved fruitless as the government has held that he was a paid civilian and Congress has as yet made no provision for pension. He was never married and left no known relatives.

He came to this section about 25 or 30 years ago and several years ago proved up on a homestead in the Pinkham country, which has been his home until recently. He was a favorite with all who knew him and many local citizens interested themselves in an effort to secure him a pension. He suffered much at times from his old wounds and these were accountable for his poor health and incapacity in later years and undoubtedly hastened his death.

In making application for a pension Mr. Anker gave the following information as to his career as a scout:

"My career as a scout on the American northwest frontier began on the eighth day of March, 1868, under General Gibbon, at Fort Ellis. I enrolled in the service as a volunteer Indian scout with quartermaster McComb, and my chief of Scouts was George Owen. On April 13,

1869, I was wounded in the battle at Fort Dobey while in the line of duty as a scout, being shot through the left lung, the bullet lodging just inside the left shoulder blade. As a result of this wound I was confined in the hospital at Fort Ellis for a period of about six months.

"In the year 1870 I was transferred to Fort George, where I served under Major Walker, serving steadily under him until the spring of 1873. During my service under Major Walker I was in five engagements or battles with the Indians. In one of them, the battle of Santee, I was wounded by a bullet in the right hip, by an arrow in the left knee and by an arrow through the left arm.

"During the years 1873-74 I served under General Custer with Charles Ranolds as chief of scouts. In 1875-76 I served under General Crook, and at the battle of Rock creek was slightly wounded twice by bullets, and was also hit by an Indian war club over the left ear, inflicting a scalp wound and causing total deafness of the left ear. From 1876 to 1881 I served under General Lugenbeal and was honorably discharged and paid off at Missoula, having served as a scout for 13 years and five months.

"During said service in those days, a scout was better known by a nickname or by a fictitious name than by his true name, and therefore, I was known as and went under the nickname of "Spotted Tail". This was for the reason that I carried the first mail into Spotted Tail, South Dakota. Also while serving under General Crook I was known by the fictitious name of Newcome."

The story of Mr. Anker is supported by various affidavits of comrades and citizens who knew him and by physicians who examined him, and his story of his life is generally accepted as true and there is no doubt but what Mr. Anker was entitled to a pension, and would probably some day have secured one if Congress passes a bill covering the services of paid civilian scouts.

DAN ANKER
By Sid Workman

The next to the last homestead on the south end of Pinkham Creek was taken by Dan Anker. He was just a little man, thin and about 5'4" who spoke with a British accent. His life span was about seventy-five years. His grave marker in the Tobacco Valley cemetery shows 1851 to 1926. He served under General Custer in the battle of the Little Big Horn as a scout. As the battle raged he was dispatched to the rear to get another mule train of ammunition. When he learned that it was all over he decided to head north and begin a different life. Sometime after leaving the battle area he camped on the prairie. In the morning he couldn't catch his saddle horse. He then tried the old trick of shooting the horse in the base of the mane to stun him. He shot too low, broke the horse's neck and he had to carry his saddle for three days before stealing another horse. What happened between the time of the battle and the time he homesteaded near my parents I have no knowledge.

Uncle Dan was not married. He was a good neighbor, living only one mile south of my parents homestead. My grandfather, Charles W. Workman, Sr., had helped him build a cabin on his place and furnished him with a team of horses. My brother Harry and family are presently living on Uncle Dan's homestead site. The original cabin is still in use after being built onto. I remember him when I was four, five, and six years old. Sometime he would leave the homestead, maybe two or three weeks at a time. Then he would ask my folks to care for his milk cow and calf until he returned. On one of these occasions my two older brothers decided they would have some fun with me and Uncle Dan's calf. They took me inside the cow corral and set me on the calf and then they insisted I pull the calves tail over my shoulder and the rodeo was on. After two or three rounds like this I saw the older brothers take off running. When I looked up I saw Uncle Dan coming toward the corral. I started to crawl toward the fence and my suspenders caught on the knotty rail fence. Well the old-timer blistered my bottom end good, convincing me to not play rodeo with his calf anymore.

In 1925 my parents moved to Leavenworth, Washington, where my father logged for about a year and Uncle Dan passed away while we were away. Some of the old-timers in this community have pictures of him.

FOUR SCORE AND SOME ODD YEARS
or
The Story of a House – (In Its Own Words)
By Bill Workman
June 1990

Four score and some odd years ago I had my humble beginnings on a hill overlooking Pinkham Crick. I'm a house – truthfully, more of a shack. You maybe never heard of my builder – one Dan Anker, but you might remember his boss – General George Custer. Lucky for me, Mr. Custer happened to send scout Anker to another company with a message, else I may have had no beginnings at all. After delivering the message Dan Anker is supposed to have told the commanding officer that "Custer is inventing Arrow shirts and won't need me any more so

I'm off to Pinkham Crick".

By and by Dan homesteaded towards the head of the crick and built me – all 14 by 20 foot – of rough cut lumber, sawdust insulation, and tarpaper and board roof. I have four windows and a door on each end. Just one room and not very fancy but Ol Dan was a bachelor and had no reason to need anything else. I wish I could tell you more about my early years, but they were so long ago I have a hard time remembering. This was rough country with tough men, so I must have seen some sights and heard some stories. But who takes things seriously, in the days of their youth.

I do know that Dan Anker sold his land and me to a neighboring homesteader by the name of Charlie Workman. Charlie had his own land and house, so he had no reason to live in me. Ever once in a while Charlie would let some family live in me for the winter or rent me for a short while but for thirty years I sat fairly quiet and mostly lonely. The Maytag repairman had nothing on me.

That all changed in the early Sixties. Harry Workman bought the ground on which I stand from his Dad, Charlie, and started coming up and doing a little fixing up and using me for a place to live while checking his traps. Like I said before, I'm not very nice looking, with the outside of me having never seen a drop of paint and the inside seeing every color at one time or another. But to a hungry, cold, tired, trapper – I always imagined I looked better than Buckingham Palace.

Every once in a while Harry would bring his wife and five kids up, and they would spend a weekend or a piece of the summer in me. Things were lookin' up or should I say – live up! The family stayed here while fixing me up some and building corrals for the stock. Then they would head down the road for school or winter, until time to come spend a few days with me.

This is not to say I never had company when the Workmans weren't around. Another family use to visit me quite a bit in between Workman visits. This was the Bear family. Mr. Bear would come in through a plastic window to see what the last visitors may have left. He would claw on the ceiling a while, bite a hole in the teakettle, open a few cans and knock the stovepipe down, then leave – sometimes through the same window he came in.

One time Mr. Bear forgot to make reservations and came barging through a window that was at the foot of the bed. This woke Harry, who had come up with youngest daughter, Alta, to do a little work and spend the night. So he pulled his .44 from under the pillow and knocked Mr. Bear back outside. This barely woke three-year old Alta and she went right back to sleep after askin' her dad what the big bang was. I don't remember how long it took for Harry to get back to sleep but I know the Bear family never came around much after that.

Just as well – the big flood of '64 got the Workman house down below damp all the way to the windows, so they moved up here for the summer. I was fairly burstin' – not just for joy but because five kids from nine down to one with Ma and Dad makes a 14x20 foot house …. well – almost burst! Put about two or three beds in and scatter kids and folks accordingly, and it can be done. Things sure weren't quiet around here any more. Besides the family there were assorted dogs, cats, horses and cows around. Everyone big 'enuff' to help out did and the others played, and all in all, it was some nice times. Sure was sorry to see them all leave for the winter.

I got good news the next spring. The Workman family was moving up for good. Things that can be stood once in a while aren't always nice for full time, so I received an eight-foot addition across one end of me. This became Harry and Claire's bedroom and kitchen. Later a porch was built across the other end and the boys slept here. Now, all of the sudden it seemed like there was lots of room. I sure was having a good time now. Oh – there were occasional times when it weren't rosy but not many. I remember getting a part of the new roof one day when Harry went outside in the morning and noticed my old one on fire. That was put out quick and I got about half of one side of my roof newly done. Got a golf ball thru one of my windows once after they were converted to glass but it's a long ways from my heart. Also had an occasional headache whenever a pack rat family moved in to the attic. They never seemed to stay too long – most all the Workmans are good shots. Sometimes it was so cold outside it was all I could do to stay cozy but the family helped out. After the stock was fed they'd pull the couch and a big chair around the fire, and Harry and Claire would read books out loud. Seemed cozy 'enuff' then. Sometimes Harry would get out his guitar and they would all sing old cowboy songs. I was damn sure country long before country wasn't cool.

Well – them old years roll along and before you know it them little kids was all growed up, at least they figured they was. Oldest daughter Darla figured she needed her own room so the porch was walled in and this became Harry and Claire's bedroom. Darla got their room but got little sister Alta in the bargain. The boys got bunkbeds in the main part of the house and since it was a change that was 'enuff.'

In 1972 the Workmans bought a big trailer house and moved it up near me. That's the end of my usefulness I figured. Wrong! – The trailer house has only two bedrooms so the boys stayed in me and I became "the bunkhouse" or as the youngest of the Workman tribe, two-year-old Chelsea puts it now – the <u>Bonk</u> house.

I began taking on a definite male atmosphere with oldest son Bill in Harry and Claire's room and Randy and Larry bedded down in the main part of me. Posters of good lookin' girls competed with Charlie Russell prints and bucking horse pictures for wall space between elk and deer horns, guns, and knives, fishin' poles and hats, and what ever else a boy has to have hangin' on his wall. I wasn't mindin' this one bit!

Through the years I've hosted the many and varied friends of the Workman boys and it has become an honor and a privilege to stay in the bunkhouse. Sometimes I've had one or two of my fellows gone for different reasons – sometimes to college, sometimes to work here or there, sometimes just to see different country but all them boys know they're really home when the get back to me. There's been times I been wall to wall boys, saddles, riggin's, assorted gear and an occasional female but I always am as big as I got to be. Of course, even then some one will still kick a spittoon over once in a while.

In '82 Bill got married and moved a good mile down the road to his great-grandpa's homestead, so his room became winter storage for the Silvertip hunting camp. This left the two younger brothers livin' in me and they were gone some for different reasons but I still had my usefulness. Hunters stay here some during the fall and I'm a good place to keep the overflow at Christmas dinners and other family gatherin's. Youngest brother, Larry, has been in college and teaching fairly steady since about then so I'm down to one more or less permanent resident. Middle brother Randy still takes care of me and I got an all brand new tin roof in 1989!

Larry got married in early 1990 and just when I figured things to become fairly quiet again – brother Bill, bein' short of space, short of coin, and some say, quite a few books short of a library decided to start building saddles in me. Randy and Bill decided Larry wouldn't need his bed no more, not that his wife wouldn't stay there – but her Ma wouldn't let her, so out it went. Down came some of the horns and gun racks, down came some certain pictures, (Not those girlie posters of yours, Larry) and in went a big sewin' machine. Up went a bigger table. Tools and hardware got nailed to the wall.

With the full cooperation of brother Randy, lots of help from wife Gail, the good supervision of daughter Chelsea, Bill now has the Workman Saddle Shop in me. With him building saddles in the daytime and Randy sawing logs at night it seems I never have any peace and quiet. Not that I'm complainin' mind you. All in all it's been a good eighty-some years. I'm looking forward to the next eighty, remind me then and I'll tell you how they went.

And they say – "if the old house could talk…"

SOME OLD ITEMS AND STORIES OF INTEREST
By Sid Workman (May 1981)

Iron Telephones

These were black cast iron telephone boxes that were installed along some of the trails in our main drainages. The iron telephone box was approximately 18" x 12" deep. This housed all the necessary equipment that any old wooden crank telephone had. They were permanently installed to a tree with lag screws. Their location was generally at two main trail junctions and was left year around with the iron weatherproof door locked. New batteries were installed by trail crews or smoke chasers or whoever came by first thing in the spring. Telephone Creek on the Rexford Ranger District was so named as a phone was installed here at the junction of trail #275 and trail #4.

Field Phone

This was another type of phone used by the packer or someone traveling a trail and who might need emergency communication. These phones were approximately 4"x6"x8", conveniently packed in a leather case. I witnessed my father using one of these one time. He would sit on the saddle horse; throw a rope over the No. 9 telephone line, which was always strung on the tree overhead along the trail. He pulled the line down anchored the rope to the saddle horn hooked up the phone and rang the station.

Another way of communicating was to use a receiver off a crank phone. One could merely hook the two wires that protruded from the bottom of it on the main No. 9 line. The trick here was to catch the line in use. When you could hear the other parties talking you needed to talk into the thing and tell them you had a message to send, but the person needed to change the receiving end from your ear to your mouth as you listened and talked. This was more effective in mid-season when the telephone traffic was heavier.

Trail Bridges

In the days when supplies were packed in by stock only the trails and stream crossings, etc., required plenty of maintenance. Trail bridges were constructed where needed. Bridges were approximately four to five feet in width and as long as each situation required. A

1,200 to 1,400 pound mule carried a load of 250 to 300 pounds and in emergencies could pack up to 400 pounds. I have seen 400 pounds packed on a 1,300-pound mule and carried for twenty miles. These bridges were vital in keeping the pack animal stable. First, stringers were placed across the stream and leveled. Then 8" to 10" logs were split lengthwise in half. These logs were placed on flat side down crosswise on the stringers. Two more stringers were cut and placed on top of the decking to the outside and were wired down with No. 9 telephone wire and were twisted tight with a small pole or husky stick, thus we had a bridge approximately four foot wide and as long as was needed to cross the swamp or stream. Some crossings with a narrower span and hard rock bottom didn't require bridges. "Burro" creek on the Rexford District was named after a pack burro at such a crossing. A trail crew of two men, Bill Hunsinger, a 6 footer and 250 pounds, and Bill Smith about 5'6" at approximately 140 pounds. It was their job to travel the trails and logout and do any hand grading that was needed. This time one of their pack burros (they had to carry the camp equipment and tools) became stubborn and decided he wouldn't cross the creek. Well, ole Bill Hunsinger couldn't pull him across by the halter rope so he walked around behind grabbed this burro's hind legs, lifted and wheel barrowed him across the creek. After the story was told it became known as Burro Creek.

Here I will add what I know about names of different places on the Rexford Ranger District:

Knife Gulch in The Big Creek Drainage

It was named after a hunting accident. John Roberts, Jr., who lived at the mouth of Big Creek at the time, downed a large blacktail buck. As he started field dressing the animal, the buck's hind leg kicked the hunting knife into his thigh and due to gangrene his leg required amputation between the knee and the hip. Hence Charlie Powell, then the District Ranger, so named the drainage Knife Gulch.

Virginia Hill

Was named after the many settlers in the Pinkham Creek drainage who migrated from Virginia and West Virginia.

Still Creek

Was named after a moonshine still found in the area during Prohibition days.

Cook's Run

This drainage was named after a homesteader from West Virginia by the name of Abraham Lincoln Cook. Here, too, a still was located and destroyed by revenue officers.

Teepee Playhouse

When I was about five years of age my father had a small canvas teepee. He used it for camping and hunting trips. One morning after my older brothers were gone to school he said, "Sid, how would you like to have the teepee for a playhouse?" Well, that suited me fine. To my amazement he dug a hole about four feet deep in the ground where the teepee was to be pitched. Then he rolled a barrel of moonshine mash out there and carefully lowered it in the hole covered it with short pieces of board and canvas then a layer of dirt. Next he gathered some scraps of wood, etc., and built a fire. This fire did away with the signs of fresh digging. Next came the teepee pitched directly over the cache. Well I moved in and was instructed to tell no one what I was living over. In the next day or two we were visited by the revenue officers who made a thorough search for moonshine or the makings. Nothing was uncovered and we all felt secure again. The barrel of mash was dug up and returned to its own place to finish brewing. I learned later that our county sheriff, Mr. Frank Baney, for forty years often times would alert the moonshiners if possible of the coming of the revenuers. In those days White Lightning was a good part of the income for the homesteaders.

Warex Mountain

Was named for being half way between the old towns of Warland and Rexford which was drowned by the Koocanusa Lake. The Warex Lookout was first manned the summer of 1936 by Ed Arnold, Jr.

Lydia Peak, Pinkham Creek, and Pinkham Mountain

Was named after Mrs. Pinkham, who homesteaded at the mouth of Pinkham Creek where it entered the Kootenai River.

Slick's Gulch

Named for homesteader Frank Slick.

Bank's Draw

Named for Victor Banks, who lived at the junction of the draw road and Pinkham Creek road. However, Mr. Banks was not the original homesteader. The homesteader here was Andrew Stacy.

Black Butte

Named after Black Lake and the highest butte in that small range.

Snow Measurement in the Past on the Rexford District

The District Ranger, who was, as a rule, the only employee at the station during the winter did the snow measurements. Bright and early in the morning about March 1 the Ranger would leave old Rexford Station with measuring equipment in the packsack and a pair of snowshoes. Once he crossed the Kootenai River and started up the Clingback Mountain trail for the Red Mountain measuring area. Approximately half-way up Clingback Mountain trail was a trapper's cabin. The District packer left a sleeping bag and a grub cache here in the previous fall. The ranger stopped here the first night. He would snowshoe up to the measurement area the next day and back to the cabin. Now it was entirely up to him if he wanted to stay a second night or go home. Mostly they stayed the second night. This trail meandered up the mountain through the area now known as Rexford Face.

Burning of the Pinkham Ranger Station

In the fall of 1922 the station was built fifteen miles up the Pinkham Creek Road. It was a beautiful lodge type cabin with concrete foundation. It was constructed entirely out of well matched peeled larch logs. It was approximately 20'x24', two rooms downstairs and with a sleeping room in the attic. It sported a full-length floored porch on the east side. It also had a matching woodshed and log outdoor toilet. Stock corrals were constructed along with approximately a thirty-acre pasture for the animals.

It was designed to be used as a work center or base camp and smokechaser's cabin. It served the purpose well until in the 1950's as more roads and better transportation took over. During the early 1950's it was left unlocked for the public to use, there being only the wood cook stove and heating stove and cupboards and tables and some other furniture. It was truly a beautiful cabin complete with brick chimney, wood shingled roof, and large window (approximately 4'x5'). The windows were divided into one foot square panes with wood frames one-half-inch wide around each pane. Gus Verdall was ranger at the Rexford District during 1956 and 1957. The Supervisor's Office decided the Forest didn't have any use for the building any longer and decided it should be destroyed. They asked Gus to burn it. The public's reaction was so severe that Gus kept putting it off. Finally, Supervisor Alskog was ready to either retire or move in February 1957. He said his last job on the Kootenai was to burn the Pinkham Ranger Station. My home is one-quarter-of-a-mile from the site. Sure enough I saw the green sedan pass my house this morning in February. I also knew, due to snow in the road, the sedan couldn't travel any farther than the station so I surmised this was the fate of Pinkham station. I walked to the site and by the time I arrived Mr. Alskog had broken out all the windows with a pulaski, opened the trapdoor into the cellar and ignited the fire. The inside of the building caught fire quickly as there was an accumulation of greasy substance on the logs and in the ceiling of the kitchen area. The heavy log stringers of the walls took several hours to burn, due to heavy snow on the roof. Needless to say the public's reaction was severe. Mr. Alskog had carried out a Forest decision and was moving as one would say "Out of sight, out of mind". Presently the District has placed a picnic table and a fire ring at the site, but the foundation is crumbling in and some of the charred pieces of the building are still visible. Recreationists are still stopping to use the facilities. I would recommend the District move in an outdoor toilet and fill and level the foundation hole and add another table if possible. I have many memories of happiness here. Part of the log outdoor toilet still stands.

Honeymoon Night in a Ranger's Residence

I doubt very much if many newlyweds have spent the first night of their honeymoon in a ranger's residence. This, by chance, happened to the wife and me. We were in Eureka, Montana, February 11, 1943. I came home on furlough from the Air Force in Illinois. We picked this day to get married, borrowed her father's car, a 1936 Chrysler, and traveled to the Libby Courthouse. The trip was slow as the snow was deep in the old Highway 37 down the Kootenai River. We reached the courthouse about 4:30 p.m., and it closed business at 5:00 p.m. The people there hurried us as best they could and the license was granted before closing time. The clerk of the court offered to go with us across the street to be our witness. By 5:30 we were married by Rev. Fort of the Methodist Church in the parsonage. The snow was coming fast and furious. We decided to head back up the river, sixty-five miles from home. We had only two days to get started back to my reporting station in Illinois. The car was puffing pretty hard by the time we arrived at the old Warland Ranger Station. It so happened my father was cooking for a crew of surveyors there that winter so we stopped to have coffee and cherry pie he had promised he would have on our way back. Snow kept falling and piling up fast. Ranger Lake heard we were in the cookhouse and he and his wife insisted they put us in their guest room for the night, as no one should be traveling on such a stormy night. We accepted the invitation. Now Mr. Lake's hobby was photography and he insisted on taking our wedding picture. After an hour and a half and a dozen different poses he finished. He had the old tripod type camera where he covered his head with a black cloth as he focused and tripped the shutters. Next we spent some time, seemed like hours, looking at his collection of wildlife pictures. He had some wonderful shots of the Ural sheep herd. He would lie in wait any length of time to get the shot he wanted of a special animal or a group of animals. Needless to say, it turned out to be a short night in the guest room. The next morning we followed the State snowplow into Rexford. Our honeymoon, as it was planned, just kept waiting.

Big Creek Cabin and Area

Big Creek Cabin, as local residents knew it, was located seven and one-half miles up Big Creek at the north and south forks. Built sometime in the late 20's or early 30's it served as a packer's base camp, smokechaser cabin, trail crew headquarters, etc. Stock corrals and feed racks were built. Many memories do the many men working the area have for the famous site, such as bears in the garbage pit, pack rats on the rafters, and of course no end to the trout that could be taken from the creek. A road was constructed in the 30's up to the cabin and before 1940 it continued on up the south fork and connected with the east fork of Pipe Creek, making it possible to drive through to Libby, Montana.

In and around 1910 mountain goats inhabited this area as told to me by my father and Wallace Butts, both early settlers here. It is believed they migrated northwest into north Idaho or British Columbia.

Some mining claims were taken in this area in the 1920's – one by Oscar Gibler, just north and west of the Big Creek Cabin. In fact the Big Creek Cabin and his cabin were side by side. Now, Oscar would stay year- round working his mine. My father, the District packer, usually the first one up the trail to the cabin, would arrive the first part of June. Oscar would, after a long winter, greet him with a hot meal and plenty of home brew. Oscar was one tickled old miner. He always said he could hear the lead mule's bray three miles down the trail.

Another claim cabin in that area was located approximately one and one-quarter miles northwest of the Big Creek Cabin. Any sign of trails have faded now and lodgepole timber covers the area. I remember a friend of mine found the remains of a miner here in the cabin by the last name of Henry. He figured the man had been dead at least thirty days.

Bob Hark, a District employee here for many years, and Ray Hanson, a local logger, visited this cabin in the 50's and picked up a 1927 calendar. I understand at that time all of the hand mining tools including the wheelbarrow were in good shape.

Too fast a communicator service and transportation put this Big Creek Cabin out of use. But instead of burning, as was the fate of the Pinkham Ranger Station, it was donated to the Historical Village in Eureka. Members of the Tobacco Valley Improvement Association (TVIA), donating their time, disassembled the cabin piece by piece and erected it in the Historical Village. Most everyone visiting the Big Creek Cabin would write, print, or scribe either names and dates in the logs on the front end and many names and initials are there.

SID WORKMAN
Employment History, Stories, and Names
Kootenai National Forest, Rexford Ranger District
May 1981, updated June 2006

During the months of July, August, and September of 1936, I was employed as temporary packer on the Rexford District. My father was a full-time packer. That summer he seemed to keep fairly busy in the Big Creek and West Kootenai areas. Road survey crews and trail crews and some other operations were active in the Sutton Creek and Pinkham Creek areas at the same time. Charlie Powell, the Rexford Ranger then, and, I might add, who is still in good health residing in Spokane, Washington, knew I could handle a small pack outfit. If he had a job I could handle in the Sutton Creek and Pinkham Creek area, he would send me word to meet him somewhere with the pack stock, or he would send the supplies to be packed, wherever. I suppose if I had added all my time together, I could have realized one months employment. I was being allowed $1.00 per day per head for a horse and saddle. I was paid $0.75 per hour, packing was considered skilled labor. Low wage on the fire line labor was $0.35 per hour. Civilian Conservation Corp (C.C.C.), boys received $1.00 per day plus room, board, and clothing.

During the summer I packed supplies to trail crews and survey crews in the Pinkham Creek and Sutton Creek areas. I moved a road survey crew camp along what is now the Sutton Ridge Road. This survey included approximately four miles of spur road into Warex Mountain Lookout. These four miles were never constructed. Only last year a road into the present Rocky Tweed timber sale followed this same survey. My youngest son, Steve, helped to saw and brush-cut this right of way while employed by Royal Logging Company.

Powell hired me and a team of my father's horses one day to skid lumber up the west side of Virginia Hill. We chained one end of the lumber on a stone boat and drug the other end. Now, this lumber was destined to build a platform for a tree lookout and frame for a tent camp. This distance was approximately one mile the way the crow flew, but I made several switchbacks getting up the hill so I traveled maybe one mile and a half. I was sure glad to see the big ponderosa pine, my destination. The tree had been carefully picked out as the only one suitable and in the right location. But lo and behold, two days later I was hired to move the lumber again. Someone had marked and topped the wrong tree. After skidding the lumber another quarter mile east up the hill, we came to the second giant ponderosa pine. This tree became known as the tree lookout on Virginia Hill. The tree was topped at about fourteen inches in diameter and a 6x6 foot platform built. It had diagonal braces back to the trunk. A sturdy guardrail was constructed around the thing, and the top was framed for a canvas roof. A trap door was cut in the floor so a man coming up the tree could push it open with his head (his hands were needed for hanging onto limbs and branches). Lightning rods of one-half-inch copper wire were installed on all four corners and run into the ground at the foot of the trees. These rods were very needful as they drew the nearby lightning during a storm and made it safer up there during a hot storm. I have witnessed blue flames two feet high entering these rods in a storm.

Four guy wires were installed on four sides of the tree for support in windy times. Some "L" shaped lag bolts were screwed into the tree trunk for steps until the limbs were reached and from then on you climbed like a monkey. The lookout fireman, who manned this place, was furnished a saddle horse for packing water and going to fires. The purpose of this lookout was to observe the Cook's Run basin to the west. None of the lookouts on the District could see into this area. In most of the 30's the summers were dry and lightning storms plentiful. Two more tree towers were built that year on the Rexford District. One was located on Lydia Peak toward the south end of Sutton Ridge, and Beartrap, located farther north on a ridge over looking most of the lower Sutton Creek Drainage.

The first week of September 1936 lightning set a fire in the Edna Creek drainage in the Ant Flat District, known today as Murphy Lake Ranger Station. A huge fire ignited, spreading 1,000 to 1,200 acres in the first twenty-four hours. Part of this fire was burning westerly toward the top of Pinkham Ridge. Early the next morning after the strike, Ranger Powell called our homestead. We had a Forest Service-installed crank telephone, as did many of the ranchers and homesteaders on the District. The main purpose of these phones was for anyone to use to report fires, etc. Charlie's message was for me to saddle a couple horses and meet him at the end of the Pinkham Creek road about three miles from home. I was sure I had enough time, as he had to drive twenty miles in a 1934 Chev pickup, but I only waited at the rendezvous a few minutes before he showed. All he said was, "We are going to recon the west side of this fire." I knew as soon as we started up Trail #4, the main trail up Pinkham Creek, that I had forgot to bring an ax. It was important to always carry an ax for clearing windfalls out of the trail if you traveled by horse. We took Trail #4, three miles south where it junctioned with Trail #274. As we rode east on 274, we encountered windfalls in the trail that could have called for an ax. We detoured some and gave others different treatment such as: Charlie, who was over six foot tall, would hold the lighter poles up so I could lead the horses under: Some, he could hold or pry down with a short pole for a lever and I would jump the horses across. Charlie was riding a bay mare by the name of Madame Queen. This mare hated these detours off the trail, she had a habit of falling down when she crossed down logs, etc., and refused to get up. On one of our detours off the trail this happened. Charlie said, "Sid, you better get that mare up, we're going to a fire." I just grinned to myself, as I had the solution from past experiences. I told Charlie to get out on the end of the halter rope. Then I went to the south end of that mare, raised her tail, and lighted a match and held it up high where there wasn't any hair. "Presto", that mare was on her feet and ready to travel.

When we reached the ridgetop the fire had spread to the trail running north and south along the ridge. Charlie said, "Let's go back down the ridge trail to the pickup," A base camp was being set up there while we were gone. By the time we had arrived where we had left the pickup in the morning, sure enough a camp was there. I saw Greyhound busloads of men, school bus loads of men, truckloads of horses, mules, hay and supplies for camp etc. We even rated a veterinarian and a blacksmith with that much stock. Charlie told me to build a manger for my horses, take good care of them, and sleep close by. The next day I was assigned four more horses to make a string of five. I was to pack drinking water to line camp at Bear Lake about a ten mile round trip. I carried thirty gallons of water per horse, that's fifteen gallon on each side. The containers were special molded heavy gauge tin that buckled to the packsaddle. I made two loads every day and sometimes three. I worked about ten days at this camp. The timekeeper would come around to inquire about time once in awhile. The first time he ask me I wasn't sure, but old Charlie was there and he said "Give Sid seventy-two hours the first three days and he will be responsible for keeping his own after that." On one night trip to the Bear Lake camp, manned by 200 C.C.C. men with Army reserve officers in charge, I arrived after dark. My saddle horse was white, so white you could almost see him at night. As I approached the camp, ole Frenchy, my horse, stopped dead in the trail and started snorting and smelling the ground in front of him.

Then, soon, I heard a lot of shouting and scuffling as men jumped out of the trail dragging sleeping bags after them. I warned them not to sleep in the trail, but the next night the same thing happened but this time everyone was screaming to his buddy "Get out of the trail. The white stallion has returned."

I also ran an ambulance service, in a way, as several times someone would ride one of the packhorses out. It was usually an injury caused by an axe cut, one with a broken arm, and I remember one man rode out with a skull fracture; his head was bound up like an Egyptian.

On June 7, 1939, I was hired as lookout fireman. I was stationed on Robinson Mountain. My father packed in the supplies and so forth. It was a seven-mile hike to from Dodge Summit north up the ridge to the lookout. My stay there was until September 7. In those ninety days two people visited me: my father brought more grub in the latter part of July and the District Ranger for an inspection about mid-August. I enjoyed watching a small covey of ptarmigan that frequented the spring where I packed my water. The spring was located one-half-mile west of the lookout. I haven't heard any reports on the ptarmigan lately to know if the little group still exists.

The season of 1940 I was employed at the Libby District. Charlie Powell, who had been transferred there from Rexford, requested Dick Clark and myself to work there that summer. He made us trail crew, telephone line maintenance crew, and a lookout of me and head smoke chaser out of Dick during the critical fire time. I spent approximately one month on a lookout on the Big Hoodoo Mountain. Except for a flurry of late June lightning strike fires, it was pretty quiet fire year. It was much wetter than the dry 30's.

Dick Clark, my foreman, was an excellent cook and a real fine fellow to work for. I remember one of our camps on Bear Creek about twenty miles south of Libby. Every now and then Dick would bake pies, biscuits, or a cake. While he was cooking I would fish right alongside our camp. We had a No. 2 galvanized washtub, which we kept at the edge of the creek and filled about half full of water. The surplus fish went into the tub to keep them fresh and cold. I told Dick one evening I wasn't fishing anymore. He said, "Just keep adding fish to that tub." The next evening we came back to camp all the fish were gone. But, lo and behold, two dozen pint bottles of home brew was floating there. It was excellent beer. You uncapped it and blue smoke rolled out of the neck of the bottle. I hadn't been aware, but Dick had prearranged this wonderful event with a friend of his in Libby. Another time we set up camp alongside a placer miner by the last name of Howard, up Libby

Creek beyond Libby old town. In those days we were paid by the month and worked five and a half days per week. Our weekend started at noon on Saturday. As one of us was required to tend camp on weekends, we took turns. Howard, the miner, hired us to wheelbarrow muck for him on weekends at $6.00 per day. We wheeled the muck out in the middle of the Creek and dumped it in a sluice box, where the water washed everything away except black sand. The sand would then be washed in the gold pan and separated from the gold flakes. Gold was selling at about $16.00 per ounce. This $6.00 on the wheelbarrows looked good compared to $3.00 per day on the trail work. Libby Creek still draws many weekenders and gold pans.

In the fall of 1940 all the crews on the Forest were assembled in one big camp on Ruby Creek in Troy District. The job here was to slash and pile and burn a fire break around an 8-mmbf white pine sale. The Diamond Match Company had purchased the sale and the Forest Service was required to construct this firebreak. It was during this job about the middle of October 1940, we were obligated to register for the draft. This meant all men twenty-one through thirty-five years of age. Each man was given a number and a time to be drafted. Dick and I both volunteered ahead of our calling for the draft. I enlisted August 22, 1941, in the Army Air Force. My tour of duty ran all through World War II until December of 1945. The only close calls I had were made by a V-2 German rocket missing me by about four city blocks in London, and spending twenty-four hours in a bomb shelter in northern England wearing a gas mask. This event took place Christmas Eve and Christmas Day of 1943 while the Germans were bombing our air base.

Dick was killed while the Allies were establishing the beachhead at Anzio, Italy, sometime in January of 1944. After my tour in the military, my employment was elsewhere and not connected with the government except for some major fires on the Forest.

In August of 1946 the Fan Creek fire cut loose after it started from two separate lightning strikes. Two fires merged into one on the ridge between Sullivan and Boulder Creeks. In today's fire class terms it could be a class E. I spent the first night crosscut sawing fallen timber out of a pack trail. My sawing partner was the late Don Sederdahl, Donna Sederdahl's father. I was assigned to blazing perimeter fire line next morning with the late Jack Skelly, Tom Skelly's uncle, from Ant Flat District. Water was dropped into camps on this fire from C-47 and C-46 planes. Ten-gallon cream cans were used for containers and were parachuted very accurately into the camps. This was the first year I recall the Forest using radios. I recall Ranger Oak Knapp burning his arms quite severely retrieving a radio that had carelessly been left in the wrong place and was surrounded by fire. These were a far cry from our portable lightweights today.

My next big fire in 1958 was the Stone Hill Fire. This fire was approximately eight miles down the Kootenai River below old Rexford. It was started by a hot box on a freight car coming up the Great Northern Railroad (since called the Burlington Railroad). This same day the same train started a fire south of Eureka called the Glen Lake Fire and another near Stryker farther up the line. Hot boxes were caused by an axle bearing running dry of lubrication. A steel box contained the axle bearing. This box was approximately eight inches square and was filled with waste cloth and oil. The oil was supposed to filter through the waste and keep the bearing lubricated. When they went dry they soon started to burn and could even melt the steel which, in turn, was scattered along the track in red-hot pieces. Many fires have been set by the hot boxes.

I hired out temporary to the Rexford Ranger District again in February of 1963 and worked in that status up to October of 1973. During this tour I managed to work the Boulder Sullivan Cutoff, the East Little North Fork, and the Pinkham Fire. The latter being man-caused, hit the community pretty hard by destroying approximately 400 acres of private timber and Christmas tree lands. About 200 acres of this fire was on National Forest. 1967 was another bad season, seemingly not our District though, as other Forests kept pulling on us for manpower and we seemed to have an asbestos Forest. The first week in October of 1967, Glenn Pershall and I were flown to St. Maries, Idaho, to work on the Shoepack Fire on the St. Joe. After a week there we were snowed out. This fire had covered approximately 1,100 acres. It had been started as a control burn.

All my time since 1963 I was employed on the Rexford Ranger District. I made many friends, too numerous to mention. Some of my older supervisors include the following: the late Bob Hark; the late Frank Bolles; the late Eldin Butts; Merrill Davis, transferred; Dave Brockmann, retired; Carl Pershall, retired; Barry Griffith, transferred; Keith Glover, private industry; Johnny Mocko, retired; George Curtis, retired; Bob Seidel, retired; and my last supervisor was Glenn Pershall, retired. This is by no means a complete list. I enjoyed working with the younger employees on the District. It seems the average age was somewhere between twenty-two and forty-two.

Rangers I have worked under are:

Charlie Powell, Rexford Ranger District and Libby Ranger District
- Ed Hendricksen, Troy Ranger District
- Oak Knapp, Rexford Ranger District
- Charles Kern, Rexford Ranger District
- John Johnson, Rexford Ranger District
- John Hossack, Rexford Ranger District
- John Bushfield, Rexford Ranger District
- Terry Moore, Rexford Ranger District
- Ed Shultz, Rexford Ranger District
- Dave Poncin, Rexford Ranger District

THE PINKHAM CREEK CLOSURE – 1924
By Sam Billings (Early Days in the Forest Service, Volume 4)

Sometimes referred to as the Pinkham Creek Insurrection or the Pinkham Creek Rebellion, the entire Federal lands in the Pinkham Creek drainage, Kootenai National Forest, were closed to entry without permit beginning about the first of August 1924 and were kept closed until the September rains.

For several years preceding this closure, the Forest Service had to contend with incendiary fires that were set within or adjacent to the drainage. These fires were believed to have been set by homesteaders in Pinkham Creek, who set the fires in order to obtain work as firefighters. In the latter part of July 1924 a rash of these fires was set – some 32 fires, if the writer remembers right, were set at one time; and the Forest Service decided to take drastic action. The Forest was closed to entry except by permit, and seven camps were established around the valley, out of which patrolmen enforced the closure. There were three men in each camp – two patrolmen and a camp tender, who did the cooking and watched camp during the day. All the patrolmen were armed and were supplied a saddle horse apiece for riding out over the trails. Wages were $100 per month and found.

This writer was one of the patrolmen and was assigned to Camp No. 1 – the first camp on the road at the lower end of Pinkham Creek. Andy Fluetsch, sent over from the then Absaroka National Forest, was the other patrolman in this camp, and Bill Hillis, from Libby, was the camp tender. Andy was a long, lean cowpuncher-type and was a fast-draw artist. Bill was short and round and bald and was a retired professional gunman who had worked for years for the Peters Arms Company, doing exhibition shooting at circuses and on the vaudeville circuit. They picked me – they told me later – because I had served in a tough outfit, the First Division, in World War I.

The people who organized this armed patrol must have thought there would be violent resistance to the closure, but there was none – only the threat of it one day. Fluetsch and I usually left camp around 8 a.m. and rode out in different directions each day, sometimes together and sometimes each in a different direction. We usually returned to camp at around 4 p.m. Bill Hillis usually stayed in camp all day, but occasionally, he would catch a ride into Rexford or Eureka on business of his own, or rarely, he would go duck hunting. One day we returned to camp around 4 p.m., as usual, and found a note on the dishup table. Bill had gone to Eureka and had not yet returned. The note read "You get to hell out of here or we will shoot up your camp," and it was signed "Pinkham Creekers." Andy and I slept on cots in one tent, and Bill slept on a cot in the cook tent where we ate our meals. Naturally, we were a little nervous for awhile after reading the note; and both Andy and I had our guns under our pillows at night. I carried a Luger 9 mm automatic, but Andy had a .38 Smith & Wesson, with an 8-inch barrel; and as stated earlier, he was a fast draw artist and practiced every morning at it before he sat down to breakfast.

The third night after receiving the note, and soon after getting to sleep some rattling of cooking utensils woke me up. There was a tarp stretched out in front of our tent and a small mix-up table under it on which Bill had stacked some pots and pans. I raised up on my elbow and looked out the tent flap and saw a pack rat rummaging around on the table and in and out of the dishes. There was a full moon – and very bright. Without arousing Andy, I pulled the Luger from under my pillow, leveled on the pack rat and fired. Andy's reaction was instantaneous. It wasn't a second before his feet hit the dirt floor and he stood there with the .38 in his hand. I don't think I ever saw a man move that fast before. Had there been someone out there, it would have been just too bad.

Bill Hillis, our camp tender, had made a profession of shooting practically all his life. As a young man, he was a market hunter in California and made his living shooting wild ducks and geese before there were any game laws. He shot them day in and day out, as long as there were any to shoot: and he became as skilled at it as anyone alive. He could do anything with a shotgun and often demonstrated his skill while we were in camp. His favorite trick was to load his pump gun full of shells and start firing into the air, and he knew how to jerk his gun while ejecting the shell so that it would fly up and ahead, and he would shoot and hit each ejected shell.

After game laws went into effect, he went to work for the Peters

Arms Company and traveled all over the United States and Europe with vaudeville companies and circuses doing trick shooting. He could take any type gun, whether he had ever had it in his hands before or not, and do amazingly accurate shooting with it.

I recall one Sunday a doctor from Eureka and his family stopped at the camp to visit. The doc had a .22 caliber rifle with him and was quite proud of his ability to shoot with it. He belonged to a rifle team and the National Rifle Association. He used a small pine knot on the tamarack flag pole we had at camp and put a very creditable group of five shots around the knot. Hillis complimented him on his marksmanship, and asked if he might try his luck. The doc said, "Sure," and handed him the rifle with five shells in it. Bill fired the five shells at the same distance at another pine knot (about the same size as a .22 bullet) in quick succession, and all holes overlapped. He apologized for the overlaps, saying his eyes were failing him.

There were two arrests made during the patrol; both for trespass on a closed area. One of the arrests was made by Fluetsch and me. We knew that one of the homesteaders, living one-half mile or so up a draw and away from the creek, had to haul water for himself and family and stock. He had none whatsoever on his place. He hauled two barrels at a time on a stone boat pulled by a team of horses. His horses, when not in use, were turned loose and grazed on the National Forest. We knew what they looked like, where they grazed, and when they were used. The homesteader had been told two different times that he could have a permit for the length of the closure and to go out and get his horses. He assured us both times that his horses never went onto Government land – he always kept them on his place and, therefore, didn't need any so-and-so permit from us. He even told us what we could do with said permit.

Our camp was near the creek and within a short distance of the willows and alders that lined the creek. We discovered tracks in the soft, moist earth that indicated possibly two barefoot boys were sneaking through the brush after dark to within hearing distance of our camp and listening in on our conversation as we sat around the campfire and discussed where we would patrol the next day. We presumed our plans were pretty well distributed among the residents up and down the creek.

So, one night we talked about our next day's plans in tones loud enough to make sure anyone could hear it out in the willows. We were to go out along some trails on the east side. At our usual bedtime, we went into our tent, lay down for a half hour or so, and then rolled up our blankets and stuffed them into packsacks along with an alarm clock and a breakfast lunch Bill Hillis had prepared for each of us. We strapped on our guns and, with packsack on our backs, we crawled out under the back end of the tent and across the creek in pitch darkness. There was no moon that night, and we had difficulty in finding the trail on the west side but finally did and without too much trouble reached the area where we knew the aforementioned horses would be grazing. They both had bells on them so they were easy to locate, and we bedded down on the trail close by after setting the alarm clock to wake us just before daybreak. When the alarm went off, we stuffed our blankets into our packsack, hid out in the brush beside the trail while we ate our sack lunch and waited for the suspect. We waited but a short while before he came up the trail with halters and a pail of oats in his hand. Andy Fluetsch jumped out into the trail with gun in hand and it scared the poor fellow to where I thought he was going to faint. We told him he was under arrest for trespassing in a closed area of the National Forest, helped him gather up his horses, and took him back to his home and thence to the U.S. Commissioner in Eureka, where he was placed under $500 bond. As far as I know, neither he nor the other man that was arrested were ever brought to trial.

    The closure ended in September with the first heavy rain, and some of us were assigned to construct the new cabin up the creek and some to build a new 72-foot lookout tower on Pinkham Ridge. After the first heavy snows, the tower job was brought to a halt, and I was assigned to go on game patrol with Charlie Hudson from the Upper Yaak country. I never knew the reason for this game patrol. Both Hudson and I were made honorary deputy game wardens, but we made no arrests or saw any evidence of poaching and very seldom saw any game.

    We were quartered in tents with the crew building the new cabin. By the time the cabin was finished in mid-November the snow around the tents was stacked up against the canvas walls to the roof line. When construction was complete, all except putting a partition through the middle, it was decided to have a dance and invite the Pinkham Creekers. Most of us had become pretty well acquainted with most of them and found them nice, friendly people; and we had a very happy party that night. Whole families came – children and all. The younger kids were put to bed in the tents.

    Our cook was a young Italian fellow, and besides being a good cook he was a good mandolin player. One of the Pinkham Creekers was a good fiddler, and he and the cook really made the folks step lively in the square dances. There was some moonshine imbibed outside between dances but none to excess. The cook had prepared a lot of food and coffee for midnight lunch after which the dance went on for another couple of hours. After everyone had gone and I crawled into my tent, I found the blankets soaked.

These people were largely from the hills of West Virginia and Kentucky and had been poverty stricken all their lives. Their ways of living back East had changed little or possibly for the worse in Pinkham Creek. The soil on most of the homesteads was a white clay too acid for the raising of most crops, and in dry summer not enough water was available for irrigating any land but that close to the creek. Some of the more able-bodied made a partial living hacking railroad ties from the tamarack and Douglas-fir stands on their homesteads and adjacent National Forest. These they hauled to the Great Northern tracks at Eureka for which they got $0.43 a tie – if they passed inspection. Some made moonshine, some had a few head of cattle and tried to raise hay. All of the land had been timber land – largely Douglas-fir and tamarack (western larch) but some ponderosa pine – and there were stumps in almost every clearing. Some clearings were also rocky, and it was the custom with some to pick up the rocks and place them on the stumps. Noticing one day that the stumps in a quite large field were pretty well rotted out, I asked the owner why he didn't get rid of them so he could raise more hay; and he replied, "Well, what in hell would I do with all of the rocks?"

All at that time lived in log cabin homes. There was no electricity in the valley nor was there telephone line except Forest Service. All farm work was by manpower or horses. No one had any powered farm machinery. There were no radios. I bought an early battery-operated Radiola with earphones – the first one in the valley – soon after the Forest Service cabin was completed.

One Sunday I invited old Mr. O'Brien, who lived a mile or so down the road, to come up and listen to a church service from a Catholic church being broadcast from Winnipeg, Canada. He had never seen a radio before, and although a devout Catholic, he had not been to church for some twenty years or more. I sat him at the table on which the radio was placed, adjusted the earphones on his head, during which process he showed considerable nervousness, and turned it on. The services had just started and were coming in real good. The old fellow sat there with both hands cupped over his cane during the full hour without moving a muscle or saying a word. When it was over he carefully removed the headphones and placed them on the table; and without saying a word, he took his cane and left. But he spent the rest of the day walking up and down the valley talking to anyone who would listen about the great miracle he had just been a party to. He had attended church in Winnipeg while sitting in the Forest Service cabin in Pinkham Creek.

Tony, our mandolin playing cook, another man whose name I can't recall but who had a good singing voice, and myself visited the O'Briens two different Sundays. The conditions under which they were living appalled us. They had no running water but dipped it out of a barrel outside; a two-lid wood-burning cook stove that was warped all out of shape; an outside toilet, the door of which wouldn't close because the top hinge was gone; a potbellied stove for heating that seemed as though it put more smoke into the room than went up the chimney; windows that you could barely see through and with two panes of glass missing and covered with paper. They did have and old foot pump organ that the old couple said was brought over from Ireland by their grandparents and was in playing condition. Their granddaughter, a girl about eighteen years old, was living with them and caring for them, and she could and did play the organ while Tony played his mandolin; and the rest of us sang from an old hymnal they had. The old folks' lives seemed to be made a little happier by these visits.

Money for my employment that year ran out the first week in December, and I left Pinkham Creek. Having just come from Massachusetts in early July, the things seen and experiences gained have remained rather vividly in my mind these fifty years. It is hoped that these recollections may add to those already placed on record by others.

PAT KEARNEY

Patrick Kearney, born in1850, came from Ireland to the U.S.A. He met and married Mary Greer of Wisconsin. Their only son, Joseph, lived with them in Standing Rock, West Virginia, in a log house. When Joe was old enough he worked with his dad in a barrel factory. At that time wooden barrels were used for shipping most everything by land or sea.

Joe married Elizabeth Hocum, also of West Virginia. They had three children, Hazel, born 1905; Roscoe, born in 1907; and Gladys, born in 1920. In 1912 both Kearney families decided to come west to seek their own land.

They came by train to Whitefish, then went to the Flathead County courthouse to file on a homestead for both Pat and Joe. Their land was located up Pinkham Creek along Cooks Run headwaters.

Pat and Joe helped each other clear land and build a log cabin to prove up on their homestead. The Kearney children attended the upper school along with Workmans and O'Briens. They all walked through the wilderness to school or to visit neighbors. The only transportation to town was by horseback.

By the summer of 1920 their hard work paid off. They were issued a patent from the General Land Office dated Sept. 28, 1920, signed by President Woodrow Wilson.

Now Pat and Joe each had 160 acres of their own. To live off the land they planted apple trees, rhubarb, and raised a big garden for stew to go along with venison and other wild meat. They picked wild berries such as serviceberries and huckleberries.

They cut the timber from their land to sell to lumber mills or make ties for the railroad. But they never used the water from the delightful little stream for making moonshine. This clear, cool spring water was essential for survival and they were thankful that it was close to their home. The water rights on their patent assured them it was theirs to use.

Pat Kearney died Oct. 10, 1922, at the age of seventy-two. He was buried in the Tobacco Valley Cemetery. His widow then lived with their son Joe. Elizabeth decided to take the children to live in town where they could attend high school. She worked as a waitress at the Eureka Cafe.

About 1925, Joe and his mother moved to the Lampton place, a homestead situated between Black Lake Road and the Pinkham Road near Gregor Lake. The little lake on the place became known as Kearney Lake as well as Turtle Lake. The sharp elbow bend in the Pinkham road was called Kearney corner.

While attending high school Roscoe was given the name "Chili" for con carne. He was also a redheaded Irishman who could set off hot sparks with his Irish temperament.

In 1933 Chili married Opal Greene, who had attended school at the Black Lake School. Their children were Luella, Carol Jeane, Lee Patrick, Michael and Lesley. They all attended school in Eureka.

Hazel Kearney married Jack Lang, lived in Spokane, and had no children. Gladys married a Gravelle and moved to Sandpoint, Idaho.

Joe let the homestead go back to the county in 1943. Roscoe paid the taxes and it became his. Then he sold it to Tobacco River Lumber Company in 1956.

Chili became a local logger and worked in the Christmas tree business. He worked for the Kirk Christmas Tree Co. for many years as a cutter and buyer for the yard, as well as load-out railroad cars.

Chili and Opal never lived on Pinkham, but it was one of their favorite recreation spots.

'PERLEY WATER OF PINKUM CRICK'

"Come to these 'perley waters of Pinkum,'"
Wrote pioneers to folks back home
"Leave ole virginny for this new land
Make Montana hills your new home."

So they came to settle Pinkham Creek
Bringing with them a familiar skill.
They found the 'perley water of Pinkum Crick'
Ideal for setting up a corn 'likker' still

They brought copper tubing and a boiler
Shipped in the sugar and the corn.
Using the 'perley waters of Pinkum Crick'
and knowledge with which they were born.

Then they sampled all the moonshine
To see which hill-billy batch was best.
"I'll taste yours and you taste mine,
We'll put this firewater to the test."

But before the testing was all done
Some other neighbors came to call.
They came in time to join the fun
Which soon turned into a brawl.

Tempers flared, fisted knuckles flashed
As old family feuds were renewed.
Names were called as hunting knives flashed
Then stopped – trouble was not to be brewed.

They made a decision, what they must do –
Was find a market for this mountain dew
Folks flocked from town with money to spend
During hard times, Pioneers made a dividend.

By Madeline Utter

JIM ROBERTS – NANCY YOUNG (SIS) ROBERTS

Jim Roberts was born in West Virginia in 1852. He and his wife had seven children before she died in a cholera epidemic the year of 1904. Their sons were Emery, Elmer and Romey and another, who died as a child. Daughters were Octavia (Lockie), Cora and Chole Ethel.

Lockie married Sylvester Stacy in West Virginia. They were already living with their family up Pinkham Creek near other relatives in Montana. Cora and Marion Perry were wed in West Virginia then came west with the rest of the family. Chole Ethel had also married in West Virginia to Clyde Ramsey. They had a son, James Albert. Emery and his wife stayed in West Virginia.

Nancy Young was born in Roan County, West Virginia, in 1861. At the age of twenty-four she married Lewis Young and they had six children. Lewis died in the 1904 Cholera epidemic and left her a widow. Besides raising her children, Nancy served as a midwife as well as other services to her neighbors. When she married Jim Roberts, half of their children were leading lives of their own.

It was 1915 that they came west to Montana with a remnant of their combined families. Nancy's children were Rufus, Charlie, Levi and Fanny, who became known as "Big Fanny." Rufus was a widower with children of his own. They were Fanny (known as "Little Fanny), Jack, Bill and Nancy Jane.

At the time the double family move to Montana, Elmer Roberts and Charlie Young were delayed in West Virginia. They had witnessed a murder there and were called to testify at the trial. The two young men traveled by train together to join the family settling up Pinkham Creek. They were just in time to help dismantle the little log school building, then put it back together again on the place that Jim and Nancy had chosen for their homestead. The land lay alongside the boundary of the Leib homestead, spanning the creek and narrow country road.

After his wife died, Rufus Young brought his young children to join the family in Montana. His sickly infant son also died and was buried in the new Leib Cemetery on Pinkham. He left Little Fanny and toddler Jane with their Grandma Roberts. He took his two sons, Jack and Bill, with him to Ural, down on the Kootenai River. There he built a double cabin with a dog trot in between. (Open space with a roof overhead) While growing up, Jack and Bill made regular treks over the hills from Ural to Pinkham to visit their Grandma Roberts. Sometimes they spent the summer there as well as part of the school year.

Romey (called Rome) Roberts and Big Fanny Young fell in love and were married in the summer of 1916. Then in October of 1916,

Rome was killed in an accident with a wagon and a runaway team of horses. Fanny gave birth to a son she named Guy James Roberts. She later married a Beutel of Eureka.

On November 16, 1916, tragedy struck again. Cora's husband, Marion Perry, passed away with a mysterious illness, leaving her a widow. Cora later remarried but never had children.

Levi Young married Melinda O'Brien, daughter of another homesteader farther up the 'crick.' They had five sons: Oscar, Gene, Robert, Richard (Dick), Harold, and daughter, Invah. Harold was destined to marry Cle Ella Stacy, daughter of Ves and Lockie Stacy.

Jim and 'Sis' Roberts soon fit in with other homesteaders up Pinkham. They built a 'lean-to' kitchen on the side of the old log school house that they set near a good spring for water. A small spring house was built around it to keep milk, cream and butter fresh, summer and winter as the even temperature of the spring kept it from freezing. Water was carried in a bucket for household use.

Men set to work to clear the flat land situated between the road and Pinkham Creek, about five acres. They used crosscut saws to fall the timber and axes to trim off limbs. Railroad ties were made to specification and hauled to the landing by team and sleigh in winter or wagon in summer. A garden spot was plowed and root crops planted plus the staple fruit of rhubarb and apple trees. A field was prepared to sow oats and timothy for livestock feed. Sis wrote back home to West Virginia of their progress and her letter was published in their local newspaper.

Sis was soon in demand as an experienced midwife as well as herb doctor. She had no formal training, but used her common sense and the knack of figuring out what ailed a person. Her cupboards served as a drug store for the neighborhood. She earned the nickname of "Physics" because if all else failed, she prescribed a physic for the cure. Some kids thought she used magic witchcraft to take off warts. By just a touch of her finger, warts disappeared in just a few days.

Jim Roberts became the dentist in the community. It was very difficult for folks to get to a dentist in town, or even have the money to pay for service. Jim had a pair of forceps that he latched onto the sore tooth with, before giving it a yank and a twist to get it out. For most folks, the tooth hurt so badly before that it was a relief to have it out. There were some folks that drank enough moonshine to deaden the pain, while others took it like a man! Jim wasn't a moonshiner himself, but he did brew up some home-made beer with hops and sugar for his own use.

Jim was remembered for his ability to make good 'ole' mountain music. Like someone said, "He could make that fiddle talk!" His playing could bring tears to the eyes of his listeners or laughter to their lips. What dancers like most, were the hand-clappin', foot stompin', hoe-downs. Jim had an ear for music and a talent to be able to pick up and play most instruments. He memorized the tunes of others and could make up tunes of his own.

Jim was in demand to do his 'stuff' at many old-time get-togethers up Pinkham. He was happy to play his fiddle from dusk to dawn, but by then he was all tuckered out. His daughter-in-law, Ovella, kept up with him on the banjo while guitar players changed about. At times, Abe Cook or Cecil Utter played their fiddles to spell each other off. Jim's fiddle is treasured by his family.

When small sawmills became popular in the Twenties and Thirties, Jim decided to have his homestead logged the easy way. He let Tom Wilke set up his sawmill on the place to cut railroad ties. A camp for workers was set up in the clearing near the spring. There were shacks built for loggers and their families, and shelters for horses. Tom Wilke made several sets up Pinkham on different homesteads, but the camp was still used for free housing, then and for many years to come.

It was in May of 1943 that Jim deeded his 160 acre homestead to his son, Elmer Roberts. Since then the place has been divided several times. Eighty acres was traded to Tom and Lucille Burch in 1950 for a $300 Jeep. The place passed on to Louis and 'Lockie' Stacy Stangle in 1958. Part of the place become "Stacy Hollow" when portions along the creek were divided up among the Stacy family.

Jim lived to be ninety-seven years old. He spent his last years in Eureka. Grandma 'Sis' Roberts lived a long life. She died in 1962 at the age of 102. Her last years were spent in a nursing home in Libby near her granddaughter, Fanny Young Hammons.

PIONEER HOME REMEDIES

Bee stings and bug bites; make paste of baking soda and water to apply directly to sting – or use mud from the meadow.

Burns Pick leaf from Aloe Vera plant, split and apply juice directly on burned area, Heals and relieves pain.

Colic and upset tummies; let baby suck on peppermint candy (candy canes have handle to hold on to) adults drink mint tea.

Cold and flu; hot whiskey tonic made with 2 T whiskey and sugar and one half lemon, juiced, stirred into a cup of very hot water was used to cut a fever as well as congestion. Patient kept covered up until a sweat broke out to cleanse the body.

Croup; make tent over boiling water on stove (laced with Vicks Vapo rub or camphor) and sick baby so child can inhale medicated steam.

Cuts and Punctures; pour on wound raw turpentine immediately to relieve pain, clean wound, and sterilize. Bandage with clean strips of old sheets, etc.

Constipation; drink large cup of hot water at night before going to bed and again when getting up in the morning.

Diarrhea; scald a cup of milk in flat pan, sprinkle in lots of black pepper, slip in a slice of toasted bread and eat with a spoon. (This is where we got the term 'milk toast' to call a wimp. When buttered toast is in hot milk, it turns limp!) Rhubarb sauce is also good to cure diarrhea.

Ear ache: warm a teaspoon of sweet oil or baby oil over a lighted kerosene lamp. Drip oil gently in ear and cover with a warm cloth. Hold in place as you rock and comfort baby.

Fever; soak feet in cool bath with dry mustard stirred in water. Apply cool, wet cloths to forehead and drink lots of liquids.

Cough and Congestion; boil 1 handful each of pennyroyal, horehound and catnip in a quart of water, strain and add sugar and lemon juice to taste. Use 2 jiggers of whiskey to preserve mixture to use as cough syrup. Also, mullien leaves simmered in water about 20 minutes stirred and strained before adding brown sugar makes a good syrup to sip. It may be bottled or boiled until thick, poured into a pan to harden and cut into pieces to use as cough drops. Another; suck on lemon drops or horehound candy.

Sore Throat and Tonsils; Warm salt water is a healing gargle or a few drops of camphor on a sugar cube gives relief. A little alum and honey in sage tea helps, also onion syrup made of sliced onions and sugar simmered on wood stove. This also makes a good chest poultice.

Spring tonic; Sulphur and molasses by a spoon full made a good tonic. A spoon full of cod liver oil was taken to ward off colds.

Toothache; remedies for relief were simply ground cloves from the kitchen spice cabinet packed in the cavity and held in with a glob of chewing wax that was used to seal canning jars, or a raisin cut in half, covered with black pepper and stuck on the tooth.

ABE COOK FAMILY

Abraham and Sarah Cook started their family in Richwood, West Virginia. Edward was their first born son to grow up there and join the Army in World War I. While in active duty in France, Ed had a heel shot off his foot. He then came home and was considered fifty percent disabled by the military.

It was in 1917 that Abe and Sarah left West Virginia to go out west. Sarah had relatives there, and they hoped to get a new start. Ed was off to war and two other sons had died. It was a good time to move on. Ovella, their only daughter, was old enough to help look after younger brothers, John, Roy, Ottis and Patrick. It took them three weeks traveling by train to get from West Virginia to Portland, Oregon. One of the little ones cried most of the way.

They were still looking for a place of their own when another son, George Washington, was born in 1919 at Gray's Harbor, Washington. After hearing that there was free land in Montana, they boarded the train again to end up in Eureka that spring. Abe filed for a 160 acre homestead on a branch stream of Pinkham Creek. This little trickle of water in the wilderness soon became known as Cook's Run. Abe was adept at running off a batch of 'hootch' to sell or trade for food or other household goods for his family.

The whole family needed to pitch in to do their share of work to prove up on a homestead. Sarah soon lost the help of her only daughter when Ovella met and married Elmer Roberts. Ovella was then the helpmate of her husband to finish proving up on his homestead. That left the young Cook boys to help build a house and clear land.

The first thing they did, after they chose the best spot for a house, was build an outhouse, the most necessary of buildings.

The log house was set on a side hill overlooking an area of flat land that was to become a garden spot and a hayfield. The small creek ran through it for sub-irrigation, making it a meadow where deer like to graze. A cellar was dug out of the side hill to store root crops. Since the house was up on a side hill from the creek, water for household use had to be packed up hill. Extra buckets were lugged on wash day, bath night or canning time.

Root cellar at the Abe Cook homestead.

    Like all homesteaders, the Cooks needed a team of horses, a milk cow, chickens and a pig to make them self sufficient. Boys did not require a saddle to ride work horses. They just jumped on bareback, maybe two or three at a time, for a horseback ride. Good trained horses would go without a bridle, only a halter rope would do. Horses also had an instinct to find their way home in the dark or during a storm.

    There was a time when John needed a horse to take him home. One winter day, when he was about eight years old, he walked the three miles to visit his sister. He was to be home before dark, but the clouds came in and the day grew short. By the time he left Elmer and Ovella's place snow flakes had started. During the storm, he became disoriented and lost. He laid down to rest, and was almost covered with snow when he was found. His big toe was frozen solid, so Sarah took her big scissors and whacked it off.

    John grew up and married Florabelle Keller. They had four girls; Ruth, Joan, Virginia and Patsy. Their only son, Kenneth, earned the Bronze Star for bravery in Vietnam. He spent seventeen and one-half years in the Marines to serve his country.

    When Ed came back after serving in World War I, he joined the family up Pinkham Creek. He met and married Lillie Kinney in August of 1921. She was a daughter to homesteaders, Albert and Grace Kinney, of Pinkham. Ed and Lillie had a family of five: three sons; Lewis, Dale and Basil and two daughters; Esther and Georgie. Lewis was killed in an accident when he was nine years old. He fell off the side of a flatbed truck and was run over by the back wheel. The family was living on Pinkham at the time.

Ed and Lillie lived in town most of the time. He was a truck diver hauling freight to and from the Flathead. He also was a good truck mechanic. Lillie and her sister, Alta Workman, liked to visit one another whenever possible. After Ed died in 1968, Lillie lived alone in a little house next to her daughter, Esther and Collis Walker in Eureka. She spent her last years at the Mountain View Manor nursing home.

Ottis served in the Army during World War II. He went to France and Italy. He was a 'runner', carrying messages between units. His first wife was Ilaf Armstrong and his second, Gladyce Stacy. Ottis couldn't seem to settle down after the war. He moved from place to place and wife to wife. He fathered four children before passing away in Wenatchee, Washington.

Patrick was killed in an airplane crash in Fretterham, England, while serving in the Air Force during World War II. He left a wife and two daughters. Pat had put his mother down as a dependant, so she also got a small pension for the rest of her life.

George Cook, the youngest son of Abe and Sarah, lied about his age so he could go work with the CCC's (Civilian Conservation Corps). He gave a portion of his money to his mother so she could pay for a place in town. George also served in the Air Force in Alaska, during World War II. After the war he worked at the Malmstrom Air Force Base in Montana. At the time of his death he was a fire chief. He left a wife and two sons, Ray and James.

During the Depression, Abe became ill, so he and Sarah moved into Eureka. He died in 1939 at age sixty-three with cancer of the liver. Abe never had enough money at one time to pay for his homestead rights. Forest officials had considered the Cooks as illegal nesters or squatters besides moonshiners, even though they were never caught in the act of running a still.

After Abe's death, funds to pay for the homestead were sent in by Marjorie Collins. She was the wife of John Collins, a nephew of Abe Cook from West Virginia. Marjorie wanted the homestead to stay in the family. But her money was not accepted. The Forest Service mailed the check back to the family. John picked up the mail, cashed the check and the homestead was lost. Marjorie was very upset over the deal, but the deed was done, with no deed for a homestead. The land reverted to the government.

Sarah spent her last years living with her son, Roy Cook. She passed away at the age of eighty-six in 1965. Roy passed away five months later in Eureka.

The Ed Cook family, photo taken in 1925.

ELMER ROBERTS

Elmer Roberts was born in West Virginia and came to Montana in 1915 along with his stepbrother, Charlie Young. Elmer was fortunate to find a homestead up Pinkham Creek that had already been claimed, but not "proved up on." Andy Stacy, brother-in-law to Elmer's sister, Lockie, was ready to give up on his claim. Elmer was happy to take over, make more improvements, and pay the required amount to claim it as his. (The land was sold for taxes to Victor Banks in September 1930.)

Elmer cleared more land and built another room on the side of the cabin. He was required to live there at least six months of the year, but the rest of the time, he traveled and worked at different jobs in various places. Then in 1919 he met Ovella Cook, the girl of his dreams. She had just moved to Pinkham with her parents, Abraham and Sarah Cook. The couple married in June and continued to travel around.

Wherever they went, Ovella took her banjo along and Elmer his fiddle. They were natural musicians and could play almost any instrument. When Ovella was a little tyke, her dad set her in a rocking chair with arms to support his fiddle. Abe then showed his daughter how to hold the bow to play a tune. She caught on fast and was soon making music. Her favorite instrument was the banjo and she had an enthusiastic audience wherever she went. Ovella and Elmer were in demand at all the Pinkham jamborees. This talent was not picked up by their kids, but was passed down to grandchildren.

Their first born, Rita Fay, was born on Pinkham in 1926. Sis Roberts served as midwife. Their son, Roy, was born in Eureka in 1932 and another daughter, Agnes (Dolly), came in 1936. Her midwives were Margie Collins and Agnes Gregor, whom she was named after. At that time, Elmer and Ovella were living in west Eureka in the Abe Cook house. The couple moved back to Pinkham to live at the Jim Roberts' homestead. Roy and Dolly attended Pinkham school while Rita Fay went to high school in Eureka.

Dolly remembers living in the logging camp shacks. They had wide plank floors that were hard to keep clean. Her mom (Ovella) would carry and heat water, add some lye soap, then scrub the boards with a good stiff broom. The floors stayed clean until someone came in with dirty boots.

Another thing Dolly recalls is hog butchering time. Neighbors would set a day to share the job. Pigs were shot at close range in a vital spot then stuck with a knife in the throat to let out the blood. The carcass was then rolled into a vat or barrel of hot water with all hands pulling ropes or pulleys. After the hog was scalded, it was scraped to get the hair off. At last, it was pulled up on a tripod to hang and cool while the belly was slit open and entrails taken out. Heart and liver were saved for gourmet eating. Everyone enjoyed liver and onions for supper that night.

Other parts of the pig used immediately were strips of fat that were cut up and rendered into lard. Eyes were pried out of the head and thrown to the cats. The tongue was taken to be boiled special and sliced for sandwiches. The head was then placed in a big kettle and boiled until the meat was falling off the bone. (Dolly thought this was icky looking stuff.) All the good meat was saved and the skull thrown out to the dogs. Hooves were boiled to get out the gelatin. It was used to seal a loaf of head cheese, which was made from good meat. This was another delicacy for sandwich filling. Kids took the bladder of a hog to blow up like a balloon. They used the tail for a whip to play with. The squeal was gone and no use to anyone.

Times were tough and pioneers had to work hard to survive. Families worked together to raise a garden for winter food. They camped in the mountains to pick huckleberries on Fitzsimmons Creek on Whitefish Range or on the Fisher River drainage near Libby. Indians camped there too, to pick berries. It was a lively camp at night with music and games. Indians had stick games. While cutting Christmas trees in the fall, the Roberts family sometimes lived in a tent near Libby Creek. On cold nights they woke up to a thick layer of frost inside the tent as well as out.

After tree season, the family packed up to go to Washington to cut ferns and cascara bark. They traveled by train to and from jobs. A trip sometimes included Christmas. Dolly remembered that Santa Claus found her on the train to add to the good memories of family togetherness.

Elmer was an excellent teamster, and skidded logs during the winter when snow was on the ground. He was well known for his kindness to animals and never abused his team of horses. He urged them to do their best without raising his voice or swearing. Elmer was also a good horse doctor. One of his pet peeves was to find a deer killed with only the hind quarters taken, leaving the rest to rot. He hunted only when the family needed meat and then they used all of it, or shared with a needy neighbor. Many times, Ovella baked hot biscuits to go with fried venison, rhubarb or applesauce. (Roy got sick of rhubarb!)

At times, Dan Anker and Johnny Long Time Star stopped by to visit. They both had been scouts for Custer and kept their old habits. Their favorite spot to sit was in the open field, back to back. Thus, they could keep and eye out in both directions, while talking.

Elmer worked for the WPA when he could, building outside toilets and road work. The Pinkham road was one of the projects for improvement. The road was so crooked that at places, travelers almost met themselves going the other way! One of these places was about four miles out of Eureka. Several jogs in the road were eliminated when gullies were filled in and the road built over. These projects used teamsters and horses to do the job. Cecil Utter was another teamster working on the road.

Eventually, Elmer and Ovella bought a small sawmill that they could run by themselves. They moved from one stand of trees to another to set up the mill and cut ties or cants. Their son, Roy, dreamed of driving truck to haul the cut stuff to town. His big dream came true when he finally owned his own logging truck and hauled logs to the big mills in the area. Roy quit high school to start driving truck which was his life-long occupation. He was taught to haul ties by Darrell Roose on a 1942 Dodge at fourteen years of age. When he was sixteen, Roy bought a 1951 used Kenworth logging truck to haul for Fred King. In 1985 Roy bought a new Kenworth to haul for Don Pluid, then retired in 1991.

Roy married Shirley Hoyt and they had two daughters, Debbie and Karla.

Dolly married Bill Treece from Oklahoma. They raised seven children: Toni, Doug, Karen, Keith and Kevin (twins) and another set of twins, Luann and Loralee Jo. They all finished high school in Eureka. Now that her children are all grown, Dolly has been working on family genealogy. She has traced both sides back to the 1700's.

Head Cheese 'Receet'

1 pigs head, scrubbed and rinsed clean. Remove snout. Save tongue and brains. Put head in large kettle and cover with water. Bring to boil, skim and simmer about 4 hours. Lift head when tender onto large platter. (Reserve liquid) Remove all rind from head and cut good meat into small pieces.

In kettle of liquid, add onion stuck with cloves, bay leaf and salt. Drop brains in liquid and simmer about 15 minutes. Remove, drain and add to meat mixture. Season with cayenne pepper, sage and nutmeg. Toss to mix well with hands. Put in a loaf pan and press firmly. Pour ½ cup cooled liquid over loaf, cover with cheese cloth and flat board. Put flat iron on top. Chill for two nights before slicing to serve. Makes hearty sandwiches with home baked bread and ground horse radish.

Rita Fay Roberts went to work for the United States Forest Service the summer she was sixteen. There was a shortage of young men to hire, as most of them were going off to war. Young ladies were hired to take their place and did the work so competently that more jobs opened up in years to come. Lula Workman, Harriet Finch and Rita Fay were all hired by the Rexford Ranger Station. All three were sent out to man lookout stations for the fire season. Lula went to Black Butte, Rita Fay to Pinkham Mountain and Harriet was sent to Red Mountain across the Kootenai River.

All three girls had their own experiences and called each other on the phone every day. Also, they each had to report to headquarters on the weather every day. Lula was the closest to town, so she had more visitors dropping in to visit and look the country over.

Harriet was more isolated and spent a lot of time reading, well supplied with canned food and was proud that she could fix a regular dinner when her folks came to visit. The main menu included canned ham and yams, with fruit for dessert. There was a little screened box attached under the tower to keep fresh food. When she heard a lot of scratching and chewing at night, she took the .22 rifle to investigate. She aimed and shot at a dark blob then heard a ker-plop – and silence. Next morning, there was a dead porcupine she found lying on the ground under the tower.

Fay slept in a little cabin on the ground but stayed in the tower during the day. She had very few visitors with a lot of time on her hands. The many windows in the tower gave good reading light. She loved ranch romances which had names and addresses of other lonely people. Fay started writing letters and was soon getting a bundle of letters tied together delivered every month. There were so many, she never did get them all answered. Some of them were from servicemen and kept coming for several months.

When World War II was over, Fay married her own sweetheart of the Army, George Miller. They both had grownup in the area and kept Eureka as their hometown. Their five children were: a son, Mike and four daughters: Sherry, Becky, Pam and Shelly.

Both Fay and Dolly remember visiting their Grandma Cook and Nancy Jane after they moved to town. They raised a bountiful garden – more than just hardy root crops. There was corn on the cob, cucumbers for pickles, fresh tomatoes and green beans to can or dry. Sarah Cook and Nancy Jane took a needle and long thread to sew the beans in a string. They then covered them with cloth and hung the string from the ceiling to dry. In winter, a kettle of these beans was put on the back of the wood stove, with chunks of salt pork, to simmer all day. This dish of beans was called 'leather britches.'

MILO AND MATTIE LEIB

Milo and Mattie Leib came to Whitefish via train from Arkansas. They brought their belongings in a boxcar, including livestock. They filed for a homestead up Pinkham Creek in 1914 and built a log house on the bank, one mile above new school. Their land included a ninety-acre strip up the hill on the east side of the creek and the rest on top of the hill to the west to make a 160 acre homestead.

Sophie Alice Leib was born in the log house perched on the bank above Pinkham Creek. She was delivered by midwife Nancy Roberts on March 5, 1916. She was the seventh child in the family, but the first to be born in Montana. Her eldest sister (Jessie) Maud claimed the right to take over the care of the new baby.

Other sisters were Winnie Mae, Annie Elizabeth and Mattie Agnes. Just older than Alice was brother Joseph Hamilton. Another brother, Robert Percy, had lived only twenty days. Those born on Pinkham after Alice were John Henry and Ella Marie.

When Alice was two years old she came down with scarlet fever. It settled in her ears, and since then she was hard of hearing. She went through school with a handicap as well as raise her family of five children. Alice ended up with hearing aids in both ears.

The Leibs had a horse named John that traveled on the train boxcar from Arkansas. When not in use, the horses were put out to pasture on the Pinkham hills. One summer day when Alice was still a tiny tot, John came home and hung his head over the pole fence. Alice decided to go for a ride, so she climbed the fence, caught hold of his mane and climbed on bareback. The horse took her for a ride, while Mama looked all around for her.

During hot weather the crick was their favorite place to play. The house was on a steep bank and the crick was just below. They made their own life vests by putting two empty one gallon syrup pails in a burlap grain sack, one to each end with room for their tummy in the middle. With the flow of the current it was easy to swim downstream but much more difficult to swim back up.

MAUDE LEIB
June/2003

I, Jesse Maude Leib was born in Russell, Arkansas, August 31, 1900, to Milo and Mattie Leib. Lora Leib Moore, Dad's sister, stayed to care for Mom and me. Mom's father, Robert Moore, was there too.

My sister, Winnie Mae Leib, was born January 27, 1903. Before Annie Elizabeth was born August 16, 1905, Father got a place near the White schoolhouse on the White River. My brother, Robert, was born December 9, 1907, and died December 29, 1907. Dad sold the farm and moved back to Russell again where my brother, Joseph Hamilton Leib, was born February 4, 1909.

Mother's brother, Percy Moore, and his wife, Jennie, lived near us. Their children were Zoma, Daphne, Floyd, Crecie and Vera. Aunt Sophie, Mom's sister, lived at Bradford. Her children were Hazel, Leon and J.W.

Dad's uncle, Captain John Leib, lived in Russell with his sister Annie. They raised Aunt Lora's oldest child Frank Moore. They had raised Aunt Lora from age 3 years. Uncle John was a Union soldier, a captain, in Co. F 48th Indiana Veteran Volunteers.

Grandpa Moore was in the South, when he returned home from the war to find his home burned, cattle all gone and his wife and mother with two small children living in a slave cabin. He was raised on a grant of land where Nashville, Tennessee, is now. Grandpa Moore was one-fourth Cherokee and three-fourths English.

In 1912 Dad moved all of his family to Montana. Bill Paddick, Dad's nephew, and Frank Moore rode in a boxcar on the railroad with the stock. Aunt Lora and her two girls, Edna and Bernice Drayton, and old Aunt Annie came to Montana with us. Uncle John had died in January of that year. We arrived at Whitefish, the latter part of October. Dad worked for the Great Northern Railroad there. Frank Moore got on there too.

My sister Agnes was born January 27, 1912, before we left Arkansas, so she came to Montana as a baby. We moved to Pinkham Creek just out of Eureka in October of 1914. We three older girls went to school in a log cabin not far from home. The next spring on April 12, 1915, my little sister Agnes died from woodtick fever and was buried on the hill above the house.

In 1915 a new school was built and Ham started to school. At a Sunday school affair there on June 4, 1916, Walter Baker asked me to marry him. We were married September 1, 1916. That was the year my baby sister, Sophia Alice, was born March 4, 1916. I took care of her as my own baby all summer. Later, John Henry was born August 2, 1918, and Ella Marie April 29, 1921.

My husband and I moved to British Columbia, Canada, in October of 1917. Our daughter, Ella Maude Baker, was born August 16, 1918 at Chase, British Columbia. We moved to Chehalis, Washington, June 23 of 1923. In 1924 we moved to Salkum, Washington.

Ella Maude Baker married William Wayne Workman on May 21, 1935, at Eureka, Montana. Their children were Alma Lee, William Rodney and Patricia Marie.

JOSEPH HAMILTON LEIB

Joseph Hamilton Leib came to Pinkham Creek with his parents, Milo and Mattie Leib, as a child of six in 1915. He was born in Russell, Arkansas, on February 4, 1909. There was a new school built on

Pinkham the year they came, but since Ham was a sickly child, his older sisters went off to school and left him at home. They became his teachers and played school with him at home until he was nine years old and a growing boy. Ham then attended the Pinkham school and finished the eighth grade when he was twelve years old. Both teacher and parents thought him too young to be out of school, so he was sent back to repeat the eighth grade.

Ham grew to be a strong young man and did his share of the work to help prove up on the homestead. At sixteen he was skidding logs with a team of horses for Beard and Harper Lumber Company at Warland. He was eighteen when his father died so he became the main breadwinner for the family that was still left at home – Alice, John, Marie and his mother.

In the early 1930's Ham worked making railroad crossties with a broadax. One blow of the ax was off just a little and he split the edge of his boot. On closer inspection he discovered that the little toe had been split down the center through all the joints. (Ham had small feet for a man, wearing only a size 6-½ boot. If it had been bigger he would have cut his toe off!)

The toe was far too tender to walk on even though it was bound to his other toe, so he constructed a "peg-leg." He cut a board to fit from his knee to his foot then strapped it to his lower leg. With his knee bent at an angle, the peg-leg fit straight down from the thigh and he was able to walk and work without crutches.

Ham met the girl of his dreams while she was attending Pinkham school. The Armstrong family was new on Pinkham having moved up from California. Olive Armstrong was third from the oldest in the family. She was the one Ham wanted and was not going to let her get away. When the Armstrong family moved to Washington seeking a better place to live, Ham followed, married her on July 24, 1931, and brought his bride back to Pinkham.

Times were tough but Ham was young and willing to do most anything. A couple didn't need much to start, a shack with a wood stove, a bedstead with a feather tick, table and bench (even if homemade), water bucket, washboard, dish pan, wash tub and scrub board plus a kerosene lantern or lamp for light. A change of clothes or coats could be hung on a nail in the wall. A frying pan and coffee pot were also essential. Sometimes these things were shared by relatives.

Ham got a job on the railroad section crew out of Eureka. He moved into the empty Fluharty place at Twin Lakes, which was halfway between town and the Leib homestead on Pinkham. There was a barn there for a team of horses and a milk cow. Water was carried from a spring on the place, which was quite handy. They were living here when their son David was born in Eureka, December 29, 1932. The next summer Marie Leib and Esther Utter remembered riding down from Pinkham on horseback to spend the day playing with the baby, staying for supper, then riding back home before dark.

When her son, John Hamilton, was born September 9, 1935, Olive was in Whitefish staying with Ham's cousins, Frank and Ann Moore. Then Laura came August 21, 1938, while Ham and Olive were living on the old Thatcher place later called Pinkham Ranch. In 1939 Great Northern Railroad put Ham on as section foreman to build new tracks near Vaughn in eastern Montana. Ham got along well with the workers. He seemed to understand their broken English speech, and they all liked him.

Ham worked wherever jobs were available and moved his family with him. They lived in old Rexford while he worked skidding logs with his team of horses up Young Creek for Columbus Clark. Ham's mother, Mattie, was alone then and in ill health, so she lived with them in Rexford. She died there in 1943 at the age of sixty-five.

Ham took his family to the small town of Warland farther on down the Kootenai River while he worked as section boss for the Great Northern Railroad. They lived in a section house furnished by the railroad company and kids went to the Warland grade school.

It was in Warland where Ham and Olive became acquainted with Art and Lucille Biegler. Eventually Ham quit the railroad and became a saw partner with Art Biegler while they worked in the woods for J. Neils Lumber Co. Their families became fast friends as they shared many activities together.

Both the Leibs and the Bieglers moved on to be near Kila, where they found a place to farm for a while. They then helped one another put up hay or go cut a load of wood somewhere.

Both the Leib boys joined the Navy, David to make a career of it, but John came home again after serving a three-year stint. Laura married a local Kila man, Edwin Schnackenberg, and moved to Libby.

Ham had a paint horse that he would ride in Lincoln County Fair parades. He was deeply tanned from working without a shirt in the hayfields and showed his Indian heritage. Ham dressed in buckskin pants and rode his paint bareback to take first place as an Indian in the parade.

Ham and Olive spent their retirement years in Eureka. They bought the lots formerly owned by Dan Utter on the hill in East Eureka. They raised a productive garden there and planted more fruit trees. They also enjoyed being close to relatives. In 1991 friends and relatives honored their 60th Anniversary with a picnic at Camp 32.

During the last years of their lives they lived in an apartment at Ksanka Court. They both ended up at the Mountain View Manor nursing home. Olive died in 1992 at the age of seventy-seven. Ham died in 1993 at age eighty-three. They were both buried in the Tobacco Valley Cemetery.

JOHN LEIB

John Henry Leib was born on August 2, 1918, the eighth child and last boy to be born to Milo and Mattie Leib. He was delivered by midwife Sis Roberts on the Leib homestead up Pinkham Creek. His birthplace was registered as Rexford, the mailing address and shopping center for Pinkham homesteaders.

John's grandfather was also a John Leib, born October 15, 1800, in Lancaster, Pennsylvania. His grandparents, Ulrick and Veronica Leib, settled there after coming from Bavaria and landing in America October 20, 1764. Milo Leib was born December 18, 1865, in Laurence County, Illinois, and later went to Russell, Arkansas, where he met and married Mattie Moore, July 1, 1899. They came to Montana in 1914.

As a boy, John loved the freedom of the outdoors, roaming the woods and watching wildlife. (There were no "Keep Out" or "Private Property" signs). His first weapon was a home-made slingshot whittled from a willow growing by the creek, tied with strips of rubber, sliced from an old inner tube and a hunk of leather cut to size. He practiced shooting pine squirrels all summer long when Pinkham school was out.

When John's dad died, he was a boy of nine. He then turned to Tom Wilson, a friend of the family and future brother-in-law, for guidance and hunting companion. Tom taught him how to handle a gun and shoot. John became a good hunter and fisherman, bringing home game to help supply family food.

At the age of seventeen, John went to work falling trees with a crosscut saw with Tom Wilson as partner. The logs were used for making ties to be sold to the Great Northern Railroad with a yard in Eureka or Rexford. After the logs were cut and limbed, they were hewed with a broadax into ties. They were then loaded on a sled or wagon to be hauled to the rail yard. Workers tried to get 100 ties a day to make $5, at a nickel a tie.

The sawyers got a nickel a tie to be split between them. A skidder with team also was paid a nickel a tie. It cost $1.20 a day to live in work camp. John thought he was making good wages because he saved enough to buy the best saddle "Monkey Ward" had priced at $52 the winter of 1935.

John met his first wife, Alma Hellickson, a good-looking blonde from Scobey, Montana. She was a pen pal of Marie, John's younger sister. When she came to Pinkham to visit Marie, John escorted her to Pinkham dances and fell in love. They were married December 30, 1938, at Scobey.

John brought his bride back to Pinkham to live in a cabin owned by Cecil Utter. Their first child, Jeri Joy, was born in October of 1939. Then in the spring of 1941, John and Alma moved to Scobey on a farm. There Maurice was born in October of 1941 and Alan arrived June 13, 1943. John was exempt from the draft, as he was a farmer.

The family left Scobey in 1950 to get back to the mountains. John and Alma then managed the Christmas Tree Tavern on Dewey Avenue in Eureka. They lived in East Eureka and all three children walked to school. But then, in 1957, John and Alma were divorced.

John married Louise Gilmore on November 27, 1957. They lived on a place near Ural Creek along the Kootenai River. John worked with a road crew blasting rock for new highways on both sides of the reservoir during the construction of Libby Dam. When they were flooded out in 1971, the Leibs moved back to Pinkham.

They bought five acres from John's brother, Ham, the only remnant left of the original homestead. The other ninety acres was sold to brother-in-law Cecil Utter. The Leib family cemetery is on the five acre piece just across the road from where John was born. Both Milo and Mattie Leib are buried there alongside their three-year-old daughter, Mattie, who died in the spring of 1915 with wood tick fever.

John and Louise moved a trailer house on the hillside near the cemetery. This was to be their permanent retirement home. John, a lover of flowers, kept a beautiful yard. He dug a hole down by the creek, put a pump in and piped water under the road and up the hill. Only on severe winters did the water freeze up until spring thaw.

John and Louise took in two of their grandkids to raise when David was seven and Dena six years old. They rode the school bus to attend school in Eureka, until their graduation from high school.

John worked part time for the USFS and spent several summers manning the old Black Butte lookout. There his friends and relatives visited him and looked the country over through high powered binoculars. John was working there when a forest fire started along the

Pinkham Road near Pinkham Ranch. It burned over the hill to Twin Lakes before it was contained.

After a few years of failing health, John died May 21, 1992. His ashes were taken to Pinkham and a headstone for him put in the Leib cemetery alongside his parents.

John's wife Louise died in 1997. Her ashes were also buried in the plot next to her husband in the little cemetery on the old Leib homestead.

JOHN LEIB RECALLS VALLEY RAILROAD TIE INDUSTRY
Tobacco Valley News, October 25, 1979

A stack of ties "higher than a house, three or four rows deep and a quarter-mile long" is one memory John Leib has of the once-flourishing railroad tie business in the Tobacco Valley.

Leib, who was born on his parents' homestead in Pinkham Creek in 1918, started his career in 1935, sawing logs and cutting ties, mostly from private sales of larch and fir, for what was a booming business in the Tobacco Valley from the 1930's into the 1950's.

Although he did not want to venture a guess at how many million ties were shipped out of the area, Leib did say that one mill in Eureka owned by Columbus Clark was producing 800-1,000 ties a day at capacity.

He said that a sawyer got "a nickel a tie" falling in the woods, and that if a worker got 100 ties a day cutting with a crosscut saw, "you thought you was making pretty good wages." And a nickel went quite a ways in those days. It cost $1.20 a day to live in the work camp, Leib said, and in the winter of 1935, he paid $52 "for the best saddle Monkey Wards sold."

Pinkham Creek was also the scene of a few tie drives, Leib said. A small dam on the upper end of the creek helped supply water, he said, and when the high water of the spring runoff came the ties were floated down to the Kootenai River and taken to where the town of Rexford was before the Kootenai River valley was flooded by Lake Koocanusa. The ties, which were used by the Great Northern for the replacement, were then sent to a treatment plant at Somers.

Leib has lived and worked most of his life in the Pinkham area. He left the area a couple of times but he "always came back." From 1941-46, he tried his hand at farming near Scobey, but he left because he did not like the wind, the flat land or the weather.

"I didn't mind summers, but them winters...," he said, leaving the thought of the freezing prairie to the imagination.

Leib also worked from 1966-71 on the Libby Dam project "from the first road job to the last one," cutting and drilling for blasting. But even though he worked, on the dam project, it and Lake Koocanusa are not a pleasant subject in the Leib household. Leib and his wife, Louise, are "kinda bitter" about the reservoir, which flooded them out of their home in the old town of Rexford, where they lived before moving to five acres remaining from his parents' original homestead, which has one of the few family cemeteries in the area. His wife said sometimes she "even thinks about an anthill that was behind their house and wonders what ever happened to the ants."

Besides the Libby Dam, Leib has seen other changes. Into the middle of the 1920's, he said, there was only one road up Pinkham Creek, the main one which is paved today. But with the arrival of the automobile, all that changed. Leib said the first car he can remember seeing was one a cousin drove up from Whitefish in 1923 or 1924.

A gradual changeover was made about 1929-30 from horse and wagon to Tin Lizzies, he said, and in 1932, Pinkham Creek was made accessible from both ends when the Forest Service put the Sutton Ridge road through to Swamp Creek. He said the road was built by 250 men from a Civilian Conservation Corps camp that was located in old Rexford. The road was built using horses he said, adding that in 1937 the finish grading work on Highway 2 between Kalispell and Libby was also done with horses.

Leib said it was the late 1930's before powered equipment was used, but that it was usually gas-fueled and underpowered. He said the Forest Service had "one old cat-a Monarch" and that "the damn thing was stuck or broke down all the time. It didn't even have a blade."

The Civilian Conservation Corp, mentioned above, was a "make-work" scheme of the Franklin Roosevelt administration to get the economy going again and pull the nation out of the Great Depression by employing people for public works. Although "everybody was broke,'" Leib said the Depression did not hit the Tobacco Valley area as hard as other areas, because just about everybody had a garden, chickens "and a pig or two." "There was plenty of bartering (trading)", since cold cash was in short supply, he said, adding that there was an abundance of game and that he "didn't even have to go off the place (the original homestead) to get a deer."

But Pinkham Creek is "overflowing with people" these days he said, and it is no longer so easy to get a deer.

He said that when he was growing up, there were no more than

100 residents in about 20 families in the Pinkham Valley, but now there are "more people moving in all the time." And while the Pinkham Valley once boasted two small schools, about 50 children from the valley now attend school in Eureka, he said. There were never any stores in the valley, with Rexford being the nearest trade center, and no bars, he said, but there were plenty of stills. Commenting on the quality of the moonshine produced, Leib said it was "alright – it never killed me."

Although the days of making ties for a nickel a piece are long gone, Leib still works in the woods, setting up timber sales for the Forest Service. And even his hobby, which is "collectin' guns, shootin' and hand-loadin'," gets him outside, and he has a couple of nice bearskins and some deer and elk racks to show for it. The latest addition to his collection is a .50 caliber muzzle loader, which he constructed from a kit given to him by his children. And even though it's not as easy as it used to be, he says he is going to try for a deer this fall with the rifle.

ALICE LEIB WILSON

Alice Wilson says her family didn't go much of anywhere as the family grew up on Pinkham Creek. They went to school Christmas programs by team and sleigh. Hot bricks were tucked in the straw to keep their feet warm while they covered up with home made quilts. They took team and wagon to attend school picnics when school let out. Every one brought food to share.

When Alice was eleven years old her father died with heart trouble. The three older girls were married by then and Ham became head of the family. Alice helped her mother. John and Marie were both in school by then too.

When Sophie Alice Leib decided to marry Tom William Wilson, Mr. Banks took them to Libby for their license. They tied the knot in Libby, August 31, 1933. Alice was seventeen years old and Tom thirty-six.

Tom had gotten some land from Cecil Utter next to the Leib homestead on the hill. He built a small house of rough lumber, with a little house out back. There was no indoor plumbing even thought of on Pinkham during the Depression. This was Alice's first home away from home, just across the fence from her mother.

Their first child, Mattie Alice, was born October 6, 1934, at the home of Anna Olson in Eureka. Dr. Keith Lowell delivered Mattie as a breach birth. Both mother and daughter did fine.

Other children followed but were delivered by Dr. Lowell at home on Pinkham. Thomas Williams Jr. arrived April 2, 1937. Julia Mae was born July 27, 1939. Mary Agnes came into the world June 12, 1941. A neighbor, Agnes Sederdahl, helped out after the last two girls' birthings. Robert Roy was delivered by Dr. Clark in a raging snowstorm January 15, 1943.

When the children became school age, they walked down the same path as their mother had to attend the Pinkham school. But in 1945, the Wilsons decided to move into town for the school term. Then in 1946 Pinkham school children were sent by school bus to Eureka. The bus went up the hill to the Wilson gate to turn around.

In 1960 Alice moved into a new modern home! Tom had sold the timber off their place and used the money for a three bedroom home, with an inside bathroom, and an electric range in the kitchen besides many cupboards and cabinets with sink and lots of hot water. There was, also, a full basement with a furnace for heat.

When Mr. Victor Banks became ill in his later years he stayed with Tom and Alice to be taken care of until his death in 1965. He deeded his place to Tom, then Pete and Esther Ransier bought it in 1968.

Tom Wilson suffered with emphysema for several years before he died in 1973. Alice was left a lonely widow in a large house. Then in 1981 she moved into the low cost housing at Ksanka Court. She became active in the Senior Citizens Center as a volunteer besides other fun activities such as dancing and playing pinochle. Alice also walked to the Lutheran Church to attend services every Sunday.

Her children all married and had families of their own. Mattie married Bob Monger to live in Anaconda. Mary and Juan Wise lived in Elgin, Oregon. Julia married Russell Blonshine to have a home in Eureka. Both the boys and their wives stayed on Pinkham.

Alice spent her last years at the Mountain View Manor. She died in 1999 at age eighty-three and was buried in the Eureka Cemetery.

MARIE LEIB ROOSE

Marie Leib Roose was the last child to be born to Milo and Mattie Leib. The baby of the family was delivered by midwife Sis Roberts on April 29, 1921. The location was a log house on the banks of Pinkham Creek.

When Marie was two, her family moved from the house on the main road to the place on the hill along the Sutton Road. She was six and ready to start school when her dad died. She walked to school with her older sister, Alice, and brother John.

The older girls in the family were all married. Maude married Walt

Baker and had a daughter, Ella Maude, who married Wayne Workman. They had three children before getting divorced. Annie married Arlie Alderman and lived in Salkum, Washington. They had one daughter, Helen. Winnie Mae married Cecil Utter.

Marie's favorite teacher was Mrs. Long, who she had from third grade until she graduated from eighth. Marie says they don't have country school teachers like her anymore. They used to have parties on Halloween and Christmas. They put on plays and sang songs. The whole community would share big potluck suppers and picnics.

Marie worked hard at home while she was growing up. There was so much to do on a homestead, that it took all hands. They had cows to milk, pigs and chickens to feed, besides sawing wood with a cross-cut saw. At spring gardening time Marie drove the horse while John held the plow. Then it was work in the garden all summer.

On wash day, Marie remembered her mama had a huge black cast iron cauldron in the yard to heat wash water. It sat on a frame, so a fire could be built under it to heat the fifteen to twenty gallons of water packed by bucket from the well. When the well went dry, water was hauled from Pinkham Creek by horse and go-devil. Clothes were washed on a rub board, wrung by hand, then hung out on a clothes line to dry in summer and winter to freeze dry.

Marie told of the time they got a wringer to fasten between the wash tubs. Marie was turning the handle of the wringer while Alice was stuffing sopping wet clothes through. Alice had long hair which followed through with the clothes. When Alice hollered, Marie turned the wringer backwards to release her hair.

Marie met Lester Roose at a dance held in the Pinkham School in June. They were married that August 12 of 1939. They had four children. Carol Dawn – March 18, 1941; Roy Edward – July 1, 1943; Daniel William – March 19, 1946; and Bonita Kay – Feb 27, 1952.

Lester was a whiz at cutting Christmas trees with an ax and using a crosscut saw. He went into the army during WWII. The couple divorced in April 1953 when Bonita was a year old.

Marie worked and raised the children as a single mother. She took in laundry, tied Christmas trees and was a hotel chamber maid. She tended bar down town for twenty years, then became janitor at Lincoln County High School for eight years. She retired at age sixty-two for a well-earned rest.

Marie made quilts, plastic crosses and other fancy work which she gave away to her family.

Marie had open heart surgery in June of 1995. She spent some time at Mountain View Manor while recuperating. She then felt good enough to attend a family reunion.

Marie again went into the Mountain View Manor to live her last years. She died in April 2003, just before her eighty-second birthday.

Casket of Milo Leib, 1926, at the Leib Cemetery.

THE LEIB CEMETERY

The Leib Cemetery, or Pinkham Creek Cemetery, on the tip of Virginia Hill is surrounded by a woven wire fence with steel gate. Rocks are used for headstones and flowers are kept on the graves the year around by family members.

Little Agnes Leib was only three years old when, that spring, she became partially paralyzed. At last two large distended woodticks were found imbedded under the hair at the base of her head; the little one died April 12, 1915, as a result. The family made a small coffin and buried their little girl in a clearing above the house.

The next burial was in 1922, the infant son of Mr. and Mrs. Marion Roberts. A third grave contained the infant son of Rufus Youngs. The three little graves lie close together on the sunny hillside.

In October of 1927, Milo Leib died of a faulty heart at the Kalispell hospital and was buried in a simple graveside service near his little daughter, Agnes. When Milo's widow, Mattie Leib, died at Ham and Olive's home in Rexford in 1943, services were held in Eureka, but her body was laid to rest at the family burial site on Pinkham near her husband and daughter.

Their surviving children were Maud Baker, Mae Utter, Annie Alderman, Joseph Hamilton Leib, Alice Wilson, John Henry Leib and Marie Roose.

Cecil and Mae Leib Utter became owners of that portion of the Leib homestead with Ham Leib reserving five acres that included the cemetery. Later John and Louise Leib bought the property and lived there in retirement. At their death their grandsons inherited the plot of land.

John Leib died in 1992 and Louise Leib in 1997. Both were buried there with a joint headstone. Marie Leib Roose died in April of 2003 and her ashes were put near the graves of her parents and little sister.

It was 2003 that another member of the family, A.G. Casey, took over the care of the cemetery. He and his wife, Melody Utter Casey, purchased the property to the north of the cemetery from her dad, Lee Utter. They are interested in preserving the family heritage with the family cemetery a priority. A new fence has been built and cement headstones engraved with names and dates put in proper positions. The cemetery now contains eight graves with headstones marking the sites. An old-fashioned yellow rose and pioneer white rose have been planted as well as other hardy perennials of the era, including a lilac bush.

WHEN BOYS WORE BIBS

When I was a boy I wore bib overalls
With pockets in front and in the back
Little pockets on bibs were so handy
To carry a pencil and note paper for facts

A deep pocket held a string around a stick
A fishhook or pin was stuck in the bib
Pockets held gopher tails at a penny apiece
My overalls told what a country boy did

On washday my mother would fret
She found snail shells, rocks from the crick,
A rubber band for shooting spit wads too
And a note from teacher about boy tricks

My jackknife was in the right front pocket
To whittle a whistle or play mumble peg
It cut a willow fish pole, make a sling shot
If I lost it, for another one I'd beg
       By *Madeline Utter*

DAN UTTER (GRANDAD)

Granddad Utter was born in Bethany, Missouri, Sept. 22, 1861. His parents were Richard and Lydia Neff Utter. They named their new son Daniel Wilson. He joined a brother Willis. Richard went off to fight in the Civil War and left his family with his wife's parents.

The Neffs had immigrated from Wales to the United States and settled in Iowa, where he made coffins for a living. She was an herbalist and used plants from the woods as well as her garden. Their grandsons learned much from them.

The boys grew and remembered that their father came home from the war on a good-looking horse before riding off again. Pat McKeever has Army records that give health information about why he probably left the kids with grandpa after the war. It also lists the children, including girls.

The brothers married young girls who were sisters. Will and his wife produced a son named Ralph.

Dan was nineteen when he married Mary Lucinda Robinson at sixteen. They both had to get permission from parents to marry Dec. 25, 1881. The couple produced ten children. After William Franklin was born in 1883, they moved from Missouri to Nebraska.

Though small in stature, Dan was a good-looking blacksmith and set up his own smithy in Ainsworth and then again in Hemingford, Alliance, Bridgeport, and Broadwater, all in Nebraska. Jesse and Amy were born in Ainsworth. Danny, Cecil and Leo were born in Hemingford. Edith was born in Alliance, Myrtle in Bridgeport, Lester in Broadwater and Lillian in Julesburg, Colorado.

As a young man, Leo was restless and came farther west on his own. On reaching Eureka, he enthusiastically wrote back to his brothers to come join him. It caused a split in the family. His mother, Lucy, stayed in Nebraska with younger children while his father, Dan, came to Montana with sons Danny and Cecil. Cecil gave up his homestead in Nebraska to bring his wife, Laura, and stepdaughter, Maxine, along. Sisters Myrtle and Amy (with husband Bob Lafollett and five children) came also. That was 1915.

The Utters found cabins in the Lick Lake area where they got a job in the Anderson-Alverson sawmill.

The children attended the Therriault Creek School, District #17. Cecil was elected to the school board and Dan became clerk.

After a couple of years the Lafolletts moved into Eureka with their family. Dan moved to Pinkham Creek with Cecil and Laura. Maxine attended the Pinkham School. They first lived in the old Young cabin below the Thatcher place.

Laura was getting tired of living in the wooded hills and longed to be back on the plains. She eventually left Cecil, took her daughter and returned to Nebraska where she procured a divorce. Dan Utter and sons, Cecil and Leo, stayed on to cut ties for a living. Dan's son Danny and the Lafolletts went west.

Myrtle married George Workman and had a daughter. Leo married Bessie Workman and had three children, Leona, Roy and Donald. Roy was killed in World War II. Cecil married Winnie Mae Leib. They had three children, Francis Lee, Esther Margalene and Robert Rae.

Dan Utter was an accomplished carpenter as well as blacksmith. He was, also, adept at using a scythe to cut grass for hay or a broad ax to hew railroad ties. He kept his tools in good condition and wherever he moved, his tools of the trade went with him. Dan hewed ties right along with his sons, Cecil and Leo, to make a living. The Great Northern Railroad had issued a circular for cross ties 8½' long. They would make #3 size 6x8 and pay 45 cents each, #4 size 7x8 and pay 53 cents each, and #5 size 7x9" for 65 cents a piece. This was in 1928, and showed a big raise in pay from before.

To make ties the men selected tall straight trees that would be about the size to make a #5 at the butt, then a #4 and a #3 from the top. The tree was cut with a crosscut saw and limbed with an ax up as far as the top tie. The top limbs were left on the tree for stability until the ties were hewed before sawing off where the ties ended.

The ties were then loaded onto a sleigh in winter or a wagon in the summer to be hauled by team to the landing in Eureka. The load brought enough money to buy a 100-pound sack of grain for the horses and a 100-pound bag of potatoes for the family, with none left over.

One fall Dan was taking home to Pinkham a wagon load of winter groceries; oats, cow feed, flour, sugar, coffee, corn meal, oatmeal, beans, rice, raisins, prunes, etc. He had also picked up the mail at the post office. When Dan was crossing the railroad tracks, he was so tired and preoccupied he didn't notice a train approaching going east. At the blast of the train whistle, the horses bolted. Dan clung to the reins and was pulled along with them. The train hit the wagon, severing it in half. Dan was still on the front seat, over the wheels. The back half of the wagon and groceries were scattered up the track as the train thundered on. Broken sacks of flour and feed made a big white pouff as they flew through the air. Dan salvaged what little he could of their winter groceries. There were a few cans of stuff to take home. He drove the team home and used the front wheels as a cart. Since he was a blacksmith, he could rebuild the wagon. So he had his winter work cut out for himself. He gave thanks to the Lord that he was still able to carry on.

In later years Dan built a one room shack on the hill in East Eureka to retire. It was on the same block on 6th Avenue where his granddaughter Esther Goff lived with her four children. When grandson Lee Utter got married they lived on the other side of him. He went every day to visit his great-grandson, Kenny. Then he got sick and died in 1947, the fall before Terry was born. Dan W. Utter was eighty-six-years old. He was interred in the Eureka Cemetery.

Cabin built by Daniel W. Utter in 1919. It was restored by his great-grandson, Ken Utter, in 1999.

CECIL UTTER FAMILY

Cecil Loren Utter and Winnie Mae Leib were wed in Eureka May 3, 1921. Their first home up Pinkham Creek was in a little log cabin with a stone chimney on the Loyd Kinney homestead. (Though the log part of the cabin burned, the chimney still stands not far from a huge lilac bush.)

Their first son, Francis Lee, was born there August 22, 1922. Dr. Long from Eureka drove up the creek to do the delivery. Cecil gave him a bottle of moonshine he got from a friend to help ease his stress.

Both father and doctor shared a nip to relax.

Since Cecil was a teamster and skidded logs with his horses for various sawmills, he moved his family when possible to be closer to the job. Esther Margalene was born in another cabin along Pinkham Creek October 31, 1923.

In 1924 Cecil bought forty acres up the hill from Amos Kinney. Grandpa Dan Utter built a sturdy log cabin 18x24 in a small clearing. Grandpa lived in the cabin several years after Cecil moved on. The cabin was moved and modernized by Ken Utter.

In July of 1925 Cecil bought the Bergette homestead and sold forty acres on the hill to Tom Wilson. Cecil and Mae moved their family into the fairly new two-story frame house set in a clearing. Water had to be carried from a spring up the hill on Amos Kinney's property. Cecil traded a Model-T Ford to Amos for five acres that included the spring and stretched down along the homestead to cross the creek.

The field was full of tamarack stumps. Cecil plowed around them with his faithful mare Brownie and white horse called Maud. He

Cecil Utter with a mule deer buck.

planted oats to be cut for hay. Grandpa Utter used the scythe to cut the grain by hand around the stumps where mowers missed. When dry, they shocked it with a fork, pitched it on a hayrack, pulled the wagon with team, and pitched it again into the barn.

During the 1930's Cecil cut hay from the vacant homesteads up the creek. He used a mower with eight-foot cycle and eight-foot rake to maneuver between the stumps. At that time they were milking ten cows by hand and needed lots of hay for the winter.

In early spring, the cows would head for Twin Lakes seeking green grass. Mae would walk after them for evening milking. Their first cream was sent by train to Spokane. A five-gallon can of cream brought $3.15.

Each spring, 100 leghorn chicks were ordered through a catalog and came by train to post office. The chicks were kept close to the heater in the house until big enough to go outside. Roosters made fried chicken by the 4th of July. Hens were kept to have eggs to use, with surplus to sell.

About 1934 Cecil Utter bought ten ewes and a ram from Alfred Peltier. They were known as "old gummers" as their teeth were getting worn down, but they still produced lambs. The small flock pastured up on the hill, where it had been logged over. In the evening, Lee brought them down to a shed for protection during the night.

Grandpa Dan Utter did the shearing of wool and butchering of the mutton. He also carded the wool, had Jessie Van Horn spin it on her loom, then knit his own wool socks. It was Grandpa Utter who taught Esther to knit socks, which she did as well as sweaters.

Grandpa was a good influence on his grandkids and spent a lot of time with them. They went for walks through the woods while he would show them the plant and wild growing herbs that were good to use. He told them which mushrooms to pick, and how to prepare them to eat.

Lee remembered pedaling like a bicycle on the grinder so Grandpa could sharpen his tools. He made whistles for the kids from willows, also walking sticks of the diamond willows.

Grandpa Utter made a bobsled one winter that all the kids in the neighborhood got to ride on. It went to school for many noon hour rides down the Slick Gulch Road, across the main road, and down between two barns on the Stacy place.

In the summertime during that era, the kids all went barefoot. Most of them got new shoes in the fall about time school started, others were hand-me-downs from those who had out grown them. Towards spring, shoes were wearing out. It was then Grandpa Utter turned into a shoe cobbler.

He had three different-sized shoe lasts – one for children, ladies, and men. Half soles were cut to fit from pieces of leather, then either tacked on or sewn on using an awl to make holes, just like he mended a piece of harness.

No one had much money to buy things so they traded. Lee was about twelve when he traded a small push-button accordion (that he got in a trade before) for an old Civil War gun. It was a 1864 Springfield 50x70 rifle. One shell came with it. Lee later had Floyd Sederdahl make another.

Lee went on his first hunting trip, when he was fourteen years old, with his dad, uncles Ham and John Leib and uncle Walt Baker, who was paralyzed from the waist down. Lee drove their '26 Chevy truck to the end of the Bear Trap Road, with Walt and John as passengers. Cecil and Ham rode their horses that far, then loaded their camp gear on one horse and Walt Baker on the other for a two-mile ride, while others walked.

They made camp over the Sutton Ridge at a bend in the trail where a spring bubbled up midst tall pine trees. It was a successful hunt with all getting their game. Walt shot his from the back of a horse. Lee and John were getting tired of waiting for a deer to show and started rolling rocks down a slide. Then three deer came around the bend, inquisitive as to the noise. Lee used his borrowed .25-35 gun from John to kill his first deer.

The year of 1936 was an eventful one for Mae Utter. That was the year she got a new Maytag washing machine. It had a square aluminum tub with a gas-powered engine. She still had to carry water from the spring to heat it on the wood cookstove, but she didn't have to scrub clothes on the washboard anymore.

The Maytag salesman was Tiny Blunt, who weighed about 300 pounds. He and his younger brother wanted to go hunting and camp out, so Cecil took them on an early fall hunt. The group, including the Blunt brothers, Slim (Frank) Utter, Cecil and son Lee, started walking up over Sutton Ridge to their favorite hunting camp, leading two pack horses. Tiny soon played out and had to ride one of the pack horses, leaving packs to pick up later. Their hunt was unsuccessful and short lived. When the Blunts heard the train whistle at Stone Hill they decided to walk down and flag the train, rather than walk back up over the hill.

The Utters were involved in Pinkham community activities. Cecil served on the school board of District 18 with Frank Slick and Helmar Johnson from 1928 to 1937. During that time, a cement foundation was put around the school grounds with metal fence posts. Woven wire was stretched and topped with barbed wire. It made a durable fence.

Lee and Esther walked to Pinkham school, crossing the creek on a

—143—

foot log and on the ice in winter. Lee's first grade teacher was Gertrude Waller. Then Mrs. Ethel Long taught the next seven years. She was acclaimed by all her students to be the best teacher ever on Pinkham.

Mrs. Long bought milk from the Utters. Lee tells the tale of when he took milk to his teacher in a half gallon tin Karo syrup pail. He thought he was returning an empty pail after school, but when his mother looked inside, she found a note from the teacher. Lee had been a bad boy in school that day. First and second graders were let out early for recess. Lee and Fay Armstrong were second graders; Esther and David Armstrong were in first. Lee had wooden matches in his jean's pocket. He used them to start a small fire under a tree up back of the schoolhouse. It was soon discovered; Mrs. Long scolded them and paddled Lee. When his mother read the note, he got spanked again.

Mr. Banks taught Lee how to catch fish from the creek by tickling them under their belly. Lee had to show off his talent to others during school picnics held at the Falls or elsewhere on the creek. Very patiently while others watched, Lee slipped his fingers under the trout while they undulated in the water. With a sudden grip behind the gills and a splash, he proved his point by landing several fish.

Cecil took his turn to play fiddle at the country dances. His young wife was popular at these affairs. She was a raven haired, brown-eyed beauty, a petite 5-2 and wore a kid size shoes. She preferred high heels, which were hard to find in ladies styles. Cecil's favorite song to sing was, "I Picked a Peach in a Garden of Lemons."

Lee and Esther remembered going to dances with their folks. They went with a team and hay in the wagon for horses to eat. During the winter, dances were held at the Pinkham school. In the summertime, they were held at people's homes. Most of the furniture was moved outside to make room for dancing inside. Everyone in the community would come to the party.

Ladies would whip up a cake from scratch to bake in the oven of their wood stove or make venison sandwiches using homemade bread. Men slipped in a bottle of moonshine to insure a good time. Kids were excited to get together again to play outside or learn to dance to hillbilly music. When tired, they went to sleep on a pile of coats or blankets heaped in a corner or under a table out of the way. It was daylight in the morning before anyone went home to do chores.

Lee also told about the time his folks took the team and sleigh way up the creek to spend Thanksgiving with the Charlie Workman family. They drove up in the morning, feasted and visited and then came back the next day. Lee and the Workman boys built snow forts and enjoyed brisk snowball fights.

The first radio that Lee ever heard was a Montgomery Ward Airline at the Charlie Workman home. It was a battery operated cabinet model that brought in reception from Chicago, Spokane, Calgary, and other far-away stations. Especially enjoyed were the Grand Ole Opry and amateur hours. Montana Slim was popular in Calgary. In 1934, the Utters got their own radio, a Sears Silvertone ordered from the catalog.

Cecil Loren Utter and Winnie Mae Leib tied the matrimonial knot on May 3, 1921. Twenty-five years later their son Francis Lee and Madeline June Rost, would be wed on their anniversary.

Mae was a petite woman with dark brown eyes and black hair showing her Indian heritage. Cecil was fair with light blue eyes. Their first son took after his dad. Mae was 5' 2" and wore size five shoe. In spite of her size she was full of energy with lots of endurance. She pampered her husband and spoiled her children.

When Cecil would come in from working outside all day, Mae would meet him at the door to help him off with his coat. While he sat in a chair, she pulled his boots off and put on his house slippers. Mae put warm water into the wash pan for him, and even combed his hair. Supper was ready and on the table in no time, with his coffee cup filled repeatedly. When it was bath time, Mae heated the water and gave her husband a bath in the washtub just like she did her kids.

In the winter time the tub was brought in from the outside nail on the wall to warm up by the wood heater. While taking a bath, you were warm on one side and cold on the other. One fellow remembers the time he stood up in the tub and bent over. His wet buttocks sizzled as they smacked the hot stove. The poor little fellow straightened up with a yowl, and couldn't sit down for several days. He has a scar to prove it.

Cecil was a good teamster. He and his team of black Percherons could do most anything from farming to putting up hay, to skidding logs in the woods. Sometimes Cecil would take a cantankerous or balky horse that belonged to someone else and put them to work with Bonny or Diamond for a while to show them how a team should work together.

During the "Thirties" it was even hard to get a paying job with a good team of horses. One year the Utter family moved out on a place along the sand hills on Highway 37 to try farming on the irrigation ditch. That year they planted ten acres of potatoes. The rest of the place was put into oats for hay. Lee and Esther had the job of picking potato bugs, and putting them into a can with kerosene in it to exterminate them. The spuds were dug and bagged in the fall and sold to a grocer in Eureka for $1.00 a hundred pounds. When two guys came to admire the patch, one called them spuds and the other referred to them as Cecil's taters. Potato bugs became spud bugs or tater bugs.`

Other pests in that era were flies, mosquitoes and bed bugs. Flies and mosquitoes are still with us, but bedbugs are mostly eradicated. Bedbugs didn't come in seasons; they were there all year long. Log cabins were exceptional good brooding areas with so many hiding places in cracks and crevices. Bedbugs also traveled from place to place in clothing or bedrolls of the lumberjacks.

Bedbugs were nocturnal predators. They came out at night after good warm bodies were snuggled in under the covers and going to sleep. They silently snuck in for a big bite of blood before getting squished by the wary. Bedbugs had a distinctive odor similar to stink bugs, but didn't leave a welt like mosquitoes. Some folks would lift the quilts and light a match to catch the crawling culprits, but they were lucky if they got one or two of the scurrying bugs before they disappeared.

Cecil Utter working his team.

Housewives put a ban on bedbugs once a year. They moved everybody outside to sleep under the stars on a warm summer night. All the bedding was washed and hung out in the sunshine to dry. The house was scrubbed with lye water and a bug bomb placed inside to do its duty all night. The family camped outside for about three days before moving back into a bug free bed.

In the Thirties during the Depression, the weather was hot and dry. There was also a plague of grasshoppers – just one more thing to test the stamina of the homesteaders. There were no steady jobs to be had and no money so folks traded with one another.

This was how Mae Utter came to get two turkey hens and a tom as we well as a pair of geese. The geese did well around the pond with their goslings. The gander was a pest and picked on people. Lee and Esther learned to keep a wary eye on him. One day the gander found his match when he pulled Bonny's tail. She kicked him in the head and sent him rolling. Lee thought he was dead, but he finally got up to stagger off, a much tamer goose after that.

The turkeys feasted on grasshoppers all summer catching them in the air as they jumped. They also liked to roost in the fir trees for shelter. During the winter the tom turkey roosted on the housetop next to the stovepipe. Utters had turkey and geese to share for holiday feasting as well as feathers to make pillows, etc.

During hard times Cecil did anything he could to earn a dollar. His faithful team of black Percheon horses was an asset to his endeavors. Bonny and Diamond got so that they eagerly stepped on to a truck bed from a bank to get a ride to the job. They knew they walked enough while working.

Cecil used his team to mow hay along roadsides, around stumps in clearings or in abandoned meadows. The hay was then raked and shocked before being pitched with a fork onto a hay wagon to be hauled to the barn and pitched off again. Neighbor helped neighbor to get these arduous jobs done.

Cecil and his team skidded logs from the forest to landings at various sawmills. He was paid $1.00 a day and his team got a dollar also. One summer was spent down on Fisher River skidding logs for Ralph Burlingham, who had a sawmill that he moved from place to place – wherever there was timber to be cut into ties. (This was much easier than hand hewing). When the summer was over Cecil still hadn't got paid his wages. That was how Cecil became owner of a sawmill. Now he had the headaches of keeping the mill going and earning a living.

His son Lee was old enough to be on the other end of a crosscut saw, use the team to skid or be the tail sawyer to catch the ties and throw the slabs in a pile. At times they had other helpers and Lee graduated to running the saw and driving truck to haul the ties to the railroad.

Everyone took time out from other work to cut Christmas trees in the fall. This was a sure harvest of young trees from logged-over land. The whole family could participate from using the ax to chop them down to dragging and loading, then hauling to a tree yard close to town. The trees brought in enough money to pay taxes, buy a few winter clothes, and stockpile staple foods.

Cecil and Mae thought their family was complete with just one boy and a girl. But then another boy came to join the family on May 29, 1934, named Robert Ray. By then Lee was twelve and Esther eleven so they were a big help. When Lee started high school the Utter family moved closer to town. They settled on the Joe Kearney place at the elbow bend in the road just three miles from school.

When Ray started first grade in 1940 Cecil bought six lots in East Eureka along 6th Street. close to school. They built a one-room shack, an outhouse, and a barn for the horses and cow. They also built a chicken coop but no pigpen. They raised a beautiful garden there and even had space for a patch of oats.

Even though they were in town now, they had no electric power hook up until later. There was water piped in so Mae finally had running cold water and a sink to take it out. Hot water was still dipped from the reservoir of the wood cook stove and kerosene lamps were used for light. Mae worked in the restaurant and saved all her money to rebuild the house, she had $500.00 saved up and someone stole it from her purse. Later, she told her friend Jennie Sederdahl that anyone silly enough to carry that money around in her purse didn't deserve a new house.

The Utters lived there until Ray graduated from high school. When Lee returned from the U.S Navy at the end of WWII he took over the major job of running the sawmill. Cecil was then offered the job of being the night watchman as well as work in Albee's sawmill. It also gave them a place to live. The little shanty did have water and electricity but it was just one room with no bathroom. Mae lived there the rest of her life until she died of heart trouble in 1956.

Cecil retired and lived in bachelor shacks for a while. His health was failing from emphysema so he spent his last years living with his daughter or son. He died the fall of 1960 at the Lee Utter home on Pinkham. Both Mae and Cecil were laid to rest side by side in the Tobacco Valley cemetery.

LEE UTTER INTERVIEW
Tobacco Valley News, November 14, 1996

Lee Utter's home on Pinkham is just a half-mile from where he was born on August 22, 1922. "I was delivered by Dr. Long," he said. Lee was the oldest child of Cecil and Mae Utter. His sister, Esther, was 14 months younger and his brother, Ray, was 12 years younger.

"We lived most of the time on Pinkham but lived two years, 1934 and 1935, on a place northwest of Eureka that Art Nutting had. I also spent two summers at Twin Lakes on the Fluharty place in 1928 and 1929."

Lee began school on Pinkham in 1929 and graduated from the eighth grade in 1937. He went two years to school in Eureka. In the summer of 1937 the Utters moved to the Kearney place, which was later owned by Loren Netzloff, from where he walked to school in Eureka.

Lee said that when he was in the seventh and eighth grades he remembered having to stay out of school for a week at a time several times to help his dad skid logs for the tie mill.

Lee joined the Navy on October 7, 1942, and spent 27 months in the South and West Pacific in motor speedboat squadrons. He was discharged on December 25, 1945. He joined the Veterans of Foreign Wars Post 6786 in October of 1946 and has been an active member for the last 50 years.

As a member of the VFW, he participates in military funerals and Memorial Day services and is a member of the Veteran's Day delegation to Canada for "Hands Across The Border" fellowship and marches in parades with the American flag.

The year 1946 is also a memorable one for Lee because it was the year he married Madeline Rost, who was then teaching school on Pinkham. "Madeline and I have six wonderful children," he said. Daughter Melody became a teacher and now lives near Spokane. Terry is a teacher and counselor and lives in Eureka. Melody lives in Eureka. Ken lived near Spokane but now has the 69 Ranch headquarters. Keith was drafted into the Army and was killed in Vietnam. Pamela is married to an Air Force man, is in the National Guard and drives the Pasco school bus. Patricia joined the Navy and is married to a Navy man who retires next year. They plan to move back to Pinkham. The Utters also have 20 grandchildren and four great-grandchildren.

In the fall of 1946, Lee bought and drove the school bus to Eureka for six years. He then sawmilled for four years, short-logged for he next 20 years, and then worked for the county, running the Eureka landfill for 12 years until he retired.

For recreation, Lee said he enjoys living and working in the woods. He still does a little short-logging, cuts wood for winter and cuts Christmas trees. When not out-of-doors, he enjoys reading.

When asked what he likes best about the Tobacco Valley, Lee simply said, "It's home."

Lee Utter's sawmill.

Lee Utter at work cutting Christmas trees, sorting in the photo at the top of the page and loading to haul to the concentration yard.

UTTERS – SENIORS OF THE YEAR

Lee and Madeline Utter have been named Lincoln County's senior citizens of the year.

The Utters have been married for many years. Both were born in Montana, where they have six children, twenty grandchildren and twenty great-grandchildren. Their large family filled a pew at the Holy Cross Lutheran Church in Eureka where they are faithful members.

Lee used his truck to haul rocks as well as pine roots for the altar when they helped build the local church. Madeline currently serves as church librarian, maintained a church history album, served as a church council officer, evangelism chairwoman and president of the Lutheran Women's Missionary League. The Utters are active in the Aid Association for Lutherans where they help with benefits for the needy. Madeline also earned the award for Aid Association for Lutherans volunteer of the year. She taught Sunday school and vacation Bible school.

Madeline accompanied youth group outings as chaperone, as well as campouts and school dances. She was also involved in the Parent Teacher Association and served as room mother.

Lee served in the U.S. Navy for three years during World War II on a PT boat in the Pacific Theater and has been an active member of the Veterans of Foreign Wars, Post 6786 of Eureka for fifty-two years. He proudly shows his patriotism by carrying the American flag in parades. Lee also transports veterans to the hospital and the Veterans Association medical bus. He participates in highway cleanup and helps set veterans tombstones at the local cemetery and has served as pallbearer for the funerals of many veterans.

Madeline helped to organize a Veterans of Foreign Wars Ladies Auxiliary in 1953 and served as president for several years. Later she served as secretary, treasurer and trustee of the same organization. She sold Buddy Poppies and Forget-me-nots and worked on committees to help needy veterans and community activities. For many years she has kept a scrapbook as historian and news reporter. She contributes food and helps in the kitchen after funerals and during fund-raisers.

They also belonged to the Stockman's Association. Madeline served as secretary to the CowBelles, an auxiliary to the Stockgrowers. She also kept a scrapbook of CowBelle history and gave it to the Historical Village. She has also taken her turn at manning the Village for tourists.

Lee and Madeline take their privilege of voting in elections seriously. Madeline served on the election board in old Rexford and new Rexford, then on to Glen Lake as precinct chairman. Lee regularly transports senior citizens and veterans to the polls to vote.

For the past twenty-five years they have devoted their time to the Tobacco Valley Senior Citizens Association and Center in Eureka. They initially became involved by bringing older citizens to the center. Then Lee was elected president and served three years. He has been delivering Meals on Wheels for over twenty years, volunteering time and expense. Madeline plans many pleasure trips and Lee is a volunteer driver of the senior bus. Madeline takes photos and preserves them in a stack of scrapbooks at the center. She also started a library of books in the back room. Lately she made chair covers and cushions out of scraps of fabric that have been donated. She recycles greeting cards to be sold as a project of the center. Lee is noted for his annual donation of a premium home grown Christmas tree to the Senior Center and Madeline helps with decorations.

Madeline is now in her third term as president of the Tobacco Valley Senior Citizens Association after serving in previous years as the secretary and also as treasurer. Madeline also served eight years as secretary to Lincoln County Council on Aging.

Both Lee and Madeline make regular visits to the local nursing home and help with their outings. They call on the sick and home bound and have been known to water many house plants when friends and neighbors are not able. Lee has accumulated over five gallons in donated blood during local blood donor drives.

Lee and Madeline are both active members of the Libby Dam Good Sam's Club. Madeline served as the vice president for two years and they are both on the entertainment committee participating in skits. They assist with highway cleanup, planning campouts and fundraisers.

Madeline is a member of the Eureka Christian Women's Club and has held a variety of offices including president, vice president and friendship Bible coffee guide and coordinator.

UTTERLEE HAVEN
January 1974

Utterlee Haven is a cabin in the trees
The scent of dewey lilacs or
wild roses on the breeze.

Utterlee Haven is clear water in the brook
the sound of sighing branches or
the raindrops on the roof.

Utterlee Haven is clean air in purity
the sight of birds a-flying and
a-nesting in the trees.

Utterlee Haven is a home for Lee and me
the touch of the one I love
living close in harmony.

Utterlee Haven is a baby on my knee
the sound of children playing
and then laughing with glee.

Utterlee Haven is knowing God cares for me
He blesses every thing that is
He made it all for you and me.

Utterlee Haven is on Pinkham Creek, Montana,
this is where we live now
and plan to live montana. **M.Utter**

ESTHER UTTER CARVEY

Esther Margalene was born on a foggy Halloween in 1923 on Pinkham Creek. A neighbor, Mrs. Ella Thatcher, served as midwife as Doc. Long was out doing another delivery. Now Cecil and Mae Utter had a boy and a girl and thought their family was complete.

Esther started school the year after her brother Lee. They walked to the Pinkham school rain, shine or freezing cold and were never absent or late. Esther was little and skinny so Cecil got a nanny goat from Mr. Banks to fatten her up on goats milk.

Mrs. Long, their teacher, drove a 1929 Model A Ford up from town to Pinkham to teach school. As a treat she took the students by turns to spend the weekend in town at her home, which later became Mr. Toland's C.P.A. office.

They marveled at her modern appliances and a switch on the wall that turned on a bright light in the ceiling. They were fascinated by turning on a faucet to get hot and cold water and having an inside toilet. Each had to have their Saturday night bath in a gleaming porcelain tub in a room by their self! The most marvelous of all was walking just over to Main Street to see their first picture show.

Esther remembers family outings to pick huckleberries. There was a good patch up Pinkham Mountain where forest fires had burned it off. The family left home early in the morning on horseback, picked berries that evening, camped all night, picked in the morning, then rode back home. Boxes with food now held berries.

Esther remembers running up the logs of windfalls with her little bucket looking for big berries. Her dad, Cecil, had a homemade huckleberry picker. It was a two-pound coffee can with a handle put on the side and knitting needles soldered along the opposite top edge. The knitting needles stripped the bushes of berries and a few leaves depositing them in the can. Cecil could fill his milk bucket fast, although it took more cleaning.

The family not only picked huckleberries in the summer, but also service berries, chokecherries, elder berries and Oregon grapes to make jams and jellies for the winter. Sometimes they would find a patch of wild strawberries or raspberries to help make a variety from rhubarb, currants and gooseberries.

For winter time fun, Esther told of the times when people got together for a taffy pull. This was a favorite was to celebrate New Years Eve and welcome in the new year. Folks gathered in a cozy cabin to set out the ingredients for the taffy candy. Everyone got involved in the process. Some to cook and stir and others to wait their turn to pull and snap the stringy ropes to make hard candy. To speed the process of cooling, the sticky mass on the baking sheet was set outside for a spell in the cold. Then young and old buttered their hands to grab a hunk to pull, stretch and fold. Little ones slipped a piece in their mouth to suck on while others made fancy braids and twists.

Molasses Taffy
1 C molasses
½ C white sugar
½ C brown sugar
1/4 C water
2 T butter
½ tsp soda
pinch salt
Combine first 4 ing.
Boil to hard ball stage
remove from heat
stir in butter and soda, salt
pour on buttered
baking sheet.

When cool enough to
handle, butter hands
and make a ball.
Pull-stretch and fold
until taffy turns light in color.
Stretch and twist into
rope 1" thick – cut
into pieces using
buttered scissors.

Esther ran off and got married when she was a freshman in high school. She and Floyd Goff tied the knot at Coeur d'Alene, Idaho, and then went to Toppenish, Washington. Floyd followed the harvest, then came back to Eureka for Louise to be born November 22, 1940. Their son Daniel was born January 24, 1942. Floyd (Buck) was born in Lewistown, Montana, June 6, 1943, and Cecil was born January 28, 1945.

Esther divorced Floyd and later married Nick Carvey, who was a widower with five kids. They raised their nine kids together as they moved from place to place so Nick could work in the woods as a sawyer with his chainsaw. He was also an avid hunter and fisherman, so Esther always had wild game to prepare for the large family. She became a successful hunter herself and filled her license every year. She cleaned and cooked deer and bear and plucked the geese she brought down with a shotgun. Esther applied for a moose permit, found one and shot it but had to have help getting it out to butcher. She never wasted any meat; she cut it up to can or freeze.

Esther suffered a minor stroke in 1996. Since Nick was fishing, Esther drove herself to Prompt Care when she felt paralysis coming on. From there, she was sent by ambulance to the Kalispell Regional Hospital. She came home and was doing fine with feeling back in her left side again.

Esther died in October 2003 due to an accident. She was hit by a vehicle while crossing Main Street in Eureka. Internment was in the Tobacco Valley Cemetery.

GEORGE AND MARY ANN CALDWELL
PAT AND HAZEL CARR

George and Mary Ann Caldwell started their married life in West Virginia. It was there that George worked in the coal mines. Their son, Joe, and two daughters, May and Ora, were born there. They left West Virginia when George got a job with the railroad for construction and maintenance of tracks. The family went with George wherever the job took him. Another daughter, Hazel, was born in Iowa.

By the time they arrived in Rexford, George was a section foreman. The family moved into a house furnished by the railroad. Their family had increased with three more girls: Ellen, Katy and Myrtle. It wasn't long before the Caldwells became acquainted with more folks from West Virginia. Most of them had a homestead in the Pinkham area so that is where the Caldwells wanted to settle. George filed for a homestead there and built a log cabin to prove up on it, but eventually he let it go back to the government.

Caldwell girls attended the Pinkham school, grew up and married local men. Ora became the wife of Amos Kinney and Ellen married Payton Piles, but later divorced. Hazel tied the knot with Pat Carr. All of these men were Pinkham homesteaders. The other Caldwell girls married men from Washington or Oregon and raised their families there. George and Mary Ann moved back to Rexford to live for a while. They spent their last years living with their daughters and their families. "Grandpa Caldwell's only request at the last" said grandson George, "was for a yard of 'chewing tobaccy' when the family went to town for occasional shopping."

Pat Carr was born at Ellis Island in New York. He came west as a young man to be independent and own his own land. He found that piece of land in Montana, up Sutton Ridge and about ten miles from Rexford. Pat filed for a homestead and took Hazel Caldwell as his wife. Together they would raise a family and prove up on the homestead.

Their first two children, Joe and Clara, were born on the homestead with local midwives in attendance. The next three, George, named after grandfather Caldwell, Mary named after grandmother Caldwell, and Henry Ford, called Hank, were born in Rexford with Dr. Long who attended home deliveries. The youngest, Jane, was born when they lived in the upper school house on Pinkham. This time it was "Aunt Sis" (Nancy Jane Roberts) who served as a midwife to bring the baby safely into the world.

Pat, like most homesteaders, worked wherever he could find a job to support his family. He used his broad ax to hew ties, sawed logs with a crosscut saw and boot-legged moonshine. Sometimes the family lived "high on the hog" while at other times they were as poor as church mice. It all depended on what he could find to do or whether he had a sale for home-brewed hooch.

The Carr family moved from place to place depending on where Pat had a job. The older children, Joe and Clara, started school on lower Pinkham and walked down from Sutton Road past the Leib homestead. George Carr remembers living in Rexford on the flat next to the Kootenai River bridge. He started school there and that's where he saw his first black and white silent movies. George remembered "Tom Mix" and "Hoot Gibson" as the features.

From there the Carrs moved back up to Pinkham. One summer was spent at the old Chisham place, the farthest one up Pinkham Creek. Then they bought the upper school house and converted it into a home. While the Carrs lived there, they were far enough away from the lower school to draw transportation money from the school district. This helped keep the family in beans and bacon during lean years.

George recalled living up Pinkham during the Depression. He said, "The summers there were real nice and lots of fun. But the winters were hard. Real Hard! Winters were long and cold. The road was not kept open and we got to school any way we could. We walked mostly. Sometimes we had a horse to double up on – sometimes two horses. We rode bareback (without a saddle), in a buggy, buckboard or sleigh in winter. We went by the Robert's place about a mile from school. Many times, Aunt Sis Roberts would take us in the house, pack us in snow, thaw out fingers and toes, then send us on to school."

"Aunt Sis flagged us down one evening and said she needed to go home with us. When we got in sight of the house we saw Mother. She was yelling at us to go back and get Sis! But Sis was already with us. Some how she knew it was time. My sister, Jane was born that night. She was named after Nancy Jane, the mid-wife, who was there during the delivery."

George said he got to know almost everyone on Pinkham. They were all good neighbors and friends. Lee and Esther Utter were near his age and he stayed over at their house several times. One winter the Carrs moved closer to the school which made it a lot easier on the children. George remembered a Miss Crowley and Mrs. Long as his teachers. At the end of each school year, a big picnic was held in the community. It left many fond memories for school kids as well as parents.

While living in the upper school house, George remembered Charlie Workman and his pack train of mules going by with supplies for the lookouts up on mountain tops. He also recalled his first radio listening experience. He went with the Kinney kids to their grandparents house where there was a battery operated radio. They listened to "Amos and Andy," then shut the radio off to save the battery.

The Carr family, like so many others, went farther west during the "dirty" Thirties and found spouses elsewhere. All except Mary; she married Elliott Holder in Eureka. They spent most of their married life in Libby.

CAMP 32 AND PINKHAM FALLS

Camp 32 on lower Pinkham Creek was so named by the Bonners Ferry Lumber Company. Their logging camps were numbered to make it easier for bookkeepers to keep track of them. There was also a Camp 19 in the vicinity that was started up earlier as land and timber became available. It was located in a draw along the old Pinkham road into Rexford in Section 25, R28W, T36N.

Early logging along Pinkham Creek was done by homesteaders themselves. They used crosscut saws to fell trees, axes to trim limbs and broad axes to shape the trunks into house logs or rail road ties. A single horse was used to skid the logs to a landing where they were rolled onto a sled or wagon to be pulled by a team of horses down to their destination. (This was called horse logging.) Hewed ties (shaped with a broad ax) were taken to Great Northern Railroad holding yards by the railroad tracks in either Rexford or Eureka.

Camp 32.

Virgin timber stands in the area were plentiful and western Montana was becoming accessible by train as well as Kootenai River traffic. Large lumber companies were licking their lips in anticipation of getting a foothold in the area while making plans to harvest the bountiful supply.

As early as 1907 the Bonners Ferry Lumber Company (B.F.L.C.) of Idaho started buying up homesteads as they became available on lower Pinkham. The first one was from Mary Brown, who had just proved up on eighty acres on November 24, 1906. She accepted the offer from the lumber company and then deeded it to them in January 1907. Waverly Brown followed suit by signing over his homestead also.

B.F.L.C. held onto this portion of timber land for future use. In just a few years more homesteaders were ready to give up the struggle of living in the wilderness. They decided to sell out and move on. In 1914 John and Christina White sold their 120 acre homestead to B.F.L.C.. Their next purchase of timber land was in 1921 from the First National Bank of Kalispell who had foreclosed on a homestead. By 1923 and 1924 the B.F.L.C. owned most of the Sections 33, 34 & 35,

Pinkham Falls.

all in Township 36N and Range 28W.

It was then that logging operations began in earnest. Workers were hired to set up camps by building horse barns, a blacksmith shop, bunk houses, a cook shack, etc. These camps were close to where logging took place as felled and limbed logs were skidded (dragged) to a landing by horses then rolled onto a wagon or sled with pee vees (tool with hook on the end) to be hauled away. It was easier hauling in winter as a sled slid on snow covered roads where as wagons clattered on rocks and bumps or mired in mud during spring break up.

Bunkhouses were not built for comfort – just a place to sleep. The bunk beds built of rough lumber were double deckers with maybe four sets along a wall with another set on the end to sleep ten men. Straw mattress pads were placed on bare boards with each man bringing their own bed roll which had at least a pillow, flannel sheet and a soogan (quilt). They kept their belongings such as comb, shaving gear and a change of clothes in a pack sack that they hung on a nail pounded into the bed supports. There was a wood heater there that had to be stoked often and a table that held a coal-oil lamp or lantern to read by or play a game of cards. There was also a spittoon as most lumberjacks chewed tobacco or snoose so they wouldn't set the woods on fire. They also wore cork boots so they could walk a log without slipping. Meals for the crew were prepared in the cook shack. A good cook and his flunky could keep a crew on the job. Board and room was subtracted from the paychecks at the end of the month.

Sawyers used long crosscut saws with a handle on each end to be grabbed to pull back each way. They worked in teams that were compatible with at least one of them adept at filing a saw correctly to make it cut into the wood. Gypo sawyers were paid by the number of logs cut in a day. Trees grow larger at the base so sawyers cut above this butt log to get less taper and a more uniform log to roll. Sometimes they chopped notches on each side of the tree to insert supports for them to do a balancing act while they were sawing above the blemishes. This took real skill in winter when snow was on the ground and everything was slippery. Tall durable tamarack stumps with notches cut into them are still standing in the vicinity of Camp 32. There is also a stump on display at the Ranger Station in Eureka.

Not all workers lived in camp. Some were local fellows who lived near by and some were married men with families. Roscoe Combs was a sawyer paired with Arley Alderman, who married Annie Leib. Walt Baker (married to Maude Leib) was also a sawyer. They lived in a shack at camp with their daughter Ella Maude. Roscoe met and married Dora Stacy, another gal from up the 'Crick.'

Teamsters furnished their own team of horses to work. Teams were paid for in addition to the teamster so they got a double paycheck. They hauled logs to a landing below Rexford on the banks of the Kootenai River. Here logs were piled until high water in spring. Then lumber jacks with cork boots climbed on the pile and again used pee vees or cant hooks to roll the logs into the rushing water. Tumbling logs were carried on flood waters over the Kootenai Falls below Libby and on to Bonners Ferry, Idaho, where they were stopped with steel cables strung across the river. They were then eased into a mill pond to go through a sawmill.

Camp 32 is located in Section 35, Township 36N, Range 28W in NW Montana. This was the location of former homesteads proved up on by Waverly and Mary Brown, John and Christina White, John and Art Mikalson and Peter McGovern. After virgin timber was taken there was no need for B.F.L.C. to keep the property. They deeded all their land holdings on lower Pinkham Creek back to the U.S. Government in 1934. Thus this land on lower Pinkham which could be private taxable land is now managed by the U.S.F.S.

Camp 32 is a popular campground for people who like out-of-the-way places yet not too far away. The camp clearing makes a spacious place for group gatherings. This spot by Pinkham Creek was used by local people before it became an official Forest Service campground. Improved toilet facilities, designated camping spots with fire pits and tables are a boon to camping as well as a pump well for drinking water. Widened gravel roads also make it more accessible for campers.

The Montana School Section 36 is located just up the creek from the campgrounds. (This section has been leased for years by Utters; first Cecil, then Lee and now Terry). The section above that is where the spectacular Pinkham Falls is located. This was once private property also as Della Cann paid for her patent for a homestead there on February 10, 1907. It was also deeded to the B.F.L.C. This spot was noted for its stand of stately ponderosa pines.

Pinkham Falls is a site to behold, especially during high water in the spring run off of melting snow. A narrow-crevice with a drop of about fifty feet almost straight down has water spewing and thundering as it rushes on down for another drop to a lower pool. This is a good swimming hole except for cold water. Many photos have been taken of this scene, some have even captured a rainbow in the mist.

A new biffy built at Camp 32
Is a comfort station for me and you
It was built by government specs.
What better service can we expect?
> **By Madeline Utter**

WATER

Water was not wasted; it was too hard to come by. Pioneers couldn't turn on the faucet to get running water instantly. They had to take a bucket and run to the creek or spring. When it rained, they propped a board at a slant up under the eaves so water would run into a rain barrel. This was soft water and good for bathing and hair washing. It was then used for scrubbing the floor before thrown out. A washtub was used for bathing, after water was heated on the stove. There was no drain for it to go down; it was carried out.

In winter, snow was dipped into a tub, then brought into the house to melt. Icicles were huge, as the cabins had no insulation and snow melted fast from the roof. Sometimes there was a solid sheet of ice from the eaves to the ground. These were broken up and brought into the house to melt for water also.

Everyone had a wash stand or bench in their kitchen. That is where the water bucket sat, with a dipper hanging on a nail on the wall above. A wash pan sat alongside with a soap dish. The towel and washcloth hung on nails above, along side a mirror. It was where the men used a straight razor to shave whiskers. A razor strap hung near by and sometimes, was used to discipline the children. Hot water was heated in a teakettle on the stove.

To go to the toilet, everyone had to trek outside to a "privy" (short for private place). There were no rolls of toilet paper; this is where the "Monkey" Ward and Sears Roebuck catalogs found their final use. A pit was dug in the ground with an "outhouse" placed over it. When the pit filled up, a new one was dug and the outhouse moved. This trek to out back wasn't bad in the summer, when days were long, but in the wintertime, it was downright miserable. Days were short and dark, snow was shoveled from the path and the seat was cold and frosty! No wonder people had a chamber pot in their bedroom, even though it had to be emptied every day.

PIONEER PRIVIES

All the places on Pinkham in the pioneer era had the proverbial little house out back. Some referred to them as the outhouse or a privy, others to toilet or "can." These little buildings were as varied as the people who owned or built them. Some were hurriedly erected out of poles or slabs with a slant roof and the seat support of poles with just a square hole. Others were as painstakingly put together by carpenters as their home with moon shape cut outs near the gabled roof for ventilation.

Family affairs had three graduated shaped holes for papa, mama and child with the little one about half the height from the floor as the others. Kids in between could take their choice of stepping on the lower seat to use a mama hole or perching precariously over the papa hole.

The standard paper roll was the 'Sears' or 'Monkey Ward' catalogs. If the family wasn't too large or if too much wasn't wasted, the periodic catalogs would 'do' until the next seasonal issue. Otherwise magazines were contributed to the cause, which made better reading material during the pause than a wipe (especially slick pages). No one wasted money on buying newspapers.

The personal family touch was varied and ideas were gotten from others to improve ones own facility. There were those that had springs on the doors to automatically swing shut like a screen door. Some had hinges made from inner tubes fastened to seat covers to hold them in place. At least one had a modern toilet seat installed salvaged from the city dump. Others had fur-lined seats for warm comfort in the winter when frost formed underneath.

Seasonal changes regulated moving the privy. In the summer lime was used to control flies and odor. Frozen build up in winter made it necessary to hunt a new location come spring. The ground was easily dug then as all the family got their turn with the shovel. The old place was filled with dirt dug from the new hole, thus the ground was fertilized and recycled. A feminine touch was added by planting flowers or vines in the loose soil. Well-planned sites with forethought were near a tree for shade or out beyond the woodpile. By using the same trail for both, an armload of wood was easily brought back to stoke the fire.

Many a fireside storyteller would be reminded of some comical happening in the outhouse. Like the time the whole family had the stomach flu at the same time and Grandpa didn't make it. He tarried too long while waiting for Ma and Sis. With a family many calls came at the same time, so then the race was on to see who got there first.

There was always someone left out in the cold. The consolation was that the seat would be warmed up by the first.

A favorite story was told by a son who had proof by the pictures he snapped. He had to chuckle just to think of it. He picked a position, camera ready, and waited for ma to come out. At the appropriate time he yelled "Hey, Maw" caught her mouth open and buttoning up at the same time. The same Maw got caught again by a camera when she appeared coming up out of the bushes while camping.

Some one else remembers a winter of deep snow when it seemed like going through a tunnel to get out back. Snow was piled shoulder high on a man at the sides of the path and above the heads of the smaller ones. It was times like this when the chamber pot under the bed was put to use.

Another recalls the summer a little brother threw a puppy down in the toilet hole. The elder sister climbed down the papa hole to rescue him and give him a bath. Luckily for her, it had been newly dug that spring.

Then there was the horse called Robin who became adept at opening privy doors. It could be disconcerting to a stranger not used to that sort of thing, as Robin took the door knob in his mouth, pulled, opened the door, looked in on the occupant, then let it go to slam shut again.

A family privy was perched on the top of a bank to save a lot of digging. One day while kids were playing at the bottom of the bank, a chamber pot was emptied down a hole. Kids scattered, as contents came rolling and splashing down the bank.

An old bachelor, suffering from a hangover, spied a rabbit in his newly excavated hole as he was about to use it. Alarmed, fearing he'd lost his mind, he called a friend to come have a look. Sure enough, hopping around the bottom was a rabbit. It had burrowed in from the side, then was too confused to find its way out again. The bachelor, sobered, had his mind eased considerably.

Most of the Pinkham pioneer privies are now obsolete. Only a few are still in use including the two behind the school house used as a community center. These two probably have their own story to tell if they could talk.

Other old-timers interviewed about their private privies said "no comment."

A lonely little Pinkham privy
Sits alone out in the woods
It is a one holer just waiting
For someone to drop the goods.

PIONEER PRIVY

It's just a little house out back
The whole family has to use it.
It's a very necessary one at that
When nature calls, they can't refuse it.

In summer, flies buzz around
In winter, frost is on the seat.
Then in the fall it starts filling up
In spring, dig a new hole about 6 feet.

Sears and "Monkey" Ward catalogs
Are contributed for the cause.
Magazines and funny papers
May be read during the pause.

On some, the door opens out
On others, the door opens in.
If in, you can kick it shut
If out, A-ha, you're caught again!
     By *Madeline Utter*

PIONEER PRIVIES

By Madeline Utter

This is a modern one, why shore,
It has green fiberglass in the door
But take a flashlight in the dark.
So you can see just where to park.

This place of rest in Sandy Draw
Once was built without a flaw.
Three graduated holes made it complete,
Even boasted of a fur-lined seat.

For this one out in the snow
Put on your coat before you go.
Take your dog along at night
If howling coyotes give a fright.

June 7-1976

A place of rest in Sandy Draw
Once was built without a flaw.
Three graduated holes made it complete
It even boasted of a fur-lined seat.

For the one out in the snow
Put on your coat before you go.
Take your dog along at night
If howling coyotes give a fright.

This is a modern one, why share
It has green fiberglass in the door.
But take a flashlight in the dark
So you can see just where to park.

These twin toilets sit behind the school
Students need permission to go – it a rule.
Right one is for boys – left is for the girls
There is toilet paper on rolls that unfurls.
To go it is only a short out door walk
These toilets could tell tales if they could talk.

WPA SPECIAL
This toilet built by the WPA
Was the best of its kind in its hey-day
The Work Projects Administration
Wanted all to have a useful station

They dug a deep hole down in the ground
Built forms and poured cement all around
The sturdy toilet sat on this foundation
It was to be a permanent accommodation.

Inside was a whole new revelation
There was only one seat in the station
It was situated right in the center
With a lid on top to lift as you enter

There was a door latch to keep it in place
So no one could surprise you face to face
If a toilet served a large family
It still had to be moved regularly

The toilet was built so sturdy and strong
A horse was needed to pull it along
To put over a new hole all dug by hand
With a shovel on a new piece of land.

Everyone is proud of this new outhouse
Though it's not like having one in your house
That you flush and wash it all down the drain
Where you never have to see or smell it again.

SATURDAY NIGHT BATH
This is one of the memories I've had
Don't know whether to call it good or bad
It was time to take Saturday night baths
We all wanted to be first – nobody last.
Water was carried and heated about right
All of us had to use it to bathe that night
As one of the eldest – I had to think fast
Or we'd have a family fight to the last.

So I picked up the baby to give the first bath
And in so doing, gave myself a spit bath (sponge)
Now the water still looked fairly clean
So the next would be the one that's seen
With the cleanest face and hands for sure
As they all stood about in their underwear.
I just got the baby diapered and in bed
He gave a grunt and dirtied from feet to head.

Then as I was bending over the next in line
He vomited all over his feet and mine.
Before I could move, my sister with a blast
Let it out both ends at once – 'fore and aft'
Embarrassed, she looked at her big brother
Who of course started to laugh – then another

Held his hand to his mouth before it came
Nobody could help it – they all felt shame

I stood where I was and reached to a chair
To unfold a newspaper that was lying there
And said "nobody move, stand where you are"
It was needless to say, we couldn't go far.
But big brother didn't heed my advice
He started to run – then slipped as on ice!
His arms propelled as he tried to dash
Then he fell – in the tub with a splash!

Water came over the side of the tub in a wave
And from our predicament we were saved.
In stunned silence I reached for the broom
Then held my breath as I swept the room
Big brother was one who didn't want a bath
Once a year was enough, at others he'd laugh
Now he was in the tub while we stood about
Couldn't help but laugh as we heard him shout
Swear words followed in a steady stream
He swore he'd get us!
        Then I woke from my dream.

VICTOR A. BANKS

    Victor A. Banks had a place east of the mountains north of Choteau. In 1930 he decided to get out of the dry, windy country and move west into the mountains. He sold his place there and bought the homestead of Elmer Roberts just below the Pinkham schoolhouse along the main road, which split the place.

    Mr. Banks was a tall, slim gentleman, very exact in his carriage. He dressed neatly in khaki pants and shirt. He was respected by his neighbors and was always referred to as Mr. Banks in the community. According to the 1930 census Mr. Banks was a veteran of the Spanish American War.

    Mr. Banks came in a Model A Ford pickup and soon purchased a nanny goat for milk. He also ground wheat to make his own whole wheat bread. When his goats multiplied he had goat meat as well as hides to use. He stretched the hides on a frame in the barn to dry.

    The little homestead cabin had a door so low that Mr. Banks had to duck his head to enter. One part of the cabin, built by Andy Stacy, still had a dirt floor. This he used for storage. The other part, built by Elmer Roberts, had a board floor where he lived.

There was a little spring in the pasture above the Pinkham road for his animals to drink. Water was scarce around the buildings. Pinkham Creek was visible but flowed through the neighbor's place. In 1936 he bought one acre from a neighbor so his land would touch the creek. He then fenced a lane from his goat pens to the creek for watering.

Mr. Banks became know as the goat man and he welcomed visitors. Young folks especially liked to visit and watch the little kids romping around and butting heads. Among them were the Utters. Lee and Esther remember when they were barefoot kids themselves and crossing the creek on a log or wading through to go see Mr. Banks. The attraction passed to the next generation.

Kenny, Terry and Keith Utter made many visits across the creek to visit Mr. Banks. They were fascinated with his goatskin covered easy chair and his hand-made goatskin moccasins with the hair turned in. He even had a goatskin-covered seat for his jeep.

One year a nanny goat died after giving birth to twins. The boys just happened to be there to bring the tiny kids home to feed on the bottle, with cow's milk, of course. Kenny packed the bigger one and Terry carried the smaller one that had little nubbins of horns. The boys had a lively summer of butting heads and playing king of the hill with their playmates.

Pam and Patsy Utter also liked to visit Mr. Banks. One spring during high water, the girls asked if they could go over. They were told to go around by the bridge and the road. But the girls decided that was too far. Daring Pam decided to walk the high log across the creek. But half way over she fell into the roaring, bumbling water and washed down the creek against some other debris where she could get out. Pam stayed away until her clothes dried and it was a long time before mother found out about it.

Victor Banks had a mare called Lightning that he kept in the pasture as his riding horse. He had made a trade to Charlie Workman for the mare that was used to being put up in the barn at school. When Lee Utter purchased the unused barn in later years he backed his truck into the garage part and fastened it down with crossbeams. Going down the road past the pasture the building looked like it had wheels and moving on its own power. Lightning took a look at the familiar barn, put up her tail and galloped away over the pasture in fright.

Victor traded his old pickup for a used Army jeep in the late 40's so he would have dependable transportation when he had to go to town for mail, etc. When his eyes became covered with cataracts he was refused a license to drive. He had to go to town occasionally so he parked the jeep by the railroad track then walked to the post office and store, which were located on the lower end of main street Eureka. He let Alice Wilson use his Jeep to learn to drive. She did quite well in his pasture steering around the stumps and learning to shift gears.

When Mr. Banks became ill later in life he stayed with Tom and Alice Wilson in their new house. Before he died in 1965 he deeded his place to Tom, then Pete and Esther Ransier bought it in 1968 to build their new home.

FINCH FAMILY

Isaiah E. and Mary Jarvis Finch lived in Pittsburgh, Pennsylvania, where they raised a large family. Isaiah worked in the coal mines and steel mills to support his family. When the younger boys were born, they decided to move to Montana and get a ranch. They settled in Big Horn County near Soap Creek at Sumatra.

After a few dry seasons they gave up on that barren country and looked for greener pastures. Their youngest son, Charles (Ed) Finch, and Jim Jenkins scouted the mountains and found homesteads for sale in the Pinkham Creek area. The Finch family bought the Frank Slick homestead as well as that of Clint Slick, Frank Pluid and John M. Harrington, all up the Slick Gulch drainage.

The Finch family moved into the big white house built by Frank Slick, the fall of 1936. They were pleased with the place. Water was piped into the house from a pond and large meadows had been cleared for grazing and raising hay. It had been logged off before but more trees were reaching maturity and young growth was developing into Christmas trees.

When the caravan of Finch vehicles came up Pinkham on moving day it seemed like a parade to the kids on the school ground. They could hear the procession coming long before it got there and lined up along the fence wide eyed to watch.

Lee Utter was one of them all a goggle as he saw a 1928 Chevy truck with an Indian head painted on the door. It turned up the Slick Gulch road and behind it in the dust was a 1928 Chevy car. He can't remember those that followed but they were all loaded down with machinery and household goods to settle on their new holdings up the gulch.

Isaiah and his sons, Jim, 40, Van, 28 and Ed, 26, all went to work to make a living from the ranch. Another son, Hadden (Tom) Finch, bought a place east of Eureka to farm and raise his family. Isaiah bought fifty head of sheep from Mae Keith who lived on the other side of Pinkham Ridge near Marl Lake. They sawed wood to sell as well as cut Christmas trees every fall. Eventually a bell sawmill was purchased to saw ties and cants to be hauled to Eureka.

John, JoAnn, Jarvis and Harriet, children of Tom and Guida (pronounced Gyda) liked to go to Pinkham to visit their grandparents and uncles. Harriet remembers their sheep dog and how he would jump in the air to catch a tossed flapjack, even when an empty hand made the same motion!!

Van Finch was elected to the school board and served as clerk for several years from 1939 through 1949 until after school ended in the one room Pinkham school. His niece Harriet Finch was hired on a permit to teach the term 1944-45. She would walk up the hill a mile from the school teacherage to visit her grandfather on weekends. One time Harriet got real homesick and walked over ten miles to visit her folks, who lived east of Eureka. She had no car so walking was her mode of transportation. Her folks gave her a ride back up to Pinkham so she could teach again the next day.

The time the stovepipe caught fire at the teacherage scared Harriet half to death. She ran down to the Roscoe Combs' place in the middle of the night and lost one of her shoes on the way. Mr. Combs just picked her up and carried her back because there was snow on the ground! He also took care of the chimney fire!

In 1942, Ed went into the Army for the duration of WWII. He was sent to England, France and Germany. By the end of the war he had met Elizabeth, a widowed German girl who became his wife. Ed was discharged from Camp McCoy, Wisconsin, in June of 1946. He started proceedings to bring Elizabeth to America and she arrived a year later.

In 1943, Van and Ed Finch had become joint owners in the ranch. Now Ed had a wife and daughter, Lisa, to share their home. Van took a trip east and brought back his wife, Ruth. The couples decided to divide the house into two apartments with another kitchen being added on the side for Ruth to use. They all shared an outside privy. Van and Ruth had a son, Bobby.

Ed and Elizabeth became the parents of three boys, Walter born in 1951, Gary in 1953 and Alfred in 1955. When Walter arrived December 23, it was in the midst of a hard winter. At 30 below zero, Ed had to build a fire under the 1937 Dodge to get it started. Heavy snow had not been plowed from the road, so Ed was stuck near the Jenkins place.

He shoveled out while Elizabeth grew closer to giving birth. At last he gave up, walked back home and harnessed up the team (to pull the car out of the snow drift. Six-year-old Lisa was in the car to keep her mother company during her labor pains. They made it to town just in time to the home of Mrs. Olson. Dr. Clarke got there for the delivery and all went well.

In 1953 Ed and Elizabeth decided the house was too small for two families. They sold their half of the place to Van and went to Denver seeking work. But they missed being in Montana so they moved back to the Eureka area in 1956. Ed found work in various small sawmills. Ed also became janitor at Eureka school until he retired, then Elizabeth took over the job of janitor.

Isaiah and Mary Finch celebrated their fiftieth anniversary in 1940. Mary grew ill and died in 1943. That same winter Isaiah had his leg crushed by a falling tree and it had to be amputated. He lived until 1951. Jim died in 1964 and Van died in 1979. Then the ranch became Bobby's until he sold it in 1988.

Ed died in 2001, Hadden died in 1977 and Elizabeth died on January 16, 2005.

(Thanks to Ed Finch and Harriet Curtiss for this information)

JENKINS

Jim and Thena Jenkins moved to Pinkham in 1936 from Big Horn County of Montana near Soap Creek. They bought the original homestead of Ves Stacy from Fred Sanderson up Slick's Gulch. The couple had no children of their own.

Jim and Thena liked their small ranch nestled in the hills. The cabin and out buildings were near the tiny stream that originated from springs above, called Slicks Creek. There was a garden patch and a cleared field for growing hay.

During summer months Jim rode the hills to check on cows and calves for ranchers who had grazing rights in the area. They raised a good garden to store food for winter. Thena wore men's clothes to work outdoors with her husband. Together they put up hay for their livestock.

In the fall there was the harvest of Christmas trees to pay taxes as well as to buy staples for the winter. Jim also cut more timber off the place to be made into railroad ties. He helped put them through the sawmill of the Finch brothers who were neighbor friends from Big Horn County.

In time Jim became clerk of the Pinkham school board. He was serving in that capacity when he came down with pneumonia before Christmas in 1945. He died in the hospital.

As a widow Thena did not give up and move out. She wasn't a beautiful woman but she had character and independence. Jim Finch came often to help her with the heavy work.

When REA lines were spreading through the rural areas Thena was afraid her livestock would get electrocuted. She refused to let them have a right of way across her land and didn't want power for herself. Thena threatened the work crew with a gun when they came to put up power poles. Her nephew, Robert Gustafson, convinced her that her livestock would be safe so she allowed them to proceed.

Through Robert Gustafson as intermediary, Dean Evans was allowed to set a sawmill on Thena's place. She was very critical of the activity and Dean had to be careful, although Dee and children were welcome to visit.

Jerry Stacy was working as a sawyer at the time. Thena thought he was trespassing and fired a shot over his head. Jerry took the hint, dropped everything and took off running over the hill as if his life depended on it.

Thena was lonely and liked having company. In summertime Madeline Utter and her girls picked peas and shelled them while Thena dug small potatoes out from under each hill. Then she made new peas and potatoes creamed for lunch. She served coffee from the pot on the stove that had been boiled, more coffee and water added, and boiled again.

In the fall of 1962, Lee Utter and his teenage sons were cutting wood on their land above the Jenkins place. They spied smoke billowing up from down below. Thena's house was on fire! They raced down the hill to help. Kenny, in the lead, got there just in time to keep Thena from going back into the inferno for her purse. Dazed and confused, she wandered around the yard in her nightgown. She mumbled, and told them to dig in her woodshed. They did, and came up with a coffee can full of money. She clasped it to her bosom and collapsed against the shed wall. She was taken into Eureka to stay with Vivian Gustafson, a sister-in-law. Thena died in 1963. She was buried along side Jim in the Tobacco Valley Cemetery.

ARMSTRONG
7/5/2003

The Armstrongs came to Montana from California after the stock market crash in 1929. There were no jobs available in Montana either but life was simple.

It was in the 1930's that the Armstrong family lived up Pinkham way. Leo and Minnie Armstrong moved onto the place originally homesteaded by Lula Mikelson, then owned by Hirem and Amos Kinney and later owned by Tom Wilson. They came just at the time in their life when daughters were at the age to choose a mate. Young men in the community were thrilled for the chance to court new girls!

There were seven children in the family, four girls and three boys. They all walked to the Pinkham school a half mile away in all kinds of weather. The girls were older and until they became married they helped look after their younger brothers. Iliff married Otis Cook and Lillie married Bill Stacy.

When Leo Armstrong couldn't find a way to support his family on Pinkham he went west to seek his fortune or hoped to anyway.

Ham Leib courted Olive, then followed the family west to Washington and brought her back as his bride. Archie did the same for Lola, the youngest girl of the family.

The three Armstrong boys were Jim, LeoFay and David. The boys grew up and made frequent visits to Montana to be close to their sisters. David Armstrong married Beatrice Burlingham and they raised a family in Montana.

FLOYD AND AGNES SEDERDAHL

Floyd was born September 15, 1896, in Centerville, Iowa, to Carl and Alma (Noorene) Sederdahl. Both parents were born in Sweden. His father, Carl, was a well respected tailor and had two shops in the area. Carl died of consumption (tuberculosis) at age 28 in 1899. Floyd was three and brother Oliver was just six months old. His wife Alma also had the disease. Alma moved back to Keokuk, Iowa, by her parents, Sophia and August Noorene. After her dad died in January of 1902, Alma's mother and sister Selma took her and the boys to New Windsor, Colorado, hoping to improve Alma's health. She died in February of 1903. Floyd was seven and Oliver was three at the time. The family stayed there until 1909.

Grandmother Sophia packed up her grandsons Floyd (14) and Oliver (9) and went to Union County, Iowa, for a short time. In 1910 she took up a homestead in Perkins County, South Dakota, on the North

Fork of the Grand River. Her daughter, Selma, and husband William Hall and family, joined them in 1912. Grandmother Sophia died in 1917. Floyd was pretty much on his own by then and Oliver stayed on with their Aunt Selma.

At an early age Floyd became quite an avid horseman, riding, breaking, and training them. He worked for ranchers in the area and broke horses for the Army. In 1917 or 1918 he won the Bronc Riding contest at Belle Fourche, South Dakota. For his win he got some cash, a silver belt buckle and a pair of silver inlaid spurs.

Agnes was born March 3, 1899, in Ossian, Iowa, to Anders and Maggie (Anderson) Quien. Both parents were born in Norway. Her mother died of consumption (tuberculosis) in 1907. In 1911 Anders sold his farm and moved his family to Minnesota. His sister, Anna Quien, accompanied them to care for the children. He decided in 1914 to sell out and move back to Iowa. He had just sold the farm when he suddenly got sick and died of pneumonia, leaving the children orphans. The younger children, Alfred and Clara, were sent to Hettinger, North Dakota, to stay with their mother's sister, Ole and Dora Severson. The older boys stayed with their Aunt Anna and bought some land in Perkins County, South Dakota, to be near Alfred and Clara. Agnes (15) was sent to Sioux Falls, South Dakota, to stay with her mother's brother Martin. She was so lonesome for her siblings they soon let her follow to live with her brothers and Aunt Anna.

Agnes took a job working on a ranch when she was about seventeen and she met this red-headed cowboy named Floyd Sederdahl. The newspapers of the time showed where he was a frequent visitor at her brother's home where she lived. When he went to serve in World War I, Floyd sold Agnes his horse, Sandy. The war ended before he had all his papers signed. He went back to South Dakota and married Agnes and as an added bonus, got his horse back!

They moved around a lot when they were first married. They lived in Hettinger, North Dakota, when son Donald was born in 1920. They moved to Hill City, South Dakota, so Floyd could work on some of the 'Eye of the Needle' road construction. About 1923 they took over the grandmother's homestead and tried to farm while still working at other jobs to supplement their income. They went to Haines, North Dakota, where Floyd worked at the coal mine. Leslie was born there in 1923. He was again working in Hettinger in 1927 when Alma was born and there acquired training as a blacksmith and mechanic. Floyd worked on the road crew for the WPA during the Depression. Agnes helped as a midwife and did a lot of the plowing and planting on the farm.

By 1934 the drought hit and everything started to dry up. There wasn't enough water for farming or cattle on the homestead. In 1935 Floyd went to McCone City, Montana, to work on the Fort Peck Dam. Agnes and the children joined him. They lived in a tent until they bought a small cabin. Like many of their neighbors, they hoped to make enough money to keep the home place and wait out the drought. Agnes and the children went back to plant crops in March 1936. The poor crop was the end of their farming and time to find a new home. Floyd and Agnes had planned to go to Oregon but a man told them about some land in Eureka that his relative wanted to sell – that's how they found their cabin on Pinkham Creek.

In 1938, Floyd and Agnes Sederdahl wrote a letter to their son Donald who was in the CCC's (Civilian Conservation Corps) at Noxon, Montana. They were getting ready to sign the papers for the piece of land near Eureka. It was twenty-three acres, had a log cabin on the creek and would cost them $100.00. The work was winding down at Fort Peck and the family could hardly wait to leave McCone City. The town was to be flooded by the dam.

A Pinkham neighbor, Mr. Banks, wrote and told them they had a nice little two room cabin. He said that they should come soon as windows, etc., had a way of disappearing in vacant houses.

On December 13, 1938, Floyd, Agnes, Leslie and Alma, arrived in Eureka after a long, cold trip, pulling their belongings in a small homemade trailer. They spent the night in a cabin in Eureka and went to Pinkham the next day. The next letter to Donald told him how much they liked it and hoped he would be home for Christmas.

Although they had been warned about the 'wild' Pinkham Crickers, they soon found that the rumors were unfounded. They made many lifelong friends and were happy with their new home.

Floyd went back to work one more season at Fort Peck. In 1941 he worked part time for the U.S. Customs as a maintenance person at Rooseville. During the war, Floyd and Agnes went to Spokane and worked at the air depot. When the war ended they hurried home to Pinkham. He went to work at Rooseville again and also had to travel to Babb on certain days. In his early fifties he had to retire when he became disabled with arthritis. He took up gunsmithing and was well known for his work. He was also a Hunter's Safety instructor for thirty years. Floyd loved to visit and never met a stranger. He would always know somebody somewhere that they knew also.

Agnes inherited her father's ability as a carpenter and was as much at home with a hammer in her hand as a frying pan. She added two bedrooms onto the little cabin and later a nice sized kitchen. She made signs, cabinets, cutting boards, picture frames and other items for gifts and to sell. She loved the outdoors and pruned and cut Christmas trees until her late seventies. The family teased her about the little electric chainsaw she stored under her bed in later years. Agnes was a very quiet person with a shy smile who never said an unkind word about anyone. No one ever stopped by their house without being served coffee and cake or cookies.

Floyd always had a special love of wildlife. When he worked for the WPA road crew in South Dakota the crew was working on the section of road that went along the homestead. There was a small pond along the road but the road dipped and the water would never get very deep. He talked them into filling in the dip in the road. Their little pond became deeper and larger. The land was later taken over by the government and became part of the Grand River National Grasslands. Floyd's little project is now a beautiful pond with waterfowl and deer in abundance and a beautiful sight to see while driving on what seems like an endless prairie road.

Donald and Leslie both served in World War II. Don enlisted in the Army Air Corps and spent most of his time in India. He survived a plane crash in the Sahara Desert. Leslie enlisted in the Navy and went to the South Pacific, New Zealand and the eastern shores of Europe including England and France.

During the war, Alma got to work on one of the first women brush crews on the Fortine Ranger District. The young women camped at Ant Flats. There was an opening and she got to go on the Edna Creek Lookout and then the Elk Mountain Lookout. Mr. Osler was her supervisor.

Donald married Jennie Eichelberger Moore. Jennie's sons, Harold and Henry, were joined by sister, Donna. Harold died in 1969 at twenty-eight from complications of diabetes. Leslie married Ann Carrotto in New Jersey and they had six sons: Dennis, Gary, Raymond, Donald, James and Kenny. Son James died in infancy. Alma married Lovell Dutton in Libby and had three children: Juanita, Russell and Clark.

Don died in 1973 of cancer at fifty-three years. Floyd passed away in 1975. Agnes lived on Pinkham until 1983 when she moved into an apartment in Eureka and then to the Mountain View Manor where she died in 1990 at age ninety. Les died of cancer at his home in Rexford in 1998.

The original cabin is still there and the two little trees Agnes planted at the end of the walkway are over seventy feet high. The place still comes to life at times in the summer when Agnes and Floyd's grandchildren and great-grandchildren join their daughter, Alma, for a few days of relaxation and fun and doing repairs on the old cabin.

GENE MCWHIRTER

Gene McWhirter tells of the eight years that he lived on Pinkham Creek. He had worked on the Fort Peck Dam along with Floyd Sederdahl until the Sederdahls moved to Pinkham. Floyd and Agnes liked living along the creek in the timbered hills so well that they invited Gene to come find a place too.

Gene bought 150 acres in 1940 from Myrtle Peters by paying her a hundred dollars and paying the back taxes to Lincoln County. The place was located on the west side of the creek (across the bridge on the Gut Creek road) and formerly homesteaded by Albert Kinney.

Buildings were situated on a high rock cliff above the creek. The original log cabin had a framed room built on to each end. Lilac bushes grew close to the house with a couple of crab apple trees nearby. Rhubarb plants grew all around where gardens had been. Gene said he hated carrying water uphill from the creek for household use or hauling it by the barrel to water the garden. He soon gave up trying to raise a garden.

Gene's mother and older stepbrother, Justis L. Fonger, came to Pinkham with him. Justis was the mechanic and Gene was an electrician and radioman. Gene built his own short wave radio for an entertaining hobby. He soon made friends with Van Finch, who had the same interests.

Gene sawed logs for Chili Kearney for a while, using his one-man crosscut saw. He rigged up a chain-held table to fit on the opposite side of the tree with a brace under it. That way Gene had a support for his saw to move from one tree to another.

One winter it snowed five feet. Gene not only shoveled a path that resembled a tunnel to the outhouse but the road as well. That meant down the hill to the creek, across the bridge and up the hill to the main road, a quarter mile away, so he could drive to town. For extra traction for the vehicle, Gene and Justis secured a bar between the rear tire chains so one wheel wouldn't spin. They were driving a 1939 Chevy coupe.

The road up the hill to the house was rough and rocky most of the year, so Gene decided to make a better one. He pounded a wedge with a sledgehammer to break the rock, then used a pick and shovel to clear it away. It took hard manual labor and most of a spring season, but he had a smooth driveway.

Gene also worked in a sawmill for Harles Bergette and for a time with Rosco Combs. During the war Gene and Justis decided to run a mill of their own and cut their own timber. They got an old steam engine for power and set it up near the springs on the place Tom Wilson has now to be close to water. They soon found it was too big and produced too much power for their mill, so they bought a 10-20 International Cat motor to run the mill.

They cut both railroad ties and rough lumber out of logs from their own place and sold to W.C. Albee in Eureka. After the war Gene's nephews, Don and Dallas Fonger, hauled them into town with their own truck. They also hauled house logs cut from Forest Service timber to Columbia Heights for the first commercial log building in that area.

Gene made good friends with John and Marjorie Collins, who had moved out of the house on Pinkham before Gene moved in. Marjorie helped care for his mother until she died in 1943. Gene cut and hauled wood for Marjorie as well as for himself. It took a lot of wood in those days, sawed by a crosscut to keep both a cook stove and a heater going through the winter.

In 1948 Gene sold out to Tom Wilson and moved to town where he went to work for Steve McCullough at the light plant. Gene wired houses in town for electricity then, and also for people up Pinkham after the REA came to rural areas. He spent several years working at the Eureka Gambles store during the rush to buy electrical appliances. Gene serviced stoves, refrigerators, washers and dryers. Then television eventually became popular back when they had good programs.

Gene retired and lived in a small trailer on the Lincoln Electric grounds until he moved into the Mountain View Manor. It became his home until his death in 1999.

THIS IS THE BRIDGE
1975

This is the bridge that spans Pinkham Crick
On the old Sutton Road where the turn is quick.
It just might be the bridge that Jack built.
It's not the Sutton Bridge the Corps had built,
Which had beauty and curving lines of grace
And no one can say this one's fair of face!

This is the bridge built close to the water.

When high, water goes over, not like it aughter,
There are no side rails as you can see.
Only a log on the side, put there by Lee.
As for passing – that's out – definitely.
The bridge is too narrow – utterly.

This is the bridge that most drivers fear
Even those coming from both far and near.
Just around the corner, going down still,
There's the bridge-then long curving hill!
It catches some people by real surprise,
They don't know whether to believe their eyes.

This is the bridge when covered with ice
On a frosty morning is not very nice.
It causes new drivers to become aware,
And gives timid ones a frightening scare.
It's so easy to drive over the icy brink
Or slip sideways and tip into the drink.

This is the bridge that causes trouble.
For people who try the hill on the double.
Their rig spins out before the top curve.
They have to back down, there's no reserve.
They have to come backwards down the hill.
Back across the bridge and pray not to spill.

This is the bridge causing mothers to gray.
When children are coasting both night and day.
Sleds start out up the hill about a mile
And they come down fast, that's their style.
They hit the bridge at a terrific speed.
They have to hit straight, they do indeed.

This is the bridge that needs rebuilt.
If some one were hurt, who'd have guilt?
There is nobody who wants to claim it
But every body who wants to shame it.
People complain about a lot of road tax.
If it doesn't build bridges, something is lax.

By Madeline Utter

Ice on Pinkham Bridge.

TOM WILSON BIOGRAPHY
By Jodi Wilson

After the Crash of '29 and during the starvation and struggle to survive throughout the country, known as the Great Depression, Thomas Wilson, Junior, was born on April 2, 1937, up Pinkham Creek without a doctor. This was very common because Eureka didn't have many doctors. When they didn't have any the community was attended by Flathead Valley doctors either part time or in an emergency. Despite the conditions he was born under, Tom grew up to become a healthy, hard-working man who loves to play jokes on his friends and family. *(History of the United States, pages 538-551)*

Tom started working at a young age. During grade school his chores were milking the cows, taking care of the cows and horses, and during the summer he helped his dad cut wood with a crosscut. This was before there were chainsaws. His dad would swamp them with an ax and then buck them into eight-foot logs and then Tom skidded them with a horse. It took skill and cooperation to use a cross cut and good sawyer teams were the ones who got the highest wages. Using horses for skidding was very different than modern logging with high-powered machines. Prize draft horses were usually used because of their size and strength. Teamsters took very good care of their horses. They often worried more about their horses than about their fellow loggers. (*The Story of the Tobacco Plains, pages 223-233*)

Tom got his second car by working for a guy for three days and he got $21 and a 1928 Chevy that took three days to get running. Part of the time during the summer he worked for John Frank Moore. He would help round up the cattle, vaccinate and brand them, and then drive them for two days from where the state game ranch is now up Sutton. He also herded cows for Bert Roe.

When he was fifteen years old Tom quit school and went to work for one of his neighbors, T.V. (Van) Finch. He sawed logs and ran cats and he did that until about 1991 when he had his first back surgery. He had a hard time for a while because you had to be eighteen to work in the woods so he would work somewhere for three or four months and then his boss would find out he wasn't old enough and then he'd have to go find a job somewhere else. He also went to work for Fred King as a choker setter but when his boss found out he was barely seventeen, he loaded Tom in the truck and took him to town. The boss would have gotten in a lot of trouble if something had happened to Tom and he wasn't even old enough to be there. He also built old woods roads and skid trails in the Libby Dam area and on Gut Creek.

He put in fire lines on the Burn and on Stone Hill when it burnt a long time ago. After his first back surgery he went to work driving a logging truck and then he had to quit that because he had another back surgery in 1996 and his doctor told him had to quit or he would end up in a wheelchair. Now he volunteers a lot at Head Start and he helps out his youngest daughter, Alice Letcher, with getting firewood and this past fall he helped her tear down and build a new deck around her house. In the winter he brings out his pickup with the plow on the front and he plows out peoples driveways and stuff like that. Last summer he and Alice coached a t-ball team that had his four youngest grandkids on it.
(Second Interview 12-17-00)

When their parents were gone one day Tom and his brother Robert and his sisters Mary, Mattie, and Julia put ropes around the necks of a couple of two- or three-year-old steers and then they hooked them up to an old dump hayrake and took them out through the field until they got going too fast and the tongue of the hay rake bounced up and the steers ran away. When Tom and one of his friends, Johnny Beckstrom, were in the sixth or seventh grade they were at the school and they saw their principal's Ford convertible parked outside the school. The keys weren't in it so they kicked it out of gear and then rolled it behind some pine trees so that he would think it was stolen. Another time they were helping the janitor at the school and they knew that the first grade teacher would always flop down into her chair after she got her class all seated. So they adjusted the spring in the chair so that the back of it would tip back like a recliner and when she flopped down in it she tipped back and her feet went up in the air and she went shooting across the room. So at the end of the day she told them there was something wrong with her chair and she was wondering if they would try to fix it. So they readjusted the spring and the teacher said, "Boy you two sure do know a lot about this chair." But they wouldn't confess so they didn't get in trouble. One day Tom and another of his friends, Keith Williams, were in the office running out tests on an old mimeograph machine and one of their teachers from Chicago came in and was giving them a bad time and telling them that they weren't doing it right so they took him down in the middle of the office and de-pantsed him and were going to throw his pants out the window onto the front lawn but another teacher came in and they had to let him up.

Tom also told all of his grandkids that the reason he only had part of one finger was that Grandma had eaten it because he didn't bring any groceries home, when really he'd lost it in a machinery accident.

Another time he was working for Bob Clarke down by the

Reservoir and Tom and Alan Garrison pulled up and picked up Dutch Truman and they saw that the car was parked and that Clarke was working on it. He somehow managed to knock the screwdriver loose that was through the link of the chain that was holding the fuel tank when he was rummaging around in the hole. So the fuel tank was kind of laying on him and his head was down in the hole so he couldn't see they were standing right in front of him. So Tom said, "Alan, it looks like Dutch broke down, we might just as well go home." And then Clarke started screaming and yelling because he thought they didn't see him and that they were all going to go home and leave him there for the night. When really they were all standing there trying not to laugh too loud. (*First Interview 10-4-00*)

But even though he loves to play jokes and is known as a bit of a prankster, he has also been a hardworking man for his entire life. This fact has been proven by him saying that one of the worst days of his life was the day he found out he couldn't drive truck any more. He continues to keep himself busy by running Jessica and Alan (his five-year-old grandchildren who have lived with him and his wife Betty since their dad died in a boating accident along with their uncle, Jim Letcher and their cousin, Bob Blonshine, in April of 1996) to school, practice, plays, and friends houses as well as volunteering his time to drive the Head Start bus and work in the class room or dress up as Santa Clause. He also goes to Canada and spends time with his two youngest grandchildren Jose, 5 and James, 4. He's always on the run going somewhere even if it's just to go visit friends. Although he is always plotting ways to make a joke or scare some poor unsuspecting person he works hard at whatever he does.

(Used by permission of Tom Wilson Jr. and granddaughter Jodi Wilson.)

Bibliography
First Interview, 10-4-00, Eureka, MT
Second Interview, 12-17-00, Eureka, MT
Thomas V. DiBacco, Lorna C. Mason, Christian G. Appy, <u>The History of the United States</u>, , Copyright 1991, Boston, MA
Dan McDonald, <u>The Story of the Tobacco Valley Country</u>, published in 1950 by "The Pioneers of the Tobacco Plains Country"

AT THE PICNIC

One stout, red-headed woman entertained a bunch
While they all stood around waiting for lunch.
Well, this bunch of old hill billy guys
Were all taken somewhat by surprise
When she said, "How many kids do I got?"
"Bet you all cain't find the whole lot."

The guys stood back and eye-balled the area
They knew her kids must be around here somewhere.
They spied a red head teen in a roadster with the top down
With him was a laughing young girl in a pretty gown.
Red headed twin boys were tied together for a
three-legged race.
Another red head was in a contest with pie on his face.

She jeered, "That only makes the count up to four."
"You all better look around for many more."
"There's a girl over there with long red hair down her back.
She's holding hands and flirting with my boy, Jack."
Another guy spit tobacco and waved at the big table
"There's a strawberry blonde, a friend of my Mable."

A freckle faced kid with front teeth missing came to Ma
He grabbed her skirt, "When do we eat? I can't find Pa."
That brought a chuckle from guys standing around.
"Now there's seven, how many more can be found?"
One old guy puffed on his pipe, looked down at the ground.
A red head toddler with a spoon was making a hole round.

Nearby on a blanket rested a cute little girl
On top of her head was a bright red curl
"There, that's two more, the count is up to nine"
They said, "Now there's no more for us to find."
She chortled, patted her fat belly and then,
Said, "There's one inside of me and that makes ten!"

Embarrassed, the men turned to go their own way.
That was enough foolishness for this holiday.

                              By Madeline Utter

EUREKA JOURNAL 1911:

J. H. O'Brien living in the Pinkham Creek country brought in some six foot oats and four foot timothy grown on his forest reserve ranch that would have made Mr. Pinchot's eyes stick out could he have seen it. This was the first crop and the timothy was sown with the oats. Oats and timothy conservation beats tamarack conservation several ways.

SCHOOL DISTRICT NO. 18. SPECIFICATIONS:

Specifications for Pinkham Creek Schoolhouse. Size of schoolhouse, 18x26: sill to be 8x8; joists to be joined in joists two feet on center; sub-floor to be of common lumber, not planed, nailed with 10-penny nails, running diagonally, and matched floor on top of sub-floor, not more than 4 inches wide, well nailed with 8-penny nails. Two windows on each side of building. One door in front, opening toward road. Building paper between sheeting and siding. Cornice to be frieze board pilantia and fatia. Shingles to be cedar, the best Star-A-Star. Brick chimney to be of lime and sand. All work to be done in neat and workmanlike manner. The contractor is to be responsible for any and all damage that may happen while building schoolhouse. Board of school directors have the right to reject any and all bids. Clerk of school board will receive bids from August 13 until August 26, 1911. Work on building to commence as soon as possible after bids are received. To be completed in September, 1911.

SUPERINTENDENT HERRIG GLEANS HISTORY ABOUT PINKHAM SCHOOL

The old photo of the Pinkham school which appeared some time ago in the Tobacco Valley News created such interest that we wrote Supt. Robert Herrig for some information on the school.

He reports that the early records were not well kept. There is no record of who the teacher was during the years 1911-12 and 1912-13. There is an entry after the year 1911-12 which appears to be Moir, which could have been the teacher's last name.

On the other hand the Hunsingers are entered twice under the year 1913-14. Perhaps they also taught during the year 1912-13.

The school district was created February 15, 1911, by order of Forrest D. Head, County Superintendent. Teacher was Estella Milnor, and trustees, appointed that same date, were: C.W. Workman, Henry Stacy, and Frank Slick. Elected April 1 were Frank Slick, C.W. Workman and Wm. Stacy, and Mrs. N. E. Workman was clerk.

Subsequent trustees and the year of election or appointment:

J.H. Stacy 1912; Maurice Harrington 1914, John O'Brien 1915, C.W. Workman, Frank J. Slick, G.W. Caldwell, Clerk Ella M. Thatcher; Alvin O. Calhoun Dec. 19, 1919, appointed; Joseph Kearney 1919, Jim Roberts 1920, Mrs. Grace Kenney, Clerk; Harry Thatcher 1921; Amos A. Kinney July 19, 1922, appointed; Mrs. Harry Thatcher, clerk.

H.C. Johnson 1927, Cecil Utter 1928, Ella M. Thatcher 1930, Nancy Roberts 1934, Maude Baker, clerk 1935; Dora Combs, J.A. Jenkins, Bill Mitchell, Clerk T.V. Finch, all 1937; Roscoe Combs and James L. Stacy 1938, Charles Workman, Elmer G. Stacy, 1939, Floyd A.C. Sederdahl appointed Jan. 23, 1940; John Leib 1940; Tom Wilson, appointed March 19, 1942; Alta Workman 1942, Lester W. Roose, appointed July 22, 1942, Clerk J.A. Jenkins, 1942.

Agnes Sederdahl 1943, T.V. Finch, appointed July 22, 1944, Ovella Roberts 1946, Harles Bergette appointed April 10, 1947; Clerk Charles E. Finch; Herman Owens 1951, Mrs. June Taylor, clerk, 1950; Vivian G. Workman clerk, 1952.

Final board of trustees was Sidney Workman 1955, Agnes Sederdahl 1954, Van Finch 1953, and Madeline Utter, clerk. The district consolidated with Eureka District on July 2, 1955, Jessie L. Fagerburg, County Superintendent.

TEACHERS OF FORTY-FOUR YEARS

Estella Milnor 1911; M.A. Hunsinger, Mrs. M.A. Hunsinger 1913-1914; Mrs. F.C. O'Gallagher, Helen M. Velton 1916-17; George L. Woodworth, Mrs. F.C. O'Gallagher 1918-1919; 1919-20 (   ); Gertrude Welling, Mary Rice 1920-21; Leslie Johnson, Lorna Johnson 1921-22; Marie Hartfield (8 mo.), Harriet Smith (1 mo.) 1922-23; Hazel Schagel 1923-24; Harriet Shenefelt 1924-25; Marjorie Preston 1925-26; Mary Lampton 1926-27;

Hazel M. Jones 1927-28; Gertrude Waller 1928-29; Irene Crowley 1929-30; Ethel Long 1930-37; Jessie Cox Seger 1937-38; George Gasahl 1938-1939; Dolphy Pohlman 1939-42; Mrs. Elsie A. Benda 1943-44; Harriet Finch 1944-45; Madeline Rost 1945-46.

PINKHAM SCHOOL HISTORY

Pinkham School District #18 was established in 1910. Trustees appointed by Lincoln County for the new district were Will Workman, Henry Stacy and Frank Slick. The clerk was N.E. Workman. A young teacher by the name of Estella Milnor was secured from Eureka for the term on a salary of $70 per month. She "lived in" as a boarder at the Will Workman home.

The school was attended by Workmans and O'Briens. It was Charlie Workman's last year of school. Previous to that year the Workman family had moved to a small cabin in the Black Lake area to attend that school during the winter months. Other students were Charlie's brother Sid, sister Lula, George, Ida, Ted and Cora. O'Brien children were Pat, Pearl and Dick.

In 1911 a new frame school with a bell tower was built in a clearing on the Andrew O'Brien homestead. The lumber was sawed out by Slick's sawmill on lower Pinkham. That fall, school opened with twenty pupils enrolled. Population along Pinkham Creek increased rapidly the next few years. People looking for a piece of land under the Homestead Act came to stake their timber and stone claims along the creek in the hills. At the time it was all virgin timber.

Just two years after the school was built on upper Pinkham, another one was needed lower down the creek. Children crowded into a log cabin on the Will Stacy homestead the fall of 1913. Both schools had all eight grades. Frank Slick's mill again sawed lumber to build a duplicate school in District 18. The old log school was carefully taken apart then rebuilt on the Jim Roberts homestead for their home. A dance was held there to celebrate the occasion with local talent and musicians.

William (Bill) and Almeda Stacy deeded one acre of land to the School District at the forks of the Pinkham road and Slick's Gulch road. Men used teams of horses with slips to level the ground. A wall of rocks was placed at the lower corner to hold the fill. Then cement was mixed and poured over the rocks to hold them secure. Both school buildings had a cement foundation with steps leading up to the covered front door. Inside the door were twin cloakrooms, one for the boys and one for the girls. The main room had a row of windows on each side with blackboards at the ends. A back door led to a woodshed and twin outbuildings for boys and girls. Outside walls of schools and privies were painted white with green trim.

Now there were sixty pupils enrolled in both schools combined. Two teachers were hired, Mr. and Mrs. Merton Hunsinger. He taught the upper school and she taught the lower. They had a homestead in between. The following year the combined enrollment climbed to seventy-two pupils. Trustees then elected were Frank Slick, Will Workman and George Caldwell with Ella Thatcher as clerk. They kept their same positions for several years.

Double schools were kept open until the year 1922. By that time, population had dwindled and a new generation was coming up. The last double teachers were Leslie and Lorna Johnson. Wayne Workman remembered attending the school during its last year and his first year. Chuck Workman bought the O'Brien homestead, intending to convert the school building into a home, but young folks camped in it one night and a fire burned it down.

HUNSINGER

It was a boon to the Pinkham community when the Hunsinger family came to Pinkham Creek to claim a homestead, as they were both school teachers with two young sons. M.A. Hunsinger was hired by the school board to teach the upper Pinkham school for three terms; in 1913-14-15. It was a three mile walk from his log cabin to school. Then, when a new lower Pinkham school was built, Evelyn Hunsinger was hired as teacher in 1915. She had one mile to hike down the wagon road to school with her two sons, Alfred and Merton.

The Hunsingers had a patent for 120 acres in Section 18 recorded in Lincoln County in 1917. M.A. Hunsinger became afflicted with crippling arthritis and they moved into Eureka, where Evelyn taught first grade. Their homestead up Pinkham was sold to Bert Roe in 1954 to be used for summer pasture for his cattle.

A notation in the *Eureka Journal* stated that Alfred Hunsinger went to work in 1928 for the Rexford Power and Light Company.

Another Hunsinger, a brother to M.A. and recorded as William Clyde Hunsinger received a patent for 160 acres in Section 19 in 1918. This place was up the creek from his brother and next to the Cook's Run road. In 1939 it was recorded in the name of Will and Marg Hunsinger. Eventually it was deeded to J. Neils of Libby in 1955.

A Bill Hunsinger had a homestead down by Twin Lakes on the way to Eureka where the primitive road twisted around points of the Lakes. He had a faithful dog that went everywhere with him, even in his old Model T truck. One day when he had a truck load of wood coming down the hill past the Utter place, the truck broke through a homemade bridge spanning Pinkham Creek. After the wood was unloaded, Cecil Utter used his team of horses to pull the truck out of the creek. Everyone then forded the creek until another bridge could be built.

Pinkham School picnic in 1916. Families from both the upper and lower schools attended the picnic depicted in this photo, which was taken by a Whitefish photograpaher.

LULA MAY MIKALSON

Another teacher-homesteader was Lula May Mikalson. Her homestead was about a mile below the lower school where she taught one term, that of 1917-1918. There were thirty-nine pupils in school that year. She proved up on forty acres in Section 4, T35N, R27W and recorded it in April 1922.

Lula had relatives in the area as there was Aaron Mikalson, who proved up on 120 acres in Section 33, T36N, R28W in 1908. This homestead was eventually deeded to Paul and Nancy Totten in 1971. John and Art Mikalson also had homesteads in Camp 32 area but were sold to Bonners Ferry Lumber Company in 1922 and reverted to the United States in 1934.

Lula met and married a woodsworker named Olson. They had three little boys when he was killed in a woods accident. Her sons were named: Ralph, Ray and Howard. They grew up and graduated from Lincoln County High School. She sold her Pinkham homestead to Hiram Kinney in October 1928.

Rural school teachers had full responsibility of the school while they were teaching. They were not only the teacher of all eight grades and all subjects, they were also the principal, bookkeeper, janitor, playground supervisor and nurse when necessary. Keeping control of all eight grades in a one room school is a challenge for an experienced teacher, however, for a young girl just out of highschool or even one year of normal teacher training, it could be a very intimidating experience.

County schools were not equipped with modern conveniences. Pinkham school had two coat rooms inside by the front door. The right one was for boys, the other girls, making a hallway between. The rooms had lower and upper hooks to hang coats and hats. A shelf underneath provided a place to set lunch pails or sit on while putting on boots. These rooms also stored cleaning supplies. There was a tall window in each for light.

The main room had four tall windows on each side with blackboards mounted on each end. A school clock on the wall between windows had to be wound once a week to keep time. There were four rows of desks with combination seats mounted on strips of wood. Each row had five desks the same size, when crowded, a desk was shared with another pupil. An extra large wood heater took up space almost in the middle, with a stovepipe overhead to the chimney built at the end. This stove took constant vigilance in winter to keep steady heat. It was banked at night to have coals to start a fire next day. Woodshed and twin toilets were out the back door. Pump-up gas lanterns made light for evening activities.

When enrollment was high (seventy-two students in both schools combined) school trustees at the time, Frank Slick, Will Workman and George Caldwell with Ella Thatcher as clerk, decided to hire men teachers for each school. F. C. O'Gallagher was put in the upper school and George Woodworth in the lower. Both schools had uneducated hillbillies that did not like to take orders or be told what to do. Teachers were instructed to be strict and not take any guff from students.

Ham Leib recalled school days when he first started. There were big boys in school that were rough and tough. The man teacher was strict and did his best to keep them in line so as not to disrupt the school. To do this, he went to the creek and cut some good strong willow switches. When needed, he used them on the big, bad boys. As switches broke or disappeared, he got bigger replacements. After three years, the older ones were gone and younger students were under control.

The number of students was gradually dwindling down to a total of thirty seven in 1921-1922. That was the last year of double schools and was taught by a married couple. Leslie Johnson took the upper school and his wife, Lorna the lower. The next year there were twenty-three pupils taught by Marie Hatfield for eight months. She was in a car accident and the last month of her term was taken over by Harriet

Smith.

For the next few years, single teachers were hired at $100 per month. Most of them boarded with a family on Pinkham. They were: Mary Rice, Hazel Schagel, Harriet Shenefelt, Marjorie Preston, Mary Lampton, Hazel Jones, Gertrude Waller, and Irene Crowley. When Mrs. Ethel Long started teaching in 1930, her salary was raised to $115 per month even though it was Depression time.

Mrs. Jessie Segar followed Mrs. Ethel Long as a teacher but no one could fill Ethel's shoes. Mrs. Segar got off on the wrong foot with some of the parents and put in a rough year. She drove a Hupmobile from town to teach only one term at $110 per month. The next year, George Gasahl was hired. He was an experienced professor but was getting older. One of his students bragged about using his bald head as a target for spit wads. Mr. Gasahl retired after that term.

People in the Pinkham community were trying to live down a bad reputation. Qualified teachers were choosing to teach elsewhere. In 1939 the school board decided to build a teacherage on the school grounds to provide housing for the teacher. Board members were Charlie Workman, Rosco Combs and Floyd Sederdahl with clerk, Van Finch. A married school teacher, Dolphy Pohlman, consented to teach and live in this little house with his wife.

The teacherage, built of logs, was placed back of the school house near the fence with outside toilets nearby. The building was about 12x16 and had a little porch out front facing west. Inside under the little window by the door, was a wash bench to hold a bucket of water and dipper beside a wash pan. In the corner, a small wooden cupboard was built to hold a few dishes and food supplies. Two stoves took up the space along the north wall, a small heater and an enamel wood burning cookstove. Their stove pipes joined together with a T before exiting the roof. A small table with two wooden chairs sat on the opposite side under the south window. A kerosene lamp sat on the table for light. A double bed filled up the corner and a small closet was built in the other. Linoleum over wooden floors, fresh pastel paint and curtains at the windows gave the little cabin a homey look.

The Pohlmans resided on the school grounds three years and made many good friends in the neighborhood before moving on to another school. The next teacher was Miss Aileen Martin who taught the term for 1942 and 1943. The following year, Mrs. Elsie Benda took over with a permit to teach at $125 per month. It was war time and teachers were scarce, so it was allowed to hire untrained teachers. Miss Harriet Finch was hired on a permit to teach the term of 1944-1945 at $130 per month. Then came the last teacher of the Pinkham School District #18. Miss Madeline Rost, who had one year of normal training at Northern Montana College in Havre, was offered $150 per month to teach the term of 1945-1946. She was married before school was out in May to a Pinkham bred native and refused the offer to teach another term

Each year at the end of school term, a community picnic was held to celebrate. School children were given their report cards for the year and then it was time for freedom until the fall term began. Everyone came to the picnic to share food and fellowship. Milk and eggs were plentiful, so cooks made custards and puddings, potato salad was popular and baked ham. There were sandwiches of homemade bread filled with egg salad or canned venison. Fresh rhubarb pies and dried apple pies were devoured as well as several varieties of cakes and cookies.

This was a special occasion and folks dressed in their best bib and tucker. Suits for the men with white starched shirts and fancy neckties were topped off with a hat. Ladies wore white blouses and long dark skirts with a pretty bonnet or fancy hat on their heads. A picture was taken by a Photographer for the first community picnic.

Deweyville Drivel — *1916*

May 11 – Last Friday was a gala day in Eureka, not only for the school children of Lincoln county, but for the grown-ups as well. Spectators and contestants for the field meet began to arrive early Thursday evening, and those from the west end of the county arrived on the dinky Friday morning. After enjoying auto rides for an hour or more the contestants were assigned to the various homes in the city for entertainment. Nearly every school in the county took part in the exercises, 125 contestants participating in the events, which were witnessed by 500 children and 200 grown-ups. The following schools entered contestants: Libby, Eureka, Fortine, Warland, Kamp Kids (L. L. Co.), Leonia, Iowa Flats, Rexford, Trego, Troy, Fisher Creek, Kolln, Glen Lake, Dahlberg School, Pinkham, Lower Phillips Creek, Upper Phillips Creek.

REMEMBERING PINKHAM SCHOOL

Teachers of the Pinkham school as well as pupils have many fond memories of those by-gone days. "Bobette" Gertrude Waller taught her first year on Pinkham as a young eighteen-year-old during the school term of 1928-1929. She remembers having a dozen pupils.

Veon Stacy was the oldest, with his sister Gladyce the youngest.

Wayne, Lynn and Sidney Workman never missed a day of school. Archie and Ervin Kinney were also very regular. Alice, John and Marie Leib walked three miles every day following the Sutton Road down across the Pinkham bridge and then up the main road to the school.

Marie as a first grader came almost every day, even in deep snow. She can remember following the footsteps of Alice and John as they took turns breaking trail. In good weather, Lee Utter liked to trail along as his aunts and uncles came by in the morning. Lee visited to see what school was like before starting the next year.

Bobette remembers parents were a help to a shaky eighteen-year-old teacher. She never forgot the time she disciplined two big boys one day, then sent a note home to their parents. The next morning she received a note saying, "If you would like help let us know."

Winter fun included young teachers. A favorite sport was sledding on the hill back of the schoolhouse. Big boys pulled a toboggan up through the orchard, then everyone piled on, teacher and all for the bumpy rough ride down through the orchard over whatever the snow may cover up. Bobette thinks the "teacher" took the outstanding spill but they all went back to school refreshed.

The Pinkham School.

Another winter incident Bobette remembers was when the older boys were bringing in wood from the shed to bank the wood stove. Wayne hurried in to whisper to the teacher that Lynn had a surprise for her but not to be scared. Lynn came in, giggling, holding out his hand for the teacher. She held out her hand for his offering. A dead mouse! When she asked if it was for her, it kind of spoiled the whole thing, but he still giggled!

Some of the other students at that time were Dorothy Kinney Owens, Doyle Stacy (in between Veon and Gladyce), the Carr kids, Joe, Clara and George, who lived up the hill from Leibs on Sutton Road. Josephine and David Pluid came from the other direction down Slick's Gulch, also Otis and George Cook.

Other teachers were Lula Mikalson Olson, Evelyn Hunsinger, Mr. Woodward, Marie Hartfield, Hazel Schagel and Mary Rice. Then Harriet Shenefelt, Mary Lampton, Marjorie Preston, Irene Crowley, Hazel Jones and Eileen Cuffe Martin.

Irene Crowley was another young teacher who taught her first year at the Pinkham school. She had her own Ford that she drove from town so she didn't board with someone on Pinkham. She taught the year 1929-1930 when Lee Utter was a first grader.

A new family had moved up the creek that year. Leo and Minnie Armstrong came from California to put six kids in school. They were Lily, Olive, Lola, Jim, Fay and David. The eldest, Ilah, soon married Otis Cook. Lily married Bill Stacy. Olive married Ham Leib and Lola married Archie Kinney. The Armstrongs definitely were soon integrated into the Pinkham community.

Most of the teachers taught for only one or two years but Mrs. Ethel Long was there for about eight years and made a good impression on students as well as parents and the community.

ETHEL LONG – TEACHER

Mrs Ethel Long, widow of Dr. George Long of Eureka who died in 1929, became the best known teacher of Pinkham School. She also had the longest tenure, from 1930 to 1937. Her experience of raising three children of her own made her well qualified to be an exceptional teacher.

Pinkham school board members Grace Kinney, Frank Slick and Nancy (Sis) Roberts along with Ella Thatcher as clerk were well pleased to procure Ether Long as teacher. They gave her $125 per month, a raise from the usual pay of $100. Mrs. Long was just as happy to get the job as she was now putting her two sons, George and Frank, through high school and then college in Missoula. Her daughter Caroline married Frank Cada.

Mrs. Long drove a 1929 Model A Ford sedan from her home in Eureka up the crooked, hilly road to teach school every day. To keep it out of the weather she talked the school board into partitioning a portion of the horse barn to make room to park her car. The narrow country road wasn't plowed out in winter by the county then, so some nights she stayed at the school house which also had a temporary partition in one corner for her convenience.

The first hot lunch program was started by Mrs. Long. She felt sorry for children coming to school with very little lunch on cold days. Some days it was only hot cocoa she made on the flat topped heater and some times parents shared a piece of meat and vegetables to make soup. Everyone was poor during the Depression and most of the children didn't know any different. There was no stigma to wear patched or mended clothing.

This teacher didn't "pick pets" or show favoritism. She was a mother as well as a teacher for all alike. She encouraged them to do well and when they did, they were praised. The school board gave her the backing she needed to use common sense in disciplining. When she thought they needed correction, she did it right then, not wait for parents to do the job. If she thought they needed a spanking or a scolding, that was the time to take care of it. She gained the respect of both pupils and parents in her fairness.

Mrs. Long had her pump organ brought up to the school house to enhance the music program. She also shared her books for the library. Spelling contests were encouraged with lively competition among the students. The playground was also improved with high jump poles installed and sawdust pits for standing broad jump and running broad jump. Students were then taken to Eureka to compete with other county schools at a track meet. Some of the other schools were Iowa Flats, Glen Lake, Black Lake, Tooley Lake, Fortine, Rexford and Trego. That gave all the schools a chance to get acquainted with one another.

Another way Mrs. Long chose to broaden the horizon for her students was to take her country kids to get a taste of town. Some of them never had a chance to go to town and were all 'goggle' eyed to see all the sites. She took two at a time to make the event more special.

One of the wonders was licking a five-cent ice cream cone at the drug store on main street. Another was watching a moving picture show just a short walk from Mrs. Long's home a block off Main Street. Her home was also full of wonders. With just a pull of a chain there was a bright light in each room. With a turn of a faucet handle there was hot or cold water and a big bath tub to soak in. There was also an indoor toilet that flushed with water. So many amazing things to report back home, that all the kids were anxious for their turn.

Thus Mrs. Long made a favorable impact on the community – when they needed it the most. She made strong characters of her students who were soon to choose a life of their own. Some were to go on to high school and some into a branch of the service to serve their country during WWII. A few went on to college to make a career. Her teaching made a difference!

PINKHAM SCHOOL CLASS PICTURE (1930-31)
Tobacco Valley News
December 17, 1970

Identification of this group as a class at the Pinkham School in 1930-31 was made by several persons after it was published a few months ago. Tom Wilson took the picture with a Brownie camera, and a number of persons also have copies of the picture, originally made postcard size.

First row: Lee Utter, David Armstrong, George Carr, Esther Utter Carvey, Leo Armstrong, Marie Leib Roose;

Second row: John Leib, Bill Young, George Cook, Fannie Young Hammons (behind); Olive Armstrong Leib, Clara Carr, Dorothy Kinney Owens;

Third row: (blurred out) Archie Kinney, Otis Cook, Alice Leib Wilson, Lillie Armstrong Stacy, Jane Young Lawson, Lola Armstrong Kinney, Jack Young, Irwin Kinney, Jim Armstrong, Joe Carr.

Identification of the above was furnished by Lillie Stacy, Marie Roose, Leo and Irene Collar, and Mr. and Mrs. Joseph Leib.

PINKHAM SCHOOL

The Pinkham school building was eighty years old in 1995. It was built in 1915 as a one room schoolhouse for all eight grades. The first school teacher to initiate the new class was Evelyn Hunsinger, who had taught two years in the little log cabin on the same premises given to School District #18 by Will Stacy.

School was held continuously until the term of 1945-46 with Madeline Rost-Utter as the last teacher. In 1955 Pinkham School District #18 was consolidated with Eureka School District #13.

People on Pinkham wanted to keep the school building to use as a community center. They organized and called themselves the Moose Horn Club. They lease the school building the for ninety-nine years for a nominal fee. Their responsibility was to use and care for the building.

Pinkham School Pupils 1945-1946:
   Grade 1 – Bessie Bergette, Marlene Zachery
   Grade 2 – Jack Workman
   Grade 3 – Dolly Roberts, Beryl Stacy
   Grade 4 – Elmer Stacy, Jerry Burch, Dennis Bergette, Beatrice Burch, Jerry Stacy
   Grade 5 – Roger Workman, Eunice Stacy
   Grade 6 –
   Grade 7 – Jiggs Stacy, Harry Workman, Roy Roberts
   Grade 8 – Duane Combs, Delores Bergette

TEACHER REMINISCES ABOUT PINKHAM SCHOOL
Tobacco Valley News
   (Miss Madeline Rost, who later became Mrs. Lee Utter, was the last teacher of the Pinkham school. At our urging, she consented to write a reminiscence of her year at the school).
By Madeline Utter

It was the fall of 1945, when I first came to Pinkham to teach school. I was young and it was my very first school. I didn't feel at all like a school teacher, but I was going to do my best. When I rang the big bell by pulling on the rope at 8:30 to call the kids to school, ran the American flag up the pole by its rope, and after we all said the pledge to the flag together, before lining up to march into school, then I knew that my school had begun.

I don't remember for sure how many were there that first day, but the three Workman boys were there. Jack a second grader, Roger in the fifth, and Harry, the seventh. Roy Roberts was also a seventh grader and little Dolly in the third. There were two Stacy families, Elmer Stacy in the fourth and Eunice, a fifth grader. Bill Stacy had Jiggs in the seventh, Jerry in the fourth, and Beryl in the third. Duane Combs came a short while in the eighth. Later, Marlene Zachery enrolled, and then I had a first grader. During the year Jerry Burch attended the fifth (but he had to go outside to chew snoose) so he took longer going out back than the others. Then his sister Beatrice came, too, in the fourth grade. There never were any sixth graders, but in the spring the Harles Bergette family moved in with Delores, an eighth grader; Dennis (Rusty) a fifth grader, and Bessie in the first grade with Marlene. That made a total of eighteen students.

I don't recall getting a school picture for remembrance, but I do have one of Marlene as she stayed with me for "babysitting."

One incident I do remember with amusement and maybe they do too. I was giving spelling words to the seventh graders with my back to the big heater. One of the smaller boys walked up to the stove beside me and popped a match head on it. I reacted immediately! Automatically jumping, whirling, I brought the spelling book down on his head, breaking the book in two. Stunned, he returned to his seat. Nobody ever tried that again, or anything else for a while!

There was no playground equipment, and so we got a ball and bat. Everyone played no matter how small or big, including the teacher, and we had a ball.

In winter when the snow got packed, we took sleds up the road back of the school about a quarter of a mile and then coasted to Mr. Banks' gate, about another quarter mile and then walked back to school. It took the whole noon hour for one ride, but then we rode almost half a mile, barring wrecks.

At Christmas time, we selected our tree from the local forest. This was an important event, as a picture taken the previous year shows. The team of donkeys pulling the dray belonged to Charlie Workman. The driver is Duane Combs but all the children had a ride on these donkeys at some time or other. Others in the picture with the tree are Harry and Roger Workman, Roy and Dolly Roberts, Mattie and Tommy Wilson.

The next step was getting the tree set up and decorated. The main decorations, like paper chains, popcorn ropes and cranberry strings were made by the pupils. As there was no electricity in rural areas yet, we didn't have any lights, not even candles, as I was afraid of fire. Our only light was a gas lantern hanging from the ceiling. But this was light enough for the shy participants of the Christmas program. We all sang Christmas songs, such as "Up On The Housetop," "Jolly Old St. Nicholas," and "Jingle Bells." Since none of us had any great instrumental abilities we accompanied ourselves with Christmas bells. Interspersing the songs, everyone had a recitation. The program was well attended by everyone in the community.

There were a few old-time dances in the fall while fiddlers played and some called for square dances. The young schoolteacher was quite popular and danced every dance. Alta Workman liked to recall those dances and talk about the good times we had. She also asked me if I wouldn't like to move in with them for the winter and share a room with Lula – one year older, and Ellagene, one year younger. I gladly accepted, as I was used to a big family and was lonesome living by myself.

This was also the first time I ever met a moose. One Monday morning in January, I left the Workman home early to build up a fire and break trail for the Workman boys who would soon be following. The snow was almost up to my knees. (I was one teacher who wore long pants to school during the long winter months, and no one objected.) At that time the road was narrow and crooked. I was very intent on my trail breaking. When rounding a curve, I saw a horse coming down the road towards me. Good! I thought, now I won't have such hard going. I can follow its tracks. So I kept going up and it kept coming down. We came closer. Gee, I said to myself, that is an odd looking horse. I've never seen one like that before. I stopped to look more closely. It stopped. I walked on. It walked on and I realized that we would meet at Mr. Banks' gate. It's not his horse, why that must be a moose. I stopped again. It would be futile to try to turn back in all that snow. I stood looking at it and it stood looking at me. It turned and went up Banks' Draw just as if that was where it intended to go all along. I went on and made use of the broken trail in the snow. (Since then, I have never been afraid of a moose and I have cut Christmas trees in the same area that a cow was browsing. Also I have pictures of them drinking from our pond and passing through our field. Although we see less and less of them).

It` was probably in the same snowstorm that I first met Lee. He had just arrived home New Years after being discharged from the Navy. One evening, he was driving up to see his friend Bob Combs, when he got stuck in the snow just above the Workman place where Lynn lived. He came down there for help and never made it any further as he joined in a card game we were playing. He ended up as my partner and we won the game. Of course he asked for a date, which was the beginning of our courtship. Ellagene was going steady with Bob Combs at the time, and Lula with Randall Richmond. There were some pretty hectic evenings if all three of us were getting ready for dates at the same time! By spring we were all married. First Bob and Ellagene, then Lula and

Randall, and last Lee and I on the third of May. The pupils had a hard time remembering to say Mrs. Utter, instead of Miss Rost.

That was the last term of school at Pinkham. Lee bid for the school bus run and got it. If I couldn't teach there any longer, he would haul them to Eureka.

Note: Madeline's experience with a country school began while attending eight grades at Swan River and then Bigfork High School. She also grew up with five brothers and a sister living in a log cabin where they all had to cope. This put her in a good position to cope with her pupils.

CHRISTMAS AT A COUNTRY SCHOOL

It was back in 1945 that the last Christmas program was held at the Pinkham Creek Schoolhouse. The whole community looked forward with great anticipation to this special event of the year. Everyone came to see the children perform and Santa Claus pass out treats.

The teacher had the responsibility to make plans far ahead of time for preparations to be complete. The date was set – Friday evening before Christmas with a two-week holiday following. Children set the mood by singing "Deck the Halls" and "Jingle Bells". Recitations were passed around for the children to learn at home and parts worked out for the play.

"Now a tree, teacher! We have to have a big tree!" So the "what" was decided upon, then came the how, who, where and when. The Workman boys volunteered their team of burros and a sled if it snowed to haul the tree. Duane Combs offered to chop the tree down. The where was anywhere up on the hill they could find one. The big tree-getting time was set for Saturday afternoon.

The day came. There was no snow, so the Workman boys brought a wagon to school with Harry driving the burros. Teacher was ready and Duane waited impatiently, anxious to get started. Roger and Jack Workman and Roy Roberts came along to do their part in selecting the tree. After all were aboard, Harry urged the team to follow a logging road up the hill. All eyes were looking for that "just right" tree along the way. They looked up, and they looked down, but the perfect tree could not be found!

At last the big decision was made. Duane chopped it down with his Christmas tree ax. Everyone helped load it on the wagon and this time Duane drove the team back to the schoolhouse. Teacher hurried ahead to get her camera for a picture of bringing in the tree before it was unloaded in the woodshed to keep it cool.

Next came the project to deck the hall and trim the tree. Teacher used the hectograph to carefully make copies of Santas for children to color, cut out, and paste on cotton whiskers. These decorated the schoolroom along with boughs and bells. All eight grades became cheerfully involved making colorful chains for the Christmas tree. They used construction paper cut into strips by the paper cutter, then pasted together in connecting circles. For variety, two paper strips were folded back and forth over one another and these were hung on the tree for danglers.

That was before electricity came up the "crick," so there were no bright lights for the tree, not even candles for fear of fire. But the children were satisfied with their efforts and their eyes glowed with delight. Tinfoil stars and bells reflected light from the gas lanterns hung on both sides of the room.

During the excitement of the last week, recitations were recited from memory and songs were sung with gusto with no musical accompaniment. Songs to be acted out were "Up On The Housetop" and "Jolly Old St. Nicholas." Opening of the program relaxed everyone with sleigh bells jingling in the background while children sang "Jingle Bells," their favorite song.

The big day finally arrived. Rows of desks were turned to face the tree in the corner and the doorway to the cloak closets which were used as dressing rooms, one for boys and for girls. Benches were arranged behind the desks for grown-ups. The teacher's desk was turned into a fireplace and stockings were hung with care for the program.

Harry Workman was Santa for the play and Eunice Stacy was Mrs. Santa. They read letters written to Santa by children earlier. During this time, elves would come in singing "Deck The Halls With Boughs Of Holly" and tack up a piece of greenery. Then "Tis The Season To Be Jolly" and Roy Roberts whistled while he worked. All sang Fa-La-Las while skipping around.

Dolly Roberts recited "ith Chrithmath" during a scene change. Then came the song "Jolly Old St. Nicholas" with actions. Roy Roberts came out with his nightcap on to recite "Twas The Night Before Christmas." (Sound effects and sleigh bells and tramping feet echoed from the hall way behind the burlap curtain). All the children sang "Up On The House Top" while Harry in his Santa suit came out to fill the stockings on the fireplace.

Then the real Santa Claus came through the back door with a big pack on his back filled with bags of candy and nuts, big oranges and apples, which he passed to everyone with his happy ho, ho, ho sending thrills through all the little ones.

Grown-ups caught the excitement. The party wasn't over. Eager hands shoved benches and desks against the wall. Another block of wood was plunged into the big heater. Bill Stacy dragged out his fiddle and Ovella Roberts the banjo. Together they struck up a fast hoedown. The teacher was a popular dancing partner for an evening of fun and frolic.

TEACHER GETS MARRIED – MADELINE ROST UTTER

Lee and I were married in May 1946 before school was out. I was the country school teacher and that fall Lee was the first Pinkham school bus driver. On our wedding day school was let out at noon on Friday so we could drive the seventy-five miles to Kalispell. Before we left Eureka, the car had a flat tire. The jack slipped while Lee was changing it and almost cut his finger off. His mother gave first aid and a bandage.

After a late start, we were in a hurry. The old '36 Chrysler huffed and puffed going up the winding Dog Creek hill and threw a rod. We were stranded. Lee thumbed a ride with an Army recruiter to take us on to Kalispell for our marriage license. We got to the courthouse after a fast ride just as they were closing the doors at 5 p.m. They took five minutes more to issue our papers with no blood tests required.

With no pre-planning our next step was to find a jeweler to get wedding rings. A close friend of mine had married Oscar Koford, so a personal phone call brought them to Main Street to open their jewelry store. We bought a set of rings and they gave a free wristwatch to me as a wedding gift. It was my very first watch! Now to find a preacher to perform the ceremony.

We walked around town, found a parsonage beside a church and soon exchanged vows in the parsonage living room. That night was spent in the Kalispell Hotel. The next day we got the Chrysler hauled to Kalispell by one of my uncles living in the Flathead. He also gave us a ride home.

It was back on the job Monday morning, me to teach school and Lee to work in the sawmill. Our home was the 12 x16 teacherage. The following Friday night we were wakened by loud banging and clanging in the schoolyard. We were being "chivareed" by Pinkham people. Such a clamor! Cowbells clanging, pots and pans banging, horns tooting, shouts, yells, hoots and ribald songs! A great farewell for the last teacher.

They took us for a wild ride in the back of a Model A Ford, dust a-flying, down the road through tall pines, over the rocky hill from Twin Lakes to Black Lake, around by the old dump ground and back up the creek again. From all the jolting, sharp turns, dust and exhaust, I was terribly carsick. I never could ride in the back seat.

Former teacher Madeline Rost Utter near the Pinham School in 1990 holding a fir tree that was planted as a seedling on Arbor Day 1940. Over the years the tree was broken off twice, once run over by a car and then, as a sapling, when attacked by a bull with its horns. The remnant limbs finally made a tree of it.

SCHOOL AND GATHERING PLACE

Pinkham Pioneers were proud of the new larger school building built in 1915. It was not only to be a learning place for their children; it also was to be a gathering place for community social events. This lower school was more centrally located for families living in the Pinkham drainage.

The delight of young and old alike was hearing the sound of the big bell! It was braced in a cupola at the peak of the roof with a rope dangling down into the front hallway. Students were greatly honored when they were chosen to take a turn to ring the bell. They gave the rope a mighty tug to hear the sound of the bell above. The bell was rung by the teacher at 8:30 a.m. and again at 9 a.m. to begin school. It could be heard a mile away in any direction. The sound urged pokey ones to hurry up and not be late. The ringing of the bell was also used to bring people to the school for special parties or church services.

After school District #18 consolidated with Eureka District #13 in 1946, the bell was taken down and moved. It was mounted on a platform in a frame built behind the Lincoln County High School. It was then rung at the beginning of hometown football games. The empty cupola remains on the top of the Pinkham school building as a reminder of bygone days.

Another plus of the new school house was the narrow hardwood flooring put in with precision. The floor was then varnished, buffed and polished, making an excellent dance floor. The community was blessed with musicians and everyone loved a lively party to offset the drudgery. This gave them a chance to dress up in their best clothes, men came in white starched shirts and women took off their aprons and donned their prettiest dresses for the occasion. Everyone brought food to share. Kids were put to bed in the cloak rooms until it was time to go home. Teams of horses were tied to hay filled wagons so they could munch while waiting.

Square dancing was in vogue with "Birdie In The Cage" one of the most popular. The caller, someone with a good strong voice, would begin the call in cadence with the beat of the music. "Let's have four couples out on the floor – Head couple, back to music, face the door – All join hands and circle to the right; Reverse that circle and do it right. Head couple – face that couple on the right – Swing that couple and hug 'em tight; Gents grab hands and ladies bow under, gents hold tight and go like thunder; Let the birdie out and take the next girl, hug her up tight and give her a whirl. (Repeat until each couple has a turn)

Gents had fun lifting the gals up off their feet as they whirled like thunder. Full skirts would billow out and sometimes dancing slippers would fall off, but all this added to the fun. After the set was done, the caller would chant "All join hands and circle to the left when you get home do the ali man left. Meet your partner with an elbow swing – then promenade the pretty little thing. Take her on home and you know where – where you go and what you do – I don't care".

Many people interviewed remember bits and pieces of the time they attended Pinkham School. One of the favorite memories is the first school party of the year. Halloween parties were usually held in the evening with whole families attending and games were for young and old alike. The galvanized wash tub half full of water and bobbing red apples was popular with the boys. They didn't mind bobbing their heads down into the water to catch an apple. Girls preferred latching onto an apple on a string hanging from the hall entrance. Those with buck teeth or even missing front teeth with prominent eye teeth, were usually the first to get a bite from their apple. Another contest was pushing peanuts across the floor with their nose to the goal line, after hands were tied behind their back.

After School Districts 18 and 13 were consolidated, there were still Halloween parties sponsored by the Moose Horn Club. Local musicians were willing to play for dancing. Prizes were given for best costumes for different age groups. One party in particular stands out in my memory.

"The costume I chose was made up of clothing from the closets of teenage daughters. I wore a short red skirt with matching pumps. A revealing white blouse and a long blond wig down my back made me look much younger. To top it all off, I wore a mask with a gruesome face. I went early and stood around just inside the room with my back to the entrance. There were very few people I could recognize. I picked out Vivian Workman, dressed as a hobo, by the way she danced. With her hair tucked up inside an old hat and baggy britches, she boldly asked ladies to dance. But she avoided me! I could hear people gathering in the hall behind me. Some guy said, "who is the blonde with the pretty red skirt?" Another voice replied, "I don't know. Why don't you ask her to dance and find out?" "No, you do it. You're the ladies man". "Let's let Ben do it." That was when I turned around to face them. They all let out an astonished gasp and fell back into each other. I left, laughing behind my mask to ask Vivian to dance with me. She reluctantly did, but soon guessed who it was and we had a great time together."

Christmas school programs and Valentines Day activities were always looked forward to a good time. Country school kids liked to cut colored construction paper into heart shapes, then paste them together or onto a square. Some talented pupils made fancy Valentines that were coveted by their special friends. All of them had a shoe box or something similar to decorate as their mail box.

This was also the time of year that box socials or pie parties were held at the school house. Ladies fixed a lunch to put in her own decorated box, which was kept as a secret. Gents then bid on the box hoping there was good food inside. The highest bidder had the privilege of sharing supper with the gal who brought the box. Sometimes this could be an exciting adventure and other times a disappointment. Money raised usually went to a special project to benefit the school. There was always music and dancing to liven up the party.

Nature walks on nice days were a delightful diversion from sitting inside. In the fall, pretty leaves were gathered to decorate the school or making patterns by laying a blank piece of paper on top of them, then rub with a broken crayon. Spring brought forth flowers and leaves to identify. Pupils of the last term of school recall a small fir tree transplanted on Arbor Day. It was taken from the surrounding forest and planted in the front school yard. The little thing was broken off three times, but survived. It grew into a sizeable tree.

All who attended the one room country school felt they benefitted from hearing lessons from other grades. From the beginning, first graders learned how to behave by following the example of the other students. Story time, when teacher read aloud, was the favorite time of day. Books from the library were chosen; "Little Women", "Jo's Boys", "Tom Sawyer", "Flicka" (a horse) and others kept their rapt attention. Older pupils could barely wait until they had a chance to read a book by themselves. Dolly Roberts was also fascinated by a full, colorful skirt worn by her teacher, that flared around the chair while she was reading.

The school became the focal point of the community. That was where elections were held and important meetings of the school board.

This 1934 picture at the Pinkham School is of a church group that met there, Rev. Swinehart's Church of God.

For fun and frolic, the schools offered a place to celebrate birthday parties, anniversaries and weddings. More serious gatherings were for funerals or farewells to friends.

The earliest church services were held at the upper school by the O'Briens, who were Catholic. They had an old pump organ for music to sing hymns. The O'Brien family alone filled up the school, but others were welcome.

Then in the 'Twenties,' Baptist missionaries came to the valley to hold services in the lower school. Almeda Stacy was one of the charter members of this group. Some folks were converted and baptized in nearby Pinkham Creek. Other missionaries came about 1930 to again involve Pinkham people in religion. One of these was Rev. Swinehart of the Church of God in Eureka.

This photo taken at the Pinkham School in 1920 is of a Baptist group.

Another one to come into the community in the 1950's was a Lutheran vicar by the name of Albert Pullmann. He became the pastor of Holy Cross Lutheran Church of Eureka. Al was a very friendly fellow and mixed well with the shy and leery people of Pinkham Creek. After teaching adult Bible classes with his helpers starting a Sunday school for a while, several families in the community became believers. They were baptized and became members of the church in Eureka.

By this time, the era of the pioneer was changing. School children were bussed to town with parents involved too. Roads that now belonged to the county were widened with heavy equipment, graveled, graded in summer and snow plowed in winter. People drove dependable vehicles with a heater for cold weather, so they could go shopping or get their mail once or twice a week instead of once a month, or only when weather permitted. Families could easily go into town to see a movie at night, with head lights to show their way home. Progress and an easier way of living was coming to the country and reaching out to the hill billies. They were ready to accept changes for the better.

Changes came to the Pinkam Ridge country. Note the power pole at the Sederahl place — a spring-time scene about 1960.

CHANGES

Our times are changing, it's true
Out goes the old, in come the new.
Old ways are now obsolete
And new ways become a treat

Pinkham people may be backwoods yet
But some things we'd like to forget
Like back in the days of the "depression"
When families had a still in possession

We had to cut wood with a cross cut saw
Then prayed to God for a January thaw
For we had to haul the wood to town
To trade for grub and pay a little down

In the good old horse and buggy days
Times were tough with dollar a day pays.
It takes some doin' to change our ways
But no one wants to keep the good old days!

We now have cars to drive good paved roads
And electricity to lighten the housewife loads
So our new maid "Miss Ready Kilowatt"
Cooks our meals in an automatic pot.

No more trips to the house out back
We've put a modern one in our shack
For water, we just turn on the faucet
We've discarded the old oaken bucket.

Radio and TV are newfangled gadgets
To take our time and money from our budgets.
Kids are bussed to a school much bigger
To learn more of the world and less to figger

Instead of going to town for our mail
We go tripping down a little trail
Give the mailbox wheel a spin
To see what new treasures lie within.

The new private telephone line
Changes your number and mine
Now we can share secrets as we talk
Our own line is the one we block.

By Madeline Utter

CHANGES

Changes started coming up the 'crick' with the next generation. When the WPA (Work Projects Administration) came to the area in the 'Thirties,' it gave men a chance to get a paying job to help support their families at $44 per month. County roads were in very poor condition, so road work was high on the priority list of improvements. The family outhouse was considered a health hazard, so new privys were built by WPA workers to government specifications. Local men also helped build a large community hall in Eureka funded by the WPA. Certain commodities of food were also available to help feed hungry families.

The CCC (Civilian Conservation Corp) was another boon to poor families struggling to survive. This Corps took young idle men and put them to work on a low paying job ($25 per month), but gave them something to do. Work camps were set up under supervision near a job site. Young men from the age of sixteen to twenty-one were chosen as part of the crew. (Although strong husky boys of fourteen or fifteen often lied their age so they could have a job.) The boys were given a set of new clothes, bedding to share a tent and free board. Each month most of their pay was sent home to their folks. They were allowed to keep $5.

The Sutton Road, which branched off from the Pinkham Road, was built by the 3 C's. Their camp was set up at Pinkham Creek just down from the Utter place. The first project was to build a sturdy bridge across the creek. The road then went up past the Utter and Leib homesteads before following along the Sutton ridge.

Tools used for road building were two-man crosscut saws to fall trees along the right of way and an ax to chop limbs or brush. A pick and shovel were used to dig out rocks and around stumps. Francis Shenefelt hired on as teamster with his team of horses to pull out stumps and smooth the surface with a scoop or slip. Lee Utter remembered his first dozer ride with Marion Miller, who was also on the job.

There were no ditches along side the roadway. Spring run off from melting snow made rivulets and soft spots in the road. Very bad sections that bog down a vehicle were filled with saplings, poles or slabs laid crosswise to form a corduroy crossing. This road became the access to timberland beyond by USFS connected by the main Sutton Road.

World War II brought more changes. Men and women both found work in factories on the West Coast building boats and airplanes. These were good paying jobs and they found places to live with modern conveniences. Young men went to war and traveled the world. They saw, they learned, and they came home with new perspectives.

After the war young men wanted to settle down and raise a family. Some took advantage of the offer from Veteran Services to get a higher education. They all wanted better living conditions and went about getting them. They wanted new homes with electric power, running water and flushing toilets. Baby boomers were born and there was a boom in the housing industry.

Sawmills were hiring extra shifts to keep up with the demand. There was Albee's Mill in Eureka and Columbus Clark had a lumber mill across the Tobacco River next to the railroad tracks. Kennedy-Steven's lumber mill was on Highway 93 north and Jim Hurst owned the mill near Fortine. All these mills bought logs or cants from smaller outfits to make planed studs or 2x4's. Small portable mills were operating on private ground for a second cutting of timber, then hauling it to the big mill to finish.

When private timber was getting depleted, the small operators had to look elsewhere for logs. Timber sales were put up for bid by the USFS but they kept getting bigger until they cost more than a small operator could afford. They were soon put out of business.

It was in the early 50's when the J. Neil Lumber Company bid the highest on timber up the Pinkham drainage. This was still a virgin forested area needing heavy equipment to extract the logs. Some of the trees were huge, a yard across at the base. New long bar chainsaws were used to fell the trees and caterpillars were used to doze trails and skid logs to a landing. Heal booms loaded the logs onto extra wide logging trucks with 12' wide bunks. These trucks needed a good wide hauling road to Rexford where logs were put on a train to Libby. The

Neil's camp was also located in Rexford. Many of those duplex houses were later moved to various places for homes.

This began the period of clear-cutting patches in the forest. Large bulldozers and huge skidders raised havoc with small trees while harvesting big timber. The mess left over was dozed into huge piles and burned. Bare hillsides were then planted with small seedlings to refurbish the forest. Select harvesting and skidding with horses became a part of the past.

The good wide road built up the Pinkham drainage was a boon to the Pinkham community. The road was straightened as well as wide enough for a boulevard, and paved! It was better than the county roads and went all the way to Rexford. The county later widened, graded and paved a portion of the road to Eureka. It was a shorter distance now to either town with no dust clouds.

The school bus driver could now drive the route without fear of scraping bus sides on a loaded truck. The new paved road also opened the way for rural mail delivery to the Pinkham area. Applications were made to both Rexford and Eureka for a mail route. Rexford responded and was glad to have an addition to the route already established up the West Kootenai. Lincoln County eventually took over the road to West Kootenai and Pinkham for upkeep and snow plowing in the winter. People in both places never had it so good to easily get where they wanted to go. The era of the horse and buggy days was over!

END OF AN ERA

WOW! What a difference a day makes. The day when rural electric power was turned on up Pinkham was a day of wonders. It was the fall of 1954 and folks could hardly believe their eyes. It was enlightening! By just a pull of a string or chain, a light bulb hanging from the ceiling brightened up the whole room. Not just one room, but it happened in every room in the house without carrying a lamp from one room to another. And there were no dark corners or flickering shadows from candle light or kerosene lamps. No more lamp chimneys to wash and polish every day or lamps to keep filled with coal oil. What a blessing!

Then there were those who put a yard light on the power pole outside. It lighted the way to the woodpile or the outside toilet. With short days of winter coming on, it was a marvel to not have to light a lantern for a trip out back. Some folks even had the foresight to put a light in the barn so they could see to milk the cow and feed after dark instead of having to carry a kerosene lantern.

Gene McWhirter, who lived on Pinkham at the time, was a handyman who tinkered with radios, clocks and small engines. He also was electrically inclined, so he was called upon by his friendly neighbors to wire their house in readiness for this special event. He advised them to put at least one plug-in outlet in each room or more, as they would eventually use them. Some doubters thought that an outlet combined with a ceiling fixture would be enough. They could get a longer cord if needed. But they soon found that Gene was right. A single wire for a light bulb was not safe as they got tangled in extra cords strung around.

The Gamble store in Eureka was soon overwhelmed with orders for electric appliances. The whole countryside was now electrified with the advantages of using electric power. Housewives were delighted to get a toaster to plug into an outlet, no more toasting bread on top of the wood stove or in the oven. Husbands were grateful for a radio that they could listen to at all times without having to worry about the battery running down.

Gene soon went to work at the Gamble Store to help with the demand for electrical appliances. He then moved to town to be closer to his job. He not only sold appliances, he instructed buyers on how to use them. Gene delivered electric refrigerators, washing machines and dryers. He helped to install pumps and pipes to wells or springs to have running water in the house.

Homes were soon remodeled or new ones built. They had to be modern with electric hot water tanks to have hot and cold water in the faucets over the kitchen sink and in the bathroom that included an indoor flushing toilet! Country folks now enjoyed the same luxuries as city dwellers. They could soak in a hot tub of water without dragging in the galvanized wash tub to heat water on the cook stove before bathing.

Old-timers who lived through the Depression were still leery of borrowing money from the bank to pay for all these "new fangled gadgets." Wives wanted to move out the cumbersome wood cookstove with a water reservoir and put in a compact, temperature adjustable electric range. Why, they even wanted electric base board heaters to get rid of the wood chips and smoke in the house. What next? Men were soon relieved to not have to saw and haul wood in their spare time to keep fires going. They also enjoyed evenly cooked meals, but they missed the warmth of a wood stove to sidle up to when they came in on a cold day.

Most of them kept the stone chimney or built a fireplace just in case the power failed or had an emergency.

Freezers that came in different sizes to preserve food were a big boon to people who provided their own meat. It was no longer necessary to put up hundreds of jars of canned meat, vegetables and fruit. The freezer held a whole beef cut up and wrapped, or a pig, chickens and wild game, besides vegetables from the garden and fruits in season. There was even room for a carton of ice cream, a delicious treat any time of year.

Not only were large electric appliances available to make life easier, there were many more that no one ever dreamed about. There were electric shavers to take the place of straight razors that had to be stropped. Hair dryers were a blessing to gals on the go with long hair, even electric curlers to make old curling irons heated in a lamp chimney obsolete. There was the popular barber set with electric clippers for home hair cuts.

Kitchens seemed to sprout and multiply with new electrical helpers. Besides the marvel of a toaster, there were mixers to take the place of egg beaters, coffee pots and tea kettles were heated quickly, while fry pans, roasters and crock pots could cook a meal without constant watching. There were timers on ovens and even electric wall clocks! Electric can openers were handy gadgets as were meat grinders and vegetable choppers. There seemed to be no end to all these marvelous things and no one dreamed that some day there would be microwave cooking too.

Young folks quickly adapted to this new mode of living while older pioneers were more skeptical and took longer to be assured it was safe to use some of these newfangled gadgets. Even though an electric blanket kept the bed warm in the back bedroom on the coldest nights, they were still leery of being electrocuted while sleeping.

It didn't take long for the guys to try to keep up to the gals. They were building shops and garages with heavy duty plug-ins and lots of them. Electric drills with various sized bits became popular as well as skill saws, grinders, paint sprayers, battery chargers and much more. Some even put a portable radio in the shop to keep them company.

Just when pioneers felt like they were living in the lap of luxury with electricity, along came promoters of rural telephone service wanting them to sign up for a phone. At first they were offered a party line, with wires attached to the power pole. The right of way was already cleared and poles were up to make it easier and cheaper. The number of people on a line would depend on how many signed up for this service.

Some country folks were skeptical of this plan and wanted to wait to see how it worked. After all, they were used to visiting their neighbors to see how they were doing. If there was an emergency, they could use their neighbors phone. News spread fairly fast just from one to another.

There were ten households on Pinkham Creek to sign up for telephones. That made two party lines with five people on each line. There were five parties on upper Pinkham and five on lower Pinkham near the school house. Each line had a limit of three minutes before being shut off. That way no one could monopolize the line. Each household had its own distinct ring – such as two short and one long or other combination to designate who should answer the phone. If a person from one line called someone on the other line it opened up the phone at all ten homes and all could join the conversation. The system frustrated teens who liked to talk a lot.

But more progress was on the way. More people were moving to the country now that there was power and phones available. More hookups made private lines affordable. And so much more! In years to come there would be television, calculators and computers! The pioneer era has come to an end for Pinkham Pioneers – another day is dawning.

THE MOOSE HORN CLUB

The Moose Horn Club was organized in 1955 by Pinkham Creek residents who wanted to preserve the Pinkham School building to be used as a community center. The school had been the focal point of bringing the families together and now it sat idle since the Pinkham School District 18 had consolidated with Eureka School District 13 in 1946.

The meeting was held at the home of Lynn and Peggy Workman and officers were elected. A delegation attended the Eureka school board meeting to get permission to use the building and a lawyer was contacted to draw up the agreement. The Moose Horn Club members were responsible for the upkeep of the grounds and building under a 100 year lease agreement for $1.00.

The community responded wholeheartedly. Their first project was a clean up day at the school with a family picnic. Pastor Pullman drove by that day so stopped to see what was going on. With his suggestion it was decided to have Bible study and Sunday school classes for the children every Sunday afternoon. This lasted about three months until days grew short and weather cold.

What the building needed was some modernization to be comfortable. The new power line went right by the school so why not have electric lights? Plans were soon made to have regular dances every other Saturday night. Local musicians were hired for $5 each for the night. The tickets at the door were $1 per couple. Supper was $0.50 per plate and coffee a dime a cup. The plate held a sandwich, a dill pickle slice and a piece of cake prepared by the ladies of the Moose Horn Club. These dances were well attended and lasted about two years until they became too rowdy and law officers had to settle the fights. Money was raised to wire the building for electricity and put insulating board on the walls and ceiling. This was a big improvement.

The club got its name from a set of moose horns found out in the forest in the vicinity. The horns were mounted and put up inside above the front entry of the school house.

Through the years the Moose Horn Club has stayed active, with the same goal – preserve the Pinkham School building. Dues for membership in the club raised from $5 per couple to $5 per person or $10 for a family. The price of power has also increased from a $4 monthly fee to $7. Different people have served as officers of the club but still the same families are involved.

Many functions as well as fund-raisers have been held at the school. There have been birthday parties, weddings for the younger generation and wedding anniversaries for the older ones. Family reunions, Halloween and Christmas parties took place there besides a few funerals and memorial dedications. The Pinkham School reunion in 1990 and 1995 brought out many old-timers to reminisce about bygone school days in a country school.

Fund-raisers have been fun as well as raising money for improvements. There have been pie socials, rummage sales, Bingo, quilt raffles, auctions and barbecues to name some of the activities. Volunteers do the work and play the music.

Improvements have been re-setting the outside toilets and re-painting them, also building a lean-to roof at the back of the building and pouring cement underneath for outdoor crowds. Painting the outside and inside of the school house as well as re-finishing the floor was another project. The two coat closets were remodeled, with the boys room made into a band stand and the girls closet, a kitchen.

The biggest project of all was getting a well dug and water piped into the building. The kitchen now has running cold water coming in as well as running out the sink drain. In past years a water cistern was installed into a little creek up the draw then piped to the school. This was always a problem of the creek drying up or pipe frozen. When the adjoining land was sold it was an even bigger problem. Now the problem was solved and no one has to haul water to the school. It's right handy!

As a community service project, Moose Horn Club members promoted getting rural mail delivery. Eureka post office refused the service where as Rexford welcomed the extra patrons to help keep their postal service. The rural route to Pinkham became an extension of the delivery route from the West Kootenai. Pinkham people had the choice of getting home delivery from Rexford or picking it up in Eureka themselves.

WORLD WAR VETERANS FROM THE PINKHAM COMMUNITY

WWI
Ed Cook
Andrew Stacy

WWII
George Carr
Ed Carr
Otis Cook
Pat Cook – Killed in Action
Bob Combs
George Cook
Bill Good
Ed Finch
David Leib
John Leib
Frank O'Brien
Fred O'Brien
Leo O'Brien
Don Sederdahl
Leslie Sederdahl
Harrell Pluid
Jim Pluid
Guy Roberts
Glen Stubbs
Bill Stacy
Don Utter
F. Lee Utter

Roy Utter – Killed in Action
Sid Workman
Harry Workman
Bill Young
Jack Young
Gene Young
Harold Young.

Vietnam
Ken Utter
Keith Utter – Killed in Action
Mike Workman
Roger Workman

PEACE OF PINKHAM CREEK

The pearly waters of Pinkham Creek
come rolling down from the hills above.
This little brook is a friendly creek
Singing a soothing sound that I love.

In spring it's like a roaring lion
In summer, tame as a cooing dove.
As it goes slipping quietly along
Making pearly ripples that I love.

The pearly waters of Pinkham Creek
Soon became noted far and wide.
People came from West Virginia
Just to settle by its side.

The favorite tune for many folks
Was to hear the water sing
It tinkled merrily in summer
and it rumbled in the spring.

The pearly waters of Pinkham Creek
Had a lure that all fishermen seek
A stream teaming with Mountain brook
Just waiting to latch onto a hook.

In fall, colorful rocks appear in the rill
Where wild animals pause to drink their fill
Hunters softly tred the hardened ground
Amongst bright fall foliage all around.

In winter the stream is muffled and quiet
All covered with ice, frosty snow and yet
A place of peace prevails when all is at rest
Waiting for a time of rebirth; to that we can attest.

By Madeline Utter